American Philosophical Society
Held at Philadelphia
For Promoting Useful Knowledge
VOL. 88, PT. 2

The Theater of Man:

J. L. Vives on Society

J. A. FERNÁNDEZ-SANTAMARÍA

American Philosophical Society
Independence Square ❧ Philadelphia
1998

ISBN:0-87169-882-X
US ISSN:0065-9746

Library of Congress Cataloging-in-Publication Data

Fernández-Santamaría, J. A., 1936–
    The theater of man : J.L. Vives on society / J.A. Fernández
—Santamaria.
        p.   cm. -- (Transactions of the American Philosophical Soci
held at Philadelphia for Promoting Useful Knowledge ; vol. 88, pt
2)
    Includes bibliographical references and index.
    ISBN 0-87169-882-X (pbk.)
    1. Vives, Juan Luis, 1492-1540--Contributions in philosophical
anthropology. 2. Vives, Juan Luis, 1492-1540--Political and soci
views. 3. Philosophical anthropology--History. 4. Political
science--Philosophy--History.   I. Title.   II. Series: Transactio
of the American Philosophical Society ; vol. 88, pt. 2.
B785.V64F475 1998
196'.1--dc21   97-52
                                                                   C

TABLE OF CONTENTS

ABBREVIATIONS FOR VIVES' WORKS

DAV   *De anima et vita*

DCD   *De concordia et discordia*

DCR   *De communione rerum*

DCVA   *De censura veri in argumentatione*

DCVE   *De censura veri in enuntiatione*

DD   *De disputatione*

DIP   *De instrumento probabilitatis*

DISP   *De initiis, sectis et laudibus philosophiae*

DPP   *De prima philosophia*

DSP   *De subventione pauperum*

DTD   *De tradendis disciplinis*

DVF   *De veritate fidei Christianae*

FH   *Fabula de homine*

IAS   *Introductio ad sapientiam*

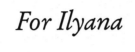

For Ilyana

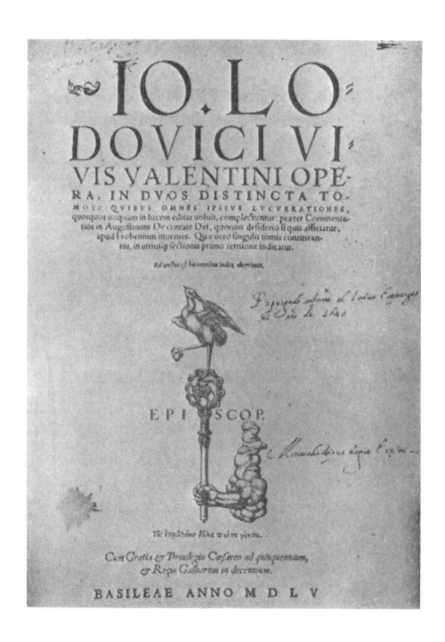

Title page of Vives' *Opera*, the Basle edition of 1555.

Preface

A FEW YEARS AGO I wrote that, thanks to the pioneering efforts of a handful of distinguished scholars, the writing of social, political, and economic Spanish history had been largely freed from the shackles that for so long had fettered its study. But even then the revolution had failed to extend its influence into the domain of the history of ideas, and we still moved within boundaries defined by the prejudices and shortcomings of old. Little, if anything, has changed since then. We know a great deal about what Spaniards did and how they acted but next to nothing concerning what they thought. And we would be hard pressed to find a more distinguished victim of the neglect that has been the lot of Spain's intellectual history than Juan Luis Vives.

The point is well worth emphasizing, because it will be a source of serious difficulties to those who in the future may at last choose to begin the systematic exploration of his thought and decide what place he deserves to occupy in the intellectual history of modern Europe. It certainly was a consideration weighing heavily on my mind as I tried to find the most effective way of structuring this, my second monograph on Vives. How to approach the thought of a man about whose ideas so little that is trustworthy has been written and whose writings are so extensive and all-encompassing? For the fact, already recorded in 1903 by Bonilla y San Martín and by Carlos G. Noreña (in his excellent *Juan Luis Vives*) in 1970, is that Vives must be counted as one of the most prolific thinkers within the northern humanist tradition, a polymath with an intellect that in terms of depth and breadth is unmatched by the mind of any among his better-known contemporaries. Given these considerations and the unfortunate circumstances made inseparable from the study of Vives by past and present neglect, there can only be one answer to the question raised above. We need a detailed understanding of his mental world. For the foreseeable future, therefore, our attention ought to be focused on producing monographic studies (Noreña's *Juan Luis Vives and the Emotions*, for example) aimed at explaining narrow and well-defined aspects of his thought. Clearly, then, it will be some time before we can hope to acquire the perspective needed to afford us, with some assurance of reliability, the opportunity to generalize about Vives' true significance as a thinker or to speculate concerning the possible impact of his ideas on the society of his time.

As my own contribution to that badly needed program of Vivesian studies, I propose to write about what I understand to be Vives' "theater of man," his conviction that man moves on a stage, mandated by God but man-made, which defines his existence as one singlemindedly devoted to restoring—at least partially— what he forfeited in a moment of insane ambition. I believe, in other words, that the one idea that ties together into a single coherent whole the extensive literary production[1] of Juan Luis Vives and informs his thought throughout is the conviction that man has the potential to recover the most important thing lost through the Fall. Man is therefore fully capable, by his own efforts alone, of attaining to that earthly *bonitas* that is the indispensable first step to be taken in the direction of everlasting salvation. But *bonitas* becomes accessible only within the context of a well-ordered society. This explains why there is no thinker during the Spanish Renaissance who applied himself more diligently to the study of the origin, evolution, nature, and reform of society than this humanist. With the last facet, the reform of society, of Vives' ideology I shall not be explicitly concerned here. I would, however, be sorely remiss if I were to move on without at least pointing out that his program for social reform has as its centerpiece the sum total of his educational works—the very fact that made Vives into one of the age's most influential educational reformers. In Vives' system, just as the arts are the sinews and building blocks of society, so a proper educational structure is the

---

[1] The chronology of the works cited in this monograph [in all cases, unless the contrary is indicated, the references will be to the *Opera omnia*, edition of Mayans y Síscar (8 vols., Valencia, 1782-1790). There is a new edition of his works currently under way by the Institució Valenciana d'Estudis I Investigació] is as follows. *Fabula de homine* (1518), *De initiis, sectis et laudibus philosophiae* (1518), *Introductio ad sapientiam* (1524), *De subventione pauperum* (1526), *De concordia et discordia in humano genere* (1529), *De disciplinis* (1531), *De communione rerum* (1535), *De anima et vita* (1538), *De veritate fidei Christianae* (1543). *De disciplinis* is an extensive work which falls naturally into two parts: *De corruptis artibus in universum* (seven books), and *De tradendis disciplinis* (five books). Also included in *De disciplinis* are: *De prima philosophia, De instrumento probabilitatis, De explanatione euiusque essentiae, De disputatione, De censura veri in enuntiatione, De censura veri in argumentatione.* For further details on Vives' works, see M. Solana, *Historia de la filosofía española. Epoca del Renacimiento* (3 vols., Madrid, 1944); F. Mateu y Llopis, *Catálogo de la Exposición Bibliográfica celebrada con motivo del IV Centenario de la muerte de Luis Vives (15 de mayo-15 de junio 1940)*; J. Esterlich, *Vives. Exposition organisée à la Bibliothèque Nationale* (Paris, January-March 1941); A. Bonilla y San Martín, *Luis Vives y la filosofía del Renacimiento* (Madrid, 1903). For this and other purposes, however, the most important work is that of C.G. Noreña, *Juan Luis Vives* (The Hague, 1970).

means of restoring them from their present corrupt and parlous state to their former and pristine vitality. The formula is straightforward: make over the educational system along the lines suggested by the humanist, and the foundations on which society stands will be correspondingly strengthened, brace up the underpinnings and society will once again become the suitable environment for men to live as "human beings ought to." In view of Vives' extraordinary interest in society in all its aspects and facets, therefore, it is no exaggeration to say that all his major works are fundamentally aimed at explaining (in terms deeply colored by Stoicism) the Aristotelian/Thomist premise that man is a social animal, fully functional only in the structured company of his peers—why in fact man is a social being, how he came to be such, how society was formed, why it became depraved—and the consequence of that premise: the inescapable obliga-tion placed upon the shoulders of each and every man to reform society, for all that he is and ought to be in this life and the next is at stake.

One final point. It is perhaps the supreme irony of a state of affairs that has condemned Vives to undeserved neglect by the accident of his place of birth that his own life is living testament to a spirit of cosmopol-itanism as great as any in the Renaissance. Born (1492) in Valencia, he attended (1508) that kingdom's university, an institution recently founded by Pope Alexander VI (in a bull of 1501) and Fernando de Aragón (*privilegio* of 1502 ordering the execution of the papal bull). He remained there until 1509, when he left for Paris and matriculated (Collège de Montaigu) at the university. His stay in Paris, however, was neither a long nor a happy one. All his life Vives retained considerable distaste for the entrenched intellectual conservatism and intolerance that characterized Parisian academic life at the time; a rather ironic twist, for it is likely at Montaigu that Vives discovered his own affinity for humanist learning. In 1512 he abandoned Paris and moved to Bruges, thus beginning the affectionate relationship with Flanders that would last to the end of the humanist's life. In Bruges he found early employ-ment as private tutor. Among his pupils were the children—one of whom, Margarita, he eventually married—of Bernardo Valdaura, a prominent member of the colony of prosperous Spanish merchants who had established themselves in the city. Soon Vives became part of Bruges' intellectual life and formed lasting friendships with some of the city's notables. In 1517 the humanist became the private tutor of Guillaume de

Croy. Nephew to the Sieur de Chièvres, king Charles' Grand Chamberlain and the most notable personage in the crowd of Flemings who arrived in Castile in the retinue of Spain's new sovereign, Croy (already bishop of Cambrai) was appointed in 1518, at the age of eighteen, to succeed Cardinal Cisneros, who had died in 1517, as archbishop of Toledo, the richest and most important see in Spain. Shortly after his own appointment Vives, following his new pupil, moved from Bruges to Louvain. By 1519 he had acquired such a reputation as a teacher that Erasmus himself recommended him—vainly, as it turned out—for the post of tutor to Ferdinand, the brother of the Spanish king. In 1520 the University of Louvain awarded him the needed license to deliver public lectures. In this fashion Vives became part of the turbulent and factious atmosphere with which the struggles between conservative theologians and the partisans of the new learning had surrounded the university.

The death of Croy and his own illness in 1521 plunged Vives into financial difficulties. A modest pension from the queen of England, Catherine of Aragón, helped out but was not sufficient to compensate for his failure to secure a post in the household of the duke of Alba. The following two years were gloomy ones for Vives. His fortune, however, soon changed for the better, and in 1523 he was invited to teach at Oxford University. The next five years were perhaps the most contented (the word "happy" rarely fits the humanist's temperament) of Vives' life. He enjoyed the patronage of the queen, the friendship of Thomas More, and the respect of the king and Cardinal Wolsey. His improved prospects persuaded him (1524) to marry Margarita Valdaura. His wife, however, remained in Bruges, a fact that partially explains Vives' repeated absences from England. By 1526, however, events in the island had taken a turn for the worse. His relations with Wolsey had cooled to the point of enmity. He was caught up in the coils of Henry's intrigues against Catherine. In 1528 Vives was forced by Wolsey to give a written account of his conversations with the queen. He was rewarded for his troubles with a month of house arrest. Shortly after his release from custody the humanist left England for the last time. Settling once more in Bruges, he spent the remaining twelve years of his life seeking influential patrons—in 1532 he was granted an imperial pension, and a few years later he became the private tutor of the duchess of Nassau—and writing. To this period belongs *De disciplinis*, Vives' greatest *opus* and certainly one of the age's most remarkable works. [2]

Acknowledgments

I should like to express my gratitude to Ms. Susan Babbitt. The care and skill with which she read the manuscript markedly improved it. Needless to say, the responsibility for any shortcomings is mine and mine alone.

---

[2] For further details on Vives' life see: R.P. Adams, *The Better Part of Valor* (Seattle, 1962); A. Bonilla y San Martín, *Luis Vives y la filosofía del Renacimiento* (Madrid, 1903); C.G. Noreña, *Juan Luis Vives* (The Hague, 1970); F. Watson, *J.L. Vives: A Scholar of the Renaissance, 1492-1540* (London, 1930).

C hapter One: *Mimus Dei*

The *Fabula de homine*

SHORTLY AFTER HIS ARRIVAL IN LOUVAIN in the employ of Guillaume
de Croy, Vives published (1518) the *Fabula de homine*. From beginning
to end the *Fabula* was conceived and executed in theatrical terms.[1] The
goddess Juno, wishing to celebrate her birthday in a manner that would
suitably impress her fellow gods, asked Jupiter to create, after the
banquet, a setting (*amphitheatrum*) and characters similar to those customarily found in the plays performed by and for mortals. Jupiter
complied with her wish and promptly caused the universe to be, placing
in the uppermost level (the heavens) of this the requested amphitheater
the abode of the gods, which for this special occasion would double as the
gallery from which they could watch the forthcoming performance. At
the bottom the Father of the gods installed the earth, namely, the stage
on which the actors, meaning the animals and everything else dwelling
on this level of Creation, would play their respective parts for the benefit
of the audience.[2] And once the actors were arranged upon the stage
Jupiter, as supreme creator and omnipotent director of the play, addressed them, imparting strict instructions to the cast never to deviate in
the slightest from the prescribed script.[3] He then gave the signal and the
festivities began. Tragedies, comedies, satires, mimes, farces and other
such were performed with unparalleled skill, to the delight of the gods.
And among the crowd of actors none pleased the divine spectators more

---

[1] See M.L. Colish's splendid article, "Vives on Man's Nature," *Journal of the History of
Ideas* 23 (1962) 3-20. Particularly interesting are the parallels drawn between Vives'
Fabula and Pico's *Oration on the Dignity of Man*. It is worth mentioning that Stoics like
Epictetus and Marcus Aurelius also used the theater as a symbol for human life, an
important fact given the Stoic flavor of Vives' ethics.

[2] FH *Opera* IV 3. Page 387 of M. Lenkeith's English translation, in *The Renaissance
Philosophy of Man*, eds. E. Cassirer, P.O. Kristeller, J.H. Randall, Jr. (Chicago, 1956)
385-93.

[3] FH *Opera* IV 3. Lenkeith 388. This is certainly an important fact to bear in mind, for
it means that man, together with all the other characters who play out the drama of life,
is not absolutely free; rather, he is irrevocably bound to perform within the rigid
boundaries established by the eternal director.

than man; a fact that greatly gratified Jupiter, for He had made that supreme imitator (*humano archmimo*) after His own image.[4]

At an early stage, then, we are shown that obviously God and man enjoy an unequaled relationship, a unique bond that leads Vives to point out that there is far more to man than merely his particularly noteworthy histrionic skills; although, to be sure, these are themselves unique by virtue of the matchless qualities of the mask (the body) that makes them possible. He is, in other words, something other than just one more member, albeit an extraordinarily talented one, of an ensemble of performing animals, because man is in point of fact both peerless and special. The statement is noteworthy in that it carries with it implications that go well beyond what would seem to be its meaning after only a cursory glance; implications, it must be understood, that become fully explicit only after we make the acquaintance of Vives' later works. Indeed, man is something unique, but only in the sense that he is both more and less than the other animals performing in Jupiter's theater. He alone was created for a purpose higher than the mere physical existence that is the inescapable lot of all other creatures; he alone fell from grace upon his willful betrayal of that purpose; and he alone still holds within himself the choice, the potential, either to redeem himself (and thus become more than the other denizens of Creation) or to wallow endlessly (thereby sinking below the animals) in the consequences attendant to the catastrophe that was the result of his tragic miscalculation. This appraisal inevitably brings Vives to the conclusion that within the nature of the human being lie buried two contradictory facets mutually and eternally at war. And this fact, in turn, is responsible for the optimism/pessimism dialectic, which at every turn stalks the student of Vives' thought. We encounter, therefore, Vives the enthusiastic believer in man's redemptive potential, the thinker who fashions (by revealing God's plan for man) the institutional and cultural fabric—and the canon of conduct indispensable to its proper functioning and continued existence—needed by man to redeem himself. But we also meet Vives the seemingly incurable pessimist who, almost perversely, will systematically hold before man the reality of a creature who sooner or later manages to debase the bounty that his creative spirit has brought forth.

The assembled gods were themselves quick to recognize that there was something unique about man. They discerned in the being peering from behind the performer's mask, which at times tantalizingly seemed on the verge of falling off to reveal the entity hidden behind it, a

---

[4] Ibid, 4; Lenkeith 388.

Jupiter-like creature who participates in the Father's immortality and shares so completely in the wisdom, prudence, and memory divines that such gifts could not possibly have been bestowed upon him except by Jupiter Himself out of His own treasury and being.[5] Their judgment was soon proven right, for they were next treated to an astonishing performance by this actor who through his virtuosity unquestionably revealed himself as Jupiter's very own pantomimist. On the stage, then, man played role after role. He first became a plant, leading a meaningless life; then he changed into a succession of fierce beasts.[6] Next, he emerged as a prudent, just, sociable model of humanity capable of obeying and commanding, fully conscious of his social and political responsibilities and willing to discharge them to the fullest.[7] In a final display of versatility the masterful actor of the *Fabula* further surprised the dazzled gods by becoming (*angelus*) one of them.[8] And just as his performance was being greeted by deafening applause and Juno, at the request of her enthusiastic peers, was preparing to ask Jupiter leave to invite the sublime mime to join his divine admirers, man once more appeared on the stage, this time as Jupiter himself. And so astonishingly skillful was his latest characterization that the amazed gods thought at first that their Father had indeed compromised His dignity by mounting the stage; in fact, some among the lesser actors participating in the drama swore that the mime on scene was in fact none other than Jupiter, an error for which they paid dearly.[9]

Vives' tale, as it unfolds in the *Fabula*, is a sketchy but nonetheless faithful anticipation of what will later become his vision of mankind's historical development. Man as *planta* and, especially, as *belua* is living the early phases of his evolution; still in the grip of the passions un-

---

[5] Ibid. Lenkeith 388-389. Here is Vives at his most optimistic; a side that is one of the two pillars upon which his life's work rests. When at his best in his earthly performance, then, man is capable of demonstrating that supreme potential that can raise him to the level of the divine. "Epictetus (said Jupiter), if it were possible I would have made your body and your possessions...free and untrammelled. But as things are—never forget this—this body is not yours, it is but a clever mixture of clay. But since I could not make it free, I gave you a portion of our divinity, this faculty or impulse to act or not to act, of will to get and will to avoid." *The Discourses of Epictetus*, trans. G. Long (London, 1977) Book I Chapter I.

[6] FH *Opera* IV 4-5; Lenkeith 389.

[7] Ibid. Lenkeith 389.

[8] Ibid. Lenkeith 389.

[9] Ibid. Lenkeith 389.

chained by his rebellion, he has not yet found himself through self-knowledge. They are phases, again the second one in particular, historically equivalent to man in a state of nature, man not yet become a social animal, facing for the first time the consequences of his transgression. And in his present situation he can do nothing but live vegetatively/bestially. Man, in other words, deprived by sin of his earlier gifts has not yet begun to integrate himself into a social mode of life. Only with the coming of society, then, does man have a choice to become something other than equal to or less than the animals. But even then (and now we experience the obverse of Vives' optimism) the demons unleashed by the Fall never let go of man completely, so it will happen that time and again man, despite the protective cocoon of society, will find himself overwhelmed by them and will revert to the beast. Finally, the last metamorphosis transforms the *vir prudens* (and, of course, *angelicus*) into Godlike, endowing him with *divina prudentia*. But it is clear from the sequel that this transformation is neither endowed with any substance nor appropriate to the circumstances; indeed, the mirage wrought by man the mime is dispelled in short order. True, Vives grants that it lies within the power of man's own will to become plant, beast, man, or even to aspire to angelic nature, the last given the sanction of reality as man takes his rightful seat among the gods. But he cannot become God while on the earthly stage; indeed, his ambition to do so under circumstances when his efforts did not enjoy God's *imprimatur* was the beginning of all his misfortunes. In Vives we find none of Giovanni Pico's extravagant notions of human greatness. The Italian humanist seeks knowledge of God by means of philosophy and, in turn, the calming of the soul's discord through divine knowledge. On the contrary, man's greatness lies in his ability to achieve to perfection the limited goals open to him; he can become great in this world, the theater of the *Fabula*, through the power of his reason and the potential of his will, but not unqualifiedly great. His true eminence (or dignity, in humanist parlance) lies in a realm beyond reason where God's grace alone avails. Vives' will is indeed free, but it is not Pico's Pelagian will. Thirty years later and, perhaps fittingly, toward the end of his life Vives once again, this time in *De anima et vita* (1538), reminds us of this central theme of the *Fabula*. Reflecting on the soul in general, Vives observes that we would like to know its essence. Granting moreover that such knowledge lies beyond man's cognitive capacity, he nevertheless insists that inasmuch as it "partakes of the divine essence" and can therefore participate in the divine nature and become one with it, the human soul can be known and defined as "the spirit through which the body to which it is united lives; a spirit able to know and love God and to unite with Him in eternal beatitude." And just as the soul descended from God to the body, so, through divine knowledge and love, it can and must ascend from the body to God. Such, Vives now emphasizes, is the very process involved in the metaphor that we call life. "In the beginning, man's existence is that of a plant, next he lives an animal's life, and lastly a human being's. After further purification man, rising above earthly things, changes into an angel. Finally achieving union with God he becomes, after a fashion, God."[10] This progressive ascent to beatitude parallels Vives' own ascending hierarchy of knowledge: "from matter to the senses, from the senses to the imagination/fantasy, then to reason, and hence to the final stage: love."[11]

The gods, spectators to man's histrionics, soon realized that they had been duped. But the discovery did not dampen their enthusiasm; on the contrary, recognizing how the superb actor had misled them with his boundless talent into thinking that their Father had indeed mounted the stage, they redoubled their efforts to have man doff his mask and join them.[12] Jupiter graciously consented to his children's' request[13] and man, now divested of his theatrical costume, joined the audience and sprang one final surprise on his admirers, for it now stood revealed that without the professional mask his nature was the twin of the gods'.[14] It was moreover at this point that Mercury chose to make his own appearance, carrying the costumes that had been used at various times during the performance, man's among them. The gods eagerly seized the opportunity to take careful and detailed stock of the latter; a mask that in fact turned out to be nothing less than the human body itself, an instrument

---

[10] But, again, with the qualifications already stated.

[11] DAV II xii *Opera* III 388.

[12] FH *Opera* IV 5; Lenkeith 388-390. As Vives lists the various roles assumed by man on the stage he headlines each of them on the margins as plant (*planta*), beast (*belua*), man (*homo*), angel/god (*angelus*), God (*Deus*). So man's acting repertoire— meaning his potential, subject to the qualifications already outlined—ranges from the vegetative to the divine.

[13] But despite appearing merely to react to the gods' enthusiasm He had already decided that man would indeed be seated among the gods.

[14] Ibid. 6; Lenkeith 390. Notice, however, that before joining the gods man had to leave his mask--his body--behind; again the constant of Vives' thought: man cannot attain to that divinity--and all attendant privileges, such as wisdom--which is his inheritance in this existence.

perfectly designed to fulfill all the functions for which it was created.[15]
It contains a mind replete with deliberation, prudence, reason; a mind so
fertile indeed that it can bring forth incredible things, and it has in fact
created cities, domesticated animals, and invented the written and spoken
language. From it have moreover issued both religion and the knowledge
of God.[16] And that very mind (the mind, in short, that we have seen
above in *De anima*, capable of yielding the knowledge that will take man
from a vegetative state to the very doorstep of God Himself), which man
alone among the creatures of Creation possesses, is proof of his close
relation to the gods. But there is still more, because the many things that
the mind can bring, and has brought, forth would be of scant value if
man did not have an additional second faculty, memory, to preserve
them as if in an immense warehouse. And these two faculties, *mens* and
memoria, united yield foreknowledge (*providentia*), which in us is like
a spark struck from that divine *scientia* capable of perceiving the future
and present; a future and present, it will eventually transpire, that the
two aspects of Vivesian *prudentia* (moral philosophy and history) place
well within the reach of man.[17]

Such, in broad strokes, is the content of the *Fabula de homine*. As
I interpret this youthful essay on man Vives offers us a brief but
panoramic sketch, couched as a metaphor (functioning here as an
instrument to aid in the elucidation of a philosophical problem: the end
of man), of what in effect will be the aim and goal of his life's work: to
reveal and to explain the nature of God's plan for man; a plan whose
essential components—the nature and purpose of man; society as the
framework that makes possible the fulfillment of that purpose; the body
of knowledge (the "arts") available to man in his present state to make
the functioning of society possible; and the prudent man, the refined
product of a well-ordered society who is ready to become, through love,
what he once had the inherited right to be—we have briefly identified
in the preceding pages. Thus in a very real sense Vives' entire literary
production is itself the product, to use the theatrical terminology of the
Fabula, of his own performance in Jupiter's play. Because Vives does
indeed act a part in the piece authored, staged, and directed by the Father
of the gods. He is the experienced drama coach privy to one fundamental
fact unknown to the performer: God's original plan, ruined by sin, has

---

[15] Ibid. 6-7; Lenkeith 391.

[16] Ibid. 7.

[17] Ibid. Lenkeith 392.

been replaced by another centered about two divine provisions: (a) knowledge as the instrument to attain man's end, and (b) society: a drama coach undertaking to teach a naturally gifted but unskilled and inexperienced actor how to realize his own potential to the end of delivering, under the guidance of a script whose every nuance he must master, the supreme performance called for by the playwright, God. Or, abandoning now the language of the theater, Vives' commitment is one of Socratic dimensions: to teach man the art of living. To that end he must explain— and let us again remember that in this role Vives alone is privy both to God's new plan and man's end[18] and function in this his worldly existence—(1) the nature of man, how that nature came to be perverted by sin, and with what consequences; (2) the wherewithal left by God to man in his now fallen state to reach the end for which he was created; and (3) the behavioral structure that man must now invent to insure success in reaching that end. But although that structure, what we call society, must indeed be created by man, he is not completely free to build as he wishes. On the contrary, he is to carry out his mandatory task constrained by certain parameters. And those parameters, the very curriculum that, after the fashion of a Platonic myth enabling us to grasp certain abstract relations, the *Fabula* is intended to convey, must be singled out for special scrutiny. To begin with, man, the sublime player, has already fallen prey to original sin; he lives, in other words, the only life possible to a nature now tarnished and burdened with the consequences of a historical event of incalculable import—the Fall. Furthermore, his performance, while brilliantly versatile and eminently suited to man's present nature and condition, is nevertheless strictly regulated at all times by a divine playbook or plan written to guide man's steps in a world profoundly altered by his rebellion. Finally, the post-Fall world is such that the production demanded by the script cannot be a solo representation; man, in other words, cannot deliver the required performance singly and independently of his fellows, because the pristine

---

[18] In another very real sense Vives' commitment parallels Socrates': he must debunk the deceitful teachings of the sophists of his own day—and it is to be noted that the term "sophist" was generously applied by contemporary controversialists to describe their intellectual opponents. It is true that Vives enjoys a distinct advantage over Socrates. Whereas the latter sought to unravel the mystery of man's end and function, the former, by virtue of his Christian faith, knows that, specifically, the end of man is to prepare himself, in this life, for the beatitude to come. But the advantage is more apparent than real, for whether the object of the search is the end and function of man or how to prepare oneself for the life to come, the result is the same: the needed--and right— knowledge must be found.

individuality of yesterday was dealt a fatal blow at the hands of original sin becoming instead, as a result, the focal point of those unruly passions and ambition that eternally threaten to thwart man's best intentions.[19] He must, instead, act at all times as a member of an ensemble housed in a theater (physically defined in the *Fabula* by the stage where the drama unfolds) to be built by man[20] guided by a rigid blueprint etched in stone by the divine script and to function as the protective cocoon that defends him from the new and hostile environment where he cannot possibly survive in isolation. Let us now turn to Vives' self-appointed Socratic task and begin with the human condition.

The Human Condition

It is clear that there are two distinct, if related, natures to the creature whose theatrical exploits are the centerpiece of the *Fabula*. First and foremost, man is said to be endowed with a divine nature[21] akin to that of the gods' (or angels', if we move from a mythological to a Christian terminology); an inner essence that stands fully revealed only once, when as a reward for his virtuosity on the stage man is invited to seat himself among the gods. But beyond the simple fact of its existence we are told nothing in the *Fabula*; the play is of course not about man's divine essence, but concerns itself exclusively with the prowess of the other nature of the human mime, his mask. This is a point to be carefully remembered, for it will be a key argument of this discussion that Vives is not unduly concerned with man's divine nature. His writings are overwhelmingly aimed at man's human side, its weaknesses and its potential. In my view this concern issues into an ethical system (but-

---

[19] The point is well worth keeping in mind, because Vives has just set the stage for the individual-society dialectic that causes him to envision, as the goal to pursue, a society along the lines of More's Utopia; a collectivity, in other words, in which the individual is ruthlessly and enthusiastically subordinated to the whole. The idea, of course, is not new. The Spanish Scholastics themselves time and again argue that only within a wholesome body social can the individual find true fulfillment. But it is unlikely that Vitoria, Soto, or Suárez ever visualized the question in terms of More's Utopian communism (of goods, mind, and spirit). Vives, we shall later see, wholeheartedly agrees that nothing can be more threatening to that happiness the Utopian state brings to its citizens through the instrument of communism (Vives, however, rejects the communism of goods) than the deviationism of unruly individualism.

[20] And Vives' own function as a Socratic teacher is to show man in what way he can best fulfill that responsibility. His function, in other words, is to outline the ethical system that will work as the instrument for man to do that for which he was created.

[21] Ibid. 4, 6.

tressed by a reforming approach to education) that paves the way for man, within the domain defined by the shortcomings of human nature, to live happily. Given, however, the import that Machiavelli's dicta on princely rule would have on the political discourse of the late sixteenth century, an important caveat must be appended. I do not mean here the sole and full measure of Greek happiness. True, Vives, in the manner of St. Thomas before him, builds on the premises of classical, that is, Aristotelian, ethics to formulate a structure of mores enabling man, again within the limitations (no flights of fantasy à la Giovanni Pico for Vives)[22] imposed upon his freedom by his condition, to reach that manner of living (social living, of course) that will make him worthy of *felicitas*. But Vives' mores carry with them the added burden of revelation, and for that reason the statement made earlier concerning his determination to formulate a secular social ethic, namely, a canon to regulate the conduct of man's mask on stage, must be carefully qualified. We may indeed discourse on society and politics with all the realism inhering to the worldly obligations that in turn are part and parcel of the travail of every social being from prince to pauper,[23] but never to the exclusion of man's essence. Vives' social and political ethic, although aimed at the mask, is at all times and irrevocably informed by the essence. And such also, of course, would be the perspective of those who like Pedro de Rivadeneira pilloried Machiavelli as the inventor of an evil reason of state. They, like Vives in this instance, would find it necessary to root their socio-political discourse in firm philosophical ground. How

---

[22] The fundamental difference between Vives' *Fabula* and Pico's *Dignity* hinges on the question of knowledge. For Vives the skeptic, man cannot reach ultimate truths; he cannot, therefore, attain to the divine essence of his own self and must be content with expressing that fundamental yearning by mimicking the Father. Pico, on the other hand, thinks that man is perfectly capable, on his own, to reach his own divine nature and become one with God. What explains the two different postures is that there is no trace of skepticism in Pico. He is, after all, the author of *Disputationes cabbalistiae*, the Christian Cabalist who seeks to strengthen Ficino's natural magic with his own–albeit superficial and incomplete—understanding of Cabala. He is, in other words, one of the founders and most important exponents of Renaissance magic. And Renaissance magicians cannot possibly countenance the possibility that knowledge, any branch of knowledge, might be beyond man's rational possibilities.

[23] It is one of the cardinal objectives—his Socratic mission, as it were—of Vives to convince his audience that the reform of society cannot be solely carried out from above. Instead he insists that each and every member of society must shoulder his fair share of the burden.

dared, then, Machiavelli plead for the amoral prince without bothering, beforehand, to build an equivalent justificatory foundation? This perceived failure of the Florentine secretary doubtless accounts for the reputation for ignorance and incompetence that he enjoyed among his Spanish detractors, who accused him of subverting man's true ethico-political universe—namely, man's true and Christian reason of state. They did not, in other words, principally object to Machiavelli's pragmatism or even his willingness to explain (perhaps endorse?) the actions of an evil ruler on the grounds of expediency. What they furiously rejected, as Vives himself most assuredly would have, was the incomplete, flawed because one-dimensional, vision of man on which his appraisal of politics rested, a vision that simply had nothing to do with human reality. To speak of man's social and political side in a metaphysical vacuum is therefore pointless because it implies either denying or ignoring the fact that man is divine and human essence, inseparable make-believe and reality. The result in both cases is identical: to outline a defective, because incomplete, portrait of man. To discourse on man's make-believe activities, namely, those things leading to his social and political behavior, is to paint merely a landscape of means; for man's socio-political activities are precisely that, a means; a means to the end of attaining *felicitas*, the Aristotelian happiness raised to an additional, spiritual plane and simultaneously transformed into an end by Christianity. It is that end that truly counts in politics and political thinking, not Machiavelli's version of success as mere survival. And it is that end that is missing in the Machiavellian perspective.

It is therefore the mask, the human body, whose Protean activities monopolize (once the above caveat is in place) Vives' attention; and it is precisely in that mask where the two faculties, mind and memory, said to be the glory of man the performer (read man the social animal) are contained. Man, it therefore transpires so far, is both reality and make-believe, substance and appearance. But, what is the nature of that human reality? And moreover, what is the actual character and concrete purpose of man's play-acting? None of these questions is fully answered in the *Fabula*. And in fact the essay is just as reticent on the subject of man's mask/body as it is taciturn when it comes to elucidating the issue of his divine essence. We catch, it is true, tantalizing glimpses but, and this is the point, their true significance emerges whole only after the *Fabula* is examined and understood (fleshed-out, as it were) from the perspective afforded by a more complete acquaintance with Vives' views as they are developed in later works. To them we must now, and for what remains of this discussion, turn our attention. And interestingly enough the most rewarding way of learning what an older Vives thinks about the human condition is by asking him about man's divine essence. The answer, however, is neither direct nor explicit, because he insists that we cannot arrive at the truth concerning that essence. The essences of things may be objects of wonder, but they are not legitimate objects of knowledge. In Vives, therefore, there will always be an important ten-sion in man, a tension arising from the relation between man's essence (his reality) and his activity (his make-believe). The latter we can study, map out, and guide; the former is not up to us to fathom. Vives will encourage the pursuit of self-knowledge; but man cannot reach to the essence of the soul and therefore the author will not consider the searching for the essence (contemplation) as falling within the scope of self-knowledge. The intrinsic nature of the soul remains hidden from us. And nowhere does the author make the point—and a basic one it is, for it significantly shapes Vives' thought—than in *De anima* when discussing what the soul is.

The soul, "a principle present in all living things and which infuses all their actions with vigor,"[24] is the most excellent of all the "creatures" under the heavens. Both good and ill are rooted in it, and for that reason nothing is worthier of being known in depth. It is the source of all our actions; knowledge of it would enable us to purify it, so that those among our actions that like tiny brooks flow therefrom would themselves be pure and crystalline. He who has not explored his own self will hardly be in a position to act righteously.[25] And yet the fact remains that man cannot have direct knowledge of this fundamentally important fount of his actions, for it happens that "only through the effects that they cause can we hope to have knowledge of things that are neither accidents— that is, ascertainable by the senses—nor involved in them."[26] And the soul itself is but the outstanding example in this category of special things. "It must be known through its workings because it cannot be perceived by the senses. The latter, however, both internal and external, do in fact tell us about the workings of the soul....We care not to know what [*quid*] the soul is, only how [*qua*] it is and its workings. He who entreated us to know ourselves meant...[understanding] of the necessary actions conducive to the moderation of our mores [prudence], in order that

---

[24] DAV I xii *Opera* III 330.

[25] Ibid. Dedication.

[26] Ibid. I xii 300.

rejecting vice we may follow the path of virtue."[27] And so what started as an inquiry aimed at ascertaining the nature of man's divine essence has, by way of the example of the soul, issued into what is one of Vives' most sweeping and consistently-held views: certain areas of knowledge are inaccessible to man's unaided reason.[28] And, in turn, this important aspect of Vives' ideology of course leaves us no choice but to ask: why can man not reach such truths as the nature of the soul or, for that matter, his own divine essence? The answer to this question is precisely the object of the present inquiry. Let us begin by finding out (1) with what gifts was man endowed upon Creation by his Master, (2) his subsequent actions, (3) the consequences of those actions.

God, Vives tells us in *De subventione pauperum* (1526), favored man with what the author chooses to call "his humanity," conferring upon him excellent health, the sharpest intellect, and a virtuous soul.[29] In *De prima philosophia* (1531), however, he is considerably more explicit, itemizing the faculties given to man by his Creator; the suitable instruments, in other words, with which he could easily have reached the goal for which he was created. He was gifted with the physical strength necessary to assert his ascendancy over all other creatures in Creation; a quick wit, swiftly to peruse over matters both divine and mundane; judgment and deliberation, to estimate the value and assess the importance of the things that were his; a sense of equity and a will, to go after whatever belonged to and was part of the ultimate Good defined by God, a Good to which man owed allegiance and obedience.[30] And man was created in this fashion so that he could fulfill a destiny uniquely his: to restore what the rebellious angels had destroyed.[31] For what would seem to have been but a fleeting moment, then, man was given the mastery of nature. And he lived in perfect harmony with it, a state in sharp contrast with the condition of perpetual tension opposite a no longer familiar and benevolently pliant nature, that would shortly be his fate to endure. But

---

[27] Ibid. 332. This idea is a variation of what Plato says about God: we may only know that He is, not what He is.

[28] It is also the fateful step that will justify Vives in no longer speculating on the matter of man's divine essence, but concentrating instead on what is indeed accessible to him: his human nature. For it is only through human nature and its proper understanding and functioning and use that man will come into his own divine essence.

[29] DSP *Opera* IV 421.

[30] DPP I *Opera* III 189.

[31] DSP *Opera* IV 421.

man decided to separate himself from nature, of which he was in the end robbed by the devil, and soon enough his actions compromised the brilliant future promised by God's munificence. Not satisfied with his own humanity and the destiny planned for him by the Father, man aspired to the very divinity of his Creator.[32] And perhaps he might have reached that goal directly from the state of nature had he first endeavored to know himself (*si se cognoscens*) and had then, mistrusting his own powers, awaited the grace of God. Misled by the devil, however, he chose to soar to heights from which he was promptly precipitated.[33] Instead of securing what he arrogantly coveted, therefore, man lost in the bargain "much of what he had been given."[34] His body weakened and he became prey to infirmity; instead of master he was now the slave of those creatures that he had been meant to rule; his wit lost its pristine agility; his counsel clouded, and his will turned depraved. Man, in short, became a degenerate creature, a mere shadow of his former self. And the cause, it must be reiterated, is well known: that original sin that in effect separated man from his God.[35] Man's ambition and its sequel, disobedience, therefore subverted everything and destroyed the order that had thereto regulated his relations with God; the passions then ceased to obey reason and the soul lost its control over the body, thus plunging man into endless, eternal strife.[36]

---

[32] Ibid. 422.

[33] DTD I *Opera* V 201-202. In 1531 (Antwerp) Vives publishes what is unquestionably his *magnum opus*: *De disciplinis*. In its first edition this truly encyclopedic work was divided into three parts. The first—for which in this study we have reserved the title *De disciplinis*—goes under the name of *De corruptis artibus in universum* and is a scathing criticism of the way in which the disciplines ("arts")—from grammar to jurisprudence—foundation of western culture became vitiated at the hands of incompetent and unscrupulous teachers. Of all the great figures that are part and parcel of the rise and development of western civilization only Socrates appears to have escaped Vives' indignation. This destructive first part is followed by a second and constructive one: *De tradendis disciplinis*, where Vives outlines the educational structure capable of reforming learning- -I will often use Foster Watson's translation: *Vives on Education* (Cambridge, 1913). The third is divided into six semi- independent logical-metaphysical tracts. The last of these tracts is *De prima philosophia*.

[34] DSP *Opera* IV 422.

[35] DPP I *Opera* III 189.

[36] The perpetual turmoil that according to Vives characterizes human society is but a necessary reflection of man's own inner disorder. Which explains why Vives will strenuously demand that before man can hope to bring harmony into the social fabric he must, through self-knowledge, first put his own house in order; that is, bring the passions

What were the consequences of this catastrophe? Four are of preeminent import to us, the four consequences that together shape the framework to which we will in turn fasten what remains of this study of Vives' vision of society. First and at the most vital level, by subverting through disobedience the order that governed his kinship with God, man effected a scission in his own hitherto whole nature that separated, irrevocably, the human from the divine. Second, man's ability to acquire knowledge, to perceive the true essence of the world that surrounds him, became flawed. And it is plain that if in his new condition man has somehow lost his former, and presumably unlimited, access to all forms of knowledge, then (a) the direct path leading to the truth (*sapientia*) that might explain his own divine essence is closed, and (b) true knowledge of nature (*scientia*) remains equally inaccessible. Clearly, as Vives takes pains to emphasize in *De prima*, this consequence fundamentally defines the human condition as that of a fallen being: one denied both direct access to God and control of nature. Third, man lost that independence that, according to Vives, he might have enjoyed before the Fall. In other words, given humanity's present circumstances no man can preserve his individuality, in terms of either personal identity or freedom of action. Intruding now again for a brief moment into the realm of politics, we might ask: what implications does this carry for Vives' ruler? Even if one is unwilling to take at face value Burckhardt's famous Renaissance individualism it is impossible to deny that there is a strong dose of it in Machiavelli's prince; he is obviously a creature loose from all institutional moorings. Italy's institutional framework had collapsed and if a prince was to be successful at surviving he must do so alone and by the sheer power of his own personality. Whatever else he may be, then, Vives' ruler can evidently not be a Machiavellian prince. Whereas the Florentine secretary's vision of contemporary Italy is precisely what compelled him to conclude that both ruler and society can survive only through the sheer individual merit of the former, for Vives such an institutional collapse would irretrievably and automatically carry with it the ruin of any prince; a conclusion that serves to underline his anguish as he witnesses the society of his own age, the society mandated by God as the only means capable of affording man another chance, tottering at the edge of the abyss. In Vives' scheme of things such denouement is impossible; society itself is the last resort, and it came into being precisely because of the failure of man's individualism. And the reason for man's

---

back under the control of reason.

loss of his earlier individuality is clear: no man is now endowed with a mind keen enough and a body vigorous enough to enable him to survive as human beings ought to.[37] Fourth, fallen man, clearly conscious of both the shortcomings attendant to his new condition and existence and the weakness to which he had now become prey, planted the seeds of something radically novel and truly revolutionary: society. Or, to say it differently, human nature, newly arisen from the shambles of the old order, created, as the only means now left to fulfill man's destiny, its own domain and field of action, its own theater/stage. The first consequence we have studied in the preceding pages. We must now explore the remaining three, beginning with the nature and potential of whatever lights were left to fallen man by his Creator.

---

[37] DSP *Opera* IV 423. To defend himself from savage beasts man sought the help of other men (*De concordia et discordia in humano genere* I *Opera* V 198). As he elaborates in the following pages of *De concordia*—a treatise devoted to proving that enmity and war are the solvents of society's bonds—both what man is and what he is not show, unerringly, that he cannot live in isolation. From the shepherd to the king, no man is an island; in fact, the further he rises in status the more he needs the aid of others. Our own frailties and strengths, God's design, nature itself: all point in the direction of mutual need; a goal that cannot possibly be fulfilled save in the presence of concord. In pages to come we shall note the great significance that Vives attaches to *caritas* and *concordia*.

*C*hapter Two: God's First Provision

Knowledge

TO START WITH, why Vives should claim that God drafted a second plan for man becomes clear if we bear in mind that his foremost preoccupation is to ascertain whether, after the loss of the faculties originally set aside for him by God, man retained or forfeited his ability to reach the end for which he had been originally created. God, Vives concludes, although punishing His errant son with considerable severity, did not disinherit him. In other words, man still has at hand the means necessary to reach the sought-after end—"God left him as much light (*lumen*) as he needs to reach *felicitas*."[1] It is difficult to overestimate the significance of this short statement. For one thing, it clearly defines Vives' position in the controversy over the true value of human reason already raging in his own lifetime. Although a skeptic, Vives is no Lutheran fideist. Man's reason, albeit deeply flawed, is far more than a mere instrument useful only to discriminate in worldly matters. And even though in many respects his thought is far removed from Aquinas' views as well as those of his sixteenth-century Spanish disciples, at least in this one instance the humanist is as one with St. Thomas: (1) *ratio practica* does indeed enable man to fathom God's desires toward him, and (2) his will is sufficient to carry them out. For another, the statement reveals the nature of God's first provision for man and as such, in my view, inspires, guides, and justifies every aspect of Vives' social and political thought; because in effect that thought is nothing more than the author's way of externalizing his abiding concern with the entire spectrum of man's activities, his triumphs and his miseries, as he marches onward, his path lighted (although, and this is a crucial theme, dimly most of the way) by the *lumen* left to him by a wrathful but not wholly unsympathetic God, toward *felicitas*. In short, and reprising now the pedagogical theme already noted above while discussing the *Fabula*, Vives, the master educator, will teach his pupil how to use that *lumen* to arrive at the worldly *ars vivendi*,

---

[1] DPP I *Opera* III 190. And it is at this moment that the theatrical representation of the *Fabula* begins. That is, it is at this moment that man will have to earn his salvation in the theater of life; the representation, that is, that the *Fabula* is all about.

which in turn is the springboard to *felicitas*. Needless to say, then, it is of the utmost importance to understand precisely what the essence of that light is.

i

Vives divides the soul, that entity about which we can know the "how" but not the "what," according to the two fundamental objectives it was created to reach: a superior part (mind or rational soul), and an inferior part or will.[2] First, the will. Man was created for eternal happiness; for that reason he was given a faculty that enables him to aspire to the good, so that in the end he may achieve union with it. That faculty is known as the will. But it is not possible to desire that which is not known, and therefore there exists a second faculty, intelligence,[3] a faculty, we are told, of awesome breadth, for "it does not confine itself to the present, but it both remembers the past and conjectures about the future."[4] In *De prima* and in the broad context of a discussion of the *vires* (potencies) or faculties that, infused by God into the *materia*, give individual things their singular characteristics and the ability to accomplish the goals for which they were created, Vives remarks that in man "the will is mistress, reason is the adviser, and the *vires* constitute the body of servants. . . . The latter can neither command nor advise, and therefore under no circumstances should they ever be in control. . . . Reason leans toward the truth and shuns falsehood, while the will seeks the good and avoids evil; good and evil, of course, as understood by reason; it is enough that it judges something to be good or true."[5] As one might well expect, however, it is in *De anima* that the will receives its most extensive treatment. "All knowledge granted to man is in function of the good." The faculty that makes this possible is the will, free and a gift of God whereby He made us His sons instead of His slaves and placed in our hands the means of molding ourselves with the aid of His favor and grace. By the will we "desire what is good and detest what is evil, with reason as our guide." Reason, although guide to and teacher of the will, "is not its mistress," for the will is free and, even though compelled to

---

[2] DAV II *Opera* III 341. Strictly speaking, there are three faculties ("functions, forces, potencies") to the soul: *voluntas, intelligentia, memoria*. And God gifted man with those faculties more with the intention that they be put to use than that we should learn about them.

[3] Ibid.

[4] Ibid. I xi 330.

[5] DPP II *Opera* III 227.

obey reason, still retains its prerogative to opt for any of the courses of action submitted to it. Furthermore, the will may, inwardly, refuse to carry out what reason counsels; and outwardly as well, because although the will might inwardly have approved of a given course of action it may simultaneously prevent its actual execution in the outside world. Still, the will is not free to choose between two actions contrary to each other since, as a faculty, it is bound to the good under any guise. In other words, at any given moment the will is free to reject any particular action because it prefers to accept another, and also good, action as more suitable; what it cannot do is reject the former in hatred. Conversely, the will is not obligated to detest a given evil action offered to it; it is, however, compelled not to love it. There are two actions to the will: approval and disapproval. Approval, applicable to the good, engenders the actions seeking to bring about what is good; disapproval, pertaining to evil, provides what is needed to either dominate or flee from it.[6]

Now for the superior or rational part of the soul.[7] It is the "seat of knowledge," a subject studied by Vives in terms of (1) the objects that can be known by man, and (2) the actual process that issues into what we call knowledge. Let us begin with the first and introduce it with a definition of knowledge taken from the author's most celebrated educational treatise. "I call knowledge that which we receive through the senses when properly used. I also call knowledge the end to which we are led either by reasoning self-evident and so intimately tied to our being that no one can possibly question it, or by reasoning simply verisimilar formed by our personal experience or those of others and confirmed by our judgment based on the probable value of the conjecture; in the former case we speak of knowledge as firm and indubitable science, in the latter we speak of *opinio*."[8] But knowledge is not open-ended, for in its path stands nature.

---

[6] DAV II xi *Opera* III 382-83.

[7] It is where the entire process of knowing develops; within its confines Vives places the operational hierarchy of intellection, and in it we shall find the answer to the question: how does the human being acquire knowledge? Here is how the author, in descending order, summarizes the course of action leading to cognition-action. "The will neither seeks nor rejects anything without first having the judging faculty declare it good or bad; no judgment can be arrived at until it has compared that which has been brought to its attention. Nothing, furthermore, can be compared without having been reflected upon and recovered by the memory, which in turn will not store the image of the object unless it has previously been received and understood." Ibid. II 342.

[8] DTD I ii *Opera* VI 251; Watson 22. It is worth remembering in this context that for Aristotle knowledge and opinion are differentiated by their objects. The former is of the necessary, the latter of the contingent. It would seem that Aristotle understood

God's creation, nature, is according to Vives the sum total of the effects whose causes only He knows; God alone, then, can go beyond nature. "We must consider nature, put together and organized by God, exactly as we would an automatic machine; a clock, for instance, is the creation of an artificer who patiently and meticulously makes it in such a way that it will move by itself and by itself alone will be able to accomplish that for which it was created."[9] From the point of view of human cognition nature is both beginning and end; we have no way of transcending it. Thus armed with a definition of knowledge and the caveat that man cannot (rationally) transcend nature, we are now in a position to understand knowledge in terms of its objects. In *De anima* we are told that things are either "mutable and temporary" or "immutable and perpetual." To deal with the latter, man needs a "supernatural light"; the resulting knowledge Vives terms *sapientia*. This is evidently the knowledge of ultimate causes alluded to in *De prima* and is thus by definition outside the purview of the human intellect. Presumably, as hinted at in *De tradendis*, this is a fideistic manner of knowing solely achieved through *pietas*. In effect, then, sapiential knowledge, knowledge of the First Cause, is withdrawn from the realm of man's rational cognitive possibilities with the noteworthy result that Vives' knowledge will refer exclusively to what is both visible and invisible within the world of nature. What we, on the other hand, know of the former (the "mutable and temporary")—both singular objects and concepts, which although general are not invariably valid ("have no unbroken constancy") but admit of some certainty (a qualified, not absolute, certainty determined by probability: the son is loved by the mother, such illness is cured with this or that herb)—"Cicero has called the realm of *verisimilitudo* or *opinio*." It is of considerable interest to point out for future reference that within this domain Vives admits that there is a great

---

philosophical knowledge or science to be divided into three categories. Speculative or theoretical knowledge is true science or knowledge pursued for knowledge's own sake, and said (*Metaphysics* VI i-ii) to consist of three branches: mathematics, physics, theology or metaphysics (the loftiest of them all); non-speculative or practical knowledge, where the ultimate purpose is action at the conduct of human life; and poetical philosophy, its goal being not action but production (the making of useful objects), and its knowledge that of the rules or theory of art.

[9] DPP I *Opera* III 212. This is obviously an early version of the clock analogy so popular in the eighteenth century. The significant difference is that with the latter goes a confidence that man, with the aid of mathematics, is able to know the inner workings of the clock, whereas for Vives the first causes that explain those workings are beyond man's abilities to fathom.

difference between the individual and the general. "Whereas from the latter we can derive rules and precepts which, in turn, form both arts and disciplines, out of the former, as they are infinite and infinitely varied, we cannot, inasmuch as the human intellect is unable to apprehend that which is numberless, create either art or discipline." Clearly, the individual, "located in the outside world, we know by means of the senses." The general are created by reason out of the sense-observation of the former; they in turn become the inductive wherewithal that will make the arts possible. Finally, there exists a third cognitive category made up of that which within "mutable nature" is both perpetual and constant: "the things which we observe remaining always the same and in the same way—such as those in the heavens—and those in the sublunar world belonging to a given genus or *forma*." Of the latter we have a glimmer "infused in us by nature; many things in the sublunar world can be inferred by reason, and their knowledge is called *scientia*. There is, moreover, a vast reservoir of natural light which can be augmented by teaching, meditation, and exercise." Given the nature of the things themselves, therefore, there are three kinds of knowledge: *sapientia*, *opinio*, and *scientia*.[10]

ii

So much for knowledge structured in terms of the objects of cognition. But what of knowledge as a creation of the rational soul? Three basic steps are involved: external knowledge, internal knowledge, and reason—"our knowledge or judgment comes from the senses, the fantasy, the mind."[11] First, the senses. The very foundation of Vives' hierarchy of knowledge is eminently sensational ("we see only what the senses allow us to see"),[12] for at the simplest and most rudimentary level there lies the knowledge derived from the senses ("the earliest . . . from it derive all the other varieties of knowledge") when they apprehend that which is both real and present ("knowledge of things present"); if the observation of things by means of the senses becomes an often-repeated process it receives the name of experience.[13] The things known as a result of this

---

[10] DAV II ix *Opera* III 379.

[11] DPP I *Opera* III 194.

[12] Ibid. 196.

[13] Aristotle notes that there are different degrees of knowledge. Animals, he points out, are born with sense-perception, and some even have memory. "Accordingly the former are more intelligent and capable of learning than those which cannot remember." But only man has experience: "the numerous memories of the same things eventually produce

manner of simple perception are singular things, an important item to remember later, when judging Vives' empiricism, inasmuch as he has already said that individual things (and so experience alone) cannot lead to art. Strictly speaking, however, the senses do not yield knowledge of the things themselves but only of their "accidents." That which is hidden inside an object cannot be known except by its external manifestations, which are apprehended by the senses.[14] On how the impressions are caused upon the latter Vives is not clear. Plainly, they are actions at a distance and strictly one-directional, namely, from the observed object to the affected sense. On at least two occasions, however, he calls them motions. The senses, then, obviously give us a simplified version of singular, individual things; and *experientia* is the repeated interaction between the senses and single objects. But since that knowledge is not of the things themselves but of their appearances, it is imperative that we understand what Vives means by *accidentiae*. To that end we must now turn to *De prima*. God created all things; from Him they received their being (*ens*), which is like an image reflecting God's own reality. As there is nothing above the *ens*, nothing can be beyond it. The name *ens* derives from "essence," while the word for "thing" (*res*) is generic for being, even though other singular meanings have been attached to it.[15] The following are the *formae* or *modi* of *ens*: the sensible, covering that which we name senses, "as we call armed the man bearing arms"; the *forma* of the *ens* itself; the *forma*, *species*, *facies*, or principles, source of all the actions of the *ens*; the *vires* or faculties emanating from the principle; the *moles* or *materia*, passive and spread throughout the universe, the receptacle that holds the *vires*. The diversity of being derives not from the *materia*, which

---

the effect of a single experience." *Metaphysics* I i 980 2-3, 981a. The Loeb Classical Library, trans. H. Tredennick (2 vols., Cambridge, Mass., 1961). To have merely experience means "to have a judgment that when Callias was suffering from this or that disease this or that benefited him, and similarly with Socrates and various other individuals." *Metaphysics* I i 981a 6. Through experience, then, we acquire, without knowing the reasons, a rule of practice. The Aristotelian man of experience, so akin to Bacon's proverbial ant, when framed against the classical and early modern medical traditions, will be the source for that typical *empírico* who became such a controversial symbol in the debate that divided seventeenth-century Spanish political thinking.

[14] DAV I ix *Opera* III 321.

[15] DPP I *Opera* III 197-99. In *De anima* Vives indicated that "to inert matter God added those *affectiones* or efficient causes which we have come to call species or forms. . . .Each, according to its own way and possibilities, shares in the divine magnificence; we may conceive them as rays emanating from His eternal and infinite light." DAV I xii *Opera* III 332-33.

is uniformly the same throughout, but from the *forma*. *Materia* can hold any *forma*.[16] Since in all natural things matter is identical the differences among them cannot originate in the latter, but in their own *vires*. For example, if *materia* is infused with the faculty of growing leaves, flowers, and fruits, we call it a tree; if the latter is low, green, red, soft, thorny, we use precisely those names that indicate the diversity of trees, not their essence. And these *modi* or *affectiones* are precisely what we call *accidentiae*. The accidents do not change the essence or *substantia* of things. They adhere to the substance and may even create other accidents. But at the foundation of it all lies the substance. Substance and accidents are so entwined that in nature there is neither accident without substance nor substance without accident. "The discussions about substance and accident have become dominated by passion instead of science, although it is clear that in this business even the latter would be of little avail, because substance and accident are so closely bound together that they cannot be told apart either by sense or thought. The reason is that our minds, locked up in our bodies, cannot reach the *imago* of naked substance stripped of its accidents."[17]

Second, the fantasy. We have already seen how all sensible things are apprehended by the senses, the source of external, immediate knowledge. But there is a second species of knowledge, internal knowledge (*cognitio interiore*), formed by an additional set of faculties within the soul. "Besides the external knowledge of these objects present it is obvious that there is another knowledge, that of absent things; for not only in dreams do we see many things but while awake, when no sensorial organ is at work, we still mull over in our thoughts what we have seen, heard, tasted, touched, and smelled earlier."[18] Therefore, just as we know that the human body has organs to receive, hold, transform, distribute, and use food, so the images external objects imprint in the senses are transmitted to the imaginative faculty or imagination. These impressions are then stored in a second faculty, memory. A third faculty, fantasy (*phantasia*), elaborates and refines them. Finally, an estimative faculty creates, on the basis of sensible perceptions, the act of judging—to determine whether they are profitable or damaging.[19] The imagination is to the soul what the eyes are to the body—"doubtless there exists a certain analogy between the

---

[16] DPP I *Opera* III 196.

[17] Ibid. This is one of the most accomplished statements of Vives' skepticism.

[18] DAV I x *Opera* III 326.

[19] Ibid. 328.

internal and external senses." The fantasy gathers the simple data received by the imaginative and puts them together into more complex arrangements. Inasmuch as "many liken the imagination to the fantasy, for they consider the function of both to be identical," Vives warns the reader that often he will use them interchangeably. Since material things are in truth but simulacra of the spiritual (themselves but images of God)—in other words, the accidents/essence mentioned earlier—none should be surprised to learn that the latter can be inferred, by means of the imagination-fantasy, from the former.[20] How much can Vives' fantasy, by itself and only with the evidence gleaned by the senses, know? It composes an image of that which is the object source of the sensation (by the form, color, size it knows the lion); out of the perceived "sensible exterior" it knows the proper *actio* of the object (dog, sheep) and the form (fire) from its action (heat). All such are called phantasms; man shares with the animals the ability to know them and, involving as they do only accidents, they are at times the source of error.[21] Now, among the animals the sum total of the internal and external faculties embodies the whole of their possibilities as sentient beings. In man, on the other hand, they are but the means to an end which only the mind can grasp; they are, in short, the instruments of man's rational life. With the aid of the data so far made available by the phantasms, the fantasy, now supported by *iudicium*,[22] infers by means of simple arguments new knowledge and comes to know "the effects from the cause, the cause from its effect, the end from the action, the action from the instruments; in brief, everything that is usually investigated and determined in the realm of outward nature by means of the subject-matter which is contained in any art."[23] But now we reach an impasse that underscores the limitations of the fantasy.

Third, the mind. Knowledge, then, is entirely constructed from actions set up from the outside or from experiences made possible by the memory. But the body can also generate its own phantasms; the fantasy is the begetting instrument ("knowledge of incorporeal things"). This is

---

[20] Ibid. 327.

[21] DPP I *Opera* III 195.

[22] DAV II v *Opera* III 362. *Iudicium*, "a manner of censoring reason and its conclusions . . . it is a norm . . . as soon as reason has carried out its task, *censura* (*censura veri* or dialectic) intervenes and judges, approving or disapproving of the results. . . . Just as reason uses dialectical formulas *quae sunt de probabilitate*, judgment's are *quae de argumentatione*. This very source, given the darkness of our minds, is responsible for the frequent errors made by *iudicium*." See below, Chapter Four.

[23] DPP I *Opera* III 195.

what happens. If the object is such that it cannot be known by the senses, the fantasy can hardly lift its image from what lies stored in the memory ("the faculty of the soul which keeps in mind that which has come to be known through one or another of the internal or external senses") inasmuch as no record of the object exists. But all is not yet lost. The mind lends a helping hand and infers that whose being or non-being cannot be reached by the senses, while the fantasy, "drawing on known things, invents an image of the object in question; as when it presents our minds with an image of God, the angels or other analogous realities."[24] The mind-fantasy collaboration, however, is not entirely a happy marriage. The fundamental difficulty lies with the fantasy itself. As a faculty responsible for elaborating internal knowledge, the fantasy is in bondage to the flesh and cannot therefore perceive clearly "the essence contained within that which is material"; in fact, it endeavors "to drag the mind toward the material." In other words, the accidents exercise a strong diversionary influence on the fantasy. For its part the mind resists, because it aims at supreme objectives understood by neither the fantasy itself nor any of the senses, meaning of course that the mind searches for the substance beyond the accidents.[25] The impasse is fortunately resolved by reason, the instrument chosen by the mind to overcome the obstacle created by the fantasy's very nature. Reason promptly goes to work on the rough image created by the fantasy and, insofar as possible, removes its fantasy-inherited character. Such, Vives claims, is the origin of universals (which means that in the domain of *opinio* internal knowledge is what generates the general concepts to be used as platform for the formulation of universals), phantasms of the mind that exist neither in nature nor in the imagination alone, for solely to the mind belongs the realm of knowledge of spiritual things (*intelligentia rerum spiritualium*).[26]

Reason: Practical and Speculative

Does the mind, "leaning on the knowledge created by the imagination-fantasy and thus rising toward knowledge of the spiritual," succeed? Herein lies the crux of Vives' scheme, the very problem with which he repeatedly tries to come to grips. We know that man cannot know the ultimate truths involved in *sapientia*. Can we, insofar as the

---

[24] DAV II i *Opera* III 344.

[25] Ibid. I xi 329.

[26] Ibid. II i 344.

natural world is concerned, learn of the less exalted but nevertheless universal truths about it? At this point Vives harbors serious doubts that the human mind is capable of accomplishing even this lesser feat. The mind "concludes that confined to this dark prison of the flesh it is kept from knowing many things, and that it can neither see nor understand clearly what it wants to know, namely, the essence or substance" hidden by the accidents.[27] If such is the limitation imposed by nature on the human mind, a comparable restriction must surely be operating on the instrument, reason. Man's cognitive ability, beyond the external and internal knowledge supplied by senses and fantasy, rests therefore squarely on an instrument whose potential is severely circumscribed from the start. Under the circumstances, it is obvious that we need to know precisely what reason is and what kind of knowledge it is capable of offering man.

i

First, some preliminary observations. Generally speaking, reason is a process or function (not a faculty) made available to man "in order that he may search for the good which shall be later adopted by the will."[28] From the start, it should be noted, reason is firmly set upon a utilitarian foundation, which is why, in the event, practical reason shall come to dominate and even monopolize the idea of reason. More specifically, reason ("a form of *discursus*") is the record left by a process of comparison as it "marches on from one thing to another, from several to one or many," denying what is false and affirming what is true. Moving from accidents to substance, then, reason extracts from concrete and obvious things learned by the senses and elaborated upon by the fantasy what is obscure and incorporeal, and makes possible the transition from the particular to the general, from the effects to the causes themselves, or, given Vives' own doubts on the subject, to how many of the causes the human mind is capable of apprehending. The fantasy is unable to put together an image that, directly or indirectly, does not have its origin in evidence provided by the senses. Reason, on the other hand, merely skims over the surface of the images; it takes nothing from the accidents of individual things. On the contrary, it avoids them altogether for fear of entangling itself in them. The senses serve the imagination, which in turn feeds the fantasy. Reason uses all of them but becomes enmeshed in none. The senses see the shadows of things; the imagination-fantasy grasps their

---

[27] Ibid. I xi 329.

[28] Ibid. II iv 355.

image; reason perceives the *forma* and the *vires*.[29] Vives next goes on to explain how reason epitomizes the very fundamental limitation that separates man from his Creator. "To God . . . the causes [the spiritual, images of God] are better and earlier known than the effects [simulacra of spiritual things] themselves, the general of things than their particulars. Men, on the other hand, as they know and infer are forced to follow the path of nature. This path is in reality not one but three, as some men are noted for their practical ability, others by a gift which inclines them toward speculation, while still others, dull of wit, are driven by a compulsion to follow the way of the senses."[30] The "path of nature" means of course the line of thinking whereby man's natural reason moves, inductively, from "the singular to the universal, the material to the spiritual, the effects to the causes, the obvious to the hidden." Such is indeed the very essence of reasoning. And having broadly defined reason and pointed out its end, Vives then proceeds to explain its inner complexities. His point of departure is the very definition of reason mentioned earlier: reason as an instrument given to man that he may search for the good to be passed on to the will. Among the animals the good is in plain sight, in their bodies; they have therefore little difficulty in seeking and finding it. But in man the good is hidden in his intelligence, to be ferreted out by reason. Furthermore, man's reason not only leads to the good but also discriminates between what is true and what is false. And this crucial characteristic unique to man's reason forces it to move in two directions leading to the fulfillment of two distinct goals. The statement is worth underlining (now and later), for it is an admission that the human being will often be forced to follow, simultaneously, two paths that sooner or later are bound to be in mutual conflict: contemplation and activity. It is a dilemma that Vives, believing that intellectual knowledge is neither hopeless nor its pursuit wholly futile, will eventually have to face. For the time being, however, he is more interested in firmly establishing the role played by reason and how it fits within the total

---

[29] Ibid. 354. We are back to the idea of fantasy as slave to the body and reason as its liberator. Taken in a vacuum the result is misleading as, ultimately, reason also depends on the senses and, therefore, despite Vives' deceptive premise (at least here, although elsewhere he clearly qualifies his statements), reason is also, but indirectly, bound to the body—"the dark cell of the mind." This is but another instance of Vives' failure to approach systematically the problem of human knowing. When defining the powers of reason he gives every indication that reason can penetrate to first principles; in practice, however, he behaves on the basis of a pessimistic view of the rational powers of man and of his ability to perform what appears to have been theoretically granted.

[30] Ibid. 355.

framework of human nature.

It seems that at one time man had been endowed with the divine quality that alone can reveal directly to the mind that which is universal—"certain norms and inclinations leading to truth and the good." There was a time, in other words, when man could simultaneously search for and reach both truth and the good. But he lost that quality and in practice "sin shrouds our minds in dense fog which perverts those instinctive norms toward rectitude given to man by God." Ignorance (meaning our inability fully to understand, and therefore work effectively with, God's norms) is responsible for the many errors committed as we judge "from those generalities on species and individual things." The opportunity to start out deductively, it would appear, was naturally passed on to us by God; man frittered it away, and what remains is the ability to go in the opposite direction, upward, through induction—"the path of nature." Enough of the original light remains in him, however, "a species of intellectual light or judgment," to enable man to garner, without assistance from either teachers (meaning authority) or experience, straight from nature itself, information that invariably, either directly or indirectly, points toward what is good and true; in other words, natural reason inductively applied. In short, man can still hope to learn the universal norms (rules not necessarily to be identified with knowledge of causes; a word of caution that will acquire its full meaning when we discuss the arts), which his own foolishness caused him to lose, and, proceeding deductively, move from them to the singular and particular.[31]

The essential mechanism that at bottom makes possible the rational activity proposed by Vives is what he calls the *anticipationes seu informationes naturales* (or *a priori* subjective forms). Given his Aristotelian assumption that all knowledge originates with the senses, Vives could hardly subscribe to the theory of innate ideas. Nevertheless, he believes in the existence of an inner "intellectual light" (to be distinguished from the "supernatural light," *pietas*, responsible for *sapientia*), which directly or indirectly points the way toward what is true and what is good. He holds that upon creation "our intelligence was endowed with an inclination toward that which is true; a practical result of this propensity was that the intellect received also certain canons or formulas which might well be said to be the seeds of all disciplines . . . in the mind of every man there lie planted principles which are the origin of the arts, wisdom, and all science. It follows that we are born apt for everything; that there is neither art nor discipline of which our mind cannot show at

---

[31] Ibid. 355-56.

least traces, however rough and imperfect at first, that could not eventually be perfected through study and practice." This is the basic premise, of clear Platonic vintage, that enables Vives to bridge the gap between the sensory and intellectual realms. Naturally enough, "some men, given the nature of their intellects, derive by this means norms which are both more numerous and certain than those ascertained by others."[32] Nevertheless, in all cases the norms or rules thus acquired can be further strengthened through practice, examination, study, and meditation.[33] This last proviso, as Vives himself hastens to add, is of some import, for all of what has been said above pertains to "knowledge of things found in nature; the others, those invented by man, cannot be learned without teachers; such is the case with languages."[34] Speech and the cult of God, for instance, are natural activities; but to speak Greek or to worship God in a given manner are human creations. In *De prima* Vives calls this species of knowledge "art and industry." "This reason, when one wishes to apply it to something . . . frequently makes provisions for both the goal to be attained and the means to be used to reach it."[35] With this we clearly have reached the point where it will be necessary to inquire into the kinds of reason envisioned by Vives.

First, there is a practical reason (*ratio practica*) whose aim is the good and that leads to the will. Some men function best as they obey the call to action; their instrument for learning how to channel that action to the good is *experientia*. Among them Vives recognizes two groups: one, men who apply their talents to the good and whose distinguishing trait is *prudentia*; another, those who employ them in function of the things that are useful to life, their singular characteristic being *ars*, although they too need experience because "as the expert acts with greater self-assurance

---

[32] "Reason is partly illumined by an innate light, though not in equal measure in all." Erasmus, "The Free Will," in *Discourse on Free Will*, trans. E.F. Winter (New York, 1961) 23. The rational inequality of man, as strong a view in humanism as it was in the Aristotelian tradition, plays an important role in the attitude of some Spanish intellectuals, notably Juan Ginés de Sepúlveda, toward the American Indians and their position in the expanded commonwealth created by the discovery of America. See my "Juan Ginés de Sepúlveda on the Nature of the American Indians," *The Americas* XXXI (April, 1975) 4: 434-51.

[33] DAV II iv *Opera* III 356. On the question of the *anticipationes naturales*, see the first book of Bacon's *Novum organon*. Vives is giving us here the classic version of humanist education: nature, art, and habit produce the finished product.

[34] Ibid. 357.

[35] DPP II *Opera* III 227.

than the sage, *scientia* alone is not enough to make either prudence or art."[36] The cognitive realm of practical reason is *opinio*, knowledge of what in nature is variable, be it singular objects or general concepts. Man, however, likes to imitate nature, and so when our mind excogitates or invents what it would do to accomplish a given end, it also searches for the suitable instruments, and finally puts them to use in the operation that creates the intended *opus*. The things in this fashion created (a form of knowledge invented by the mind) embrace the arts and disciplines, private and public administration, geometry, arithmetic, and music. The more the mind is sharpened by experience, of course, the greater the knowledge thus created.[37] Second, we have speculative reason (*ratio speculativa*): its end is truth, and its practitioners are men who think better about what is true than they do about what ought to be done. There are in turn two kinds of speculative reasoning. One, *ratio speculativa inferior* (strictly speaking, understanding or *mens*), operates on perceptions transmitted by the senses and/or elaborated by the imagination/fantasy, and it is to all appearances the sphere of knowledge derived from things that in the sublunar world of nature are unchanging (*scientia*). The other, *ratio speculativa superior*, acts on concepts both absolute and holden, higher than the objects of *scientia*, and presumably constitutes the realm of *sapientia*.[38] The operation of the *ratio speculativa inferior* Vives explains as follows. The mind acquires further knowledge, beyond that generated by the imagination/fantasy, when, "boldly and by any and all means direct or indirect, it rises above the senses and discovers not only that something is but the reason for its being or non-being as well. To this category of knowledge belong God, the angels, demons, the soul, immortality, virtue, vice, science, prudence, happiness and all the others that do not fall under the influence of the senses"; namely, immaterial and spiritual things ("they proceed from nature, but they depend on us and without us they would be meaningless"), meaning that they rest on the foundation of nature and are not the sole creation of our intellect or our actions.[39]

Vives soon makes practical reason the sole heir to the definition cited earlier. It is now practical reason that must accomplish the task of

---

[36] DAV II iv *Opera* III 355.

[37] DPP I *Opera* III 195.

[38] DAV II iv *Opera* III 355.

[39] DPP I *Opera* III. In addition Vives speaks of two more cognitive categories involving (1) fictional things exclusively created by us (honor, calamity) and endowed with a reality given to them by our minds alone; and (2) things also imagined by us but totally devoid of any reality (centaurs).

creating the wherewithal needed by the will; a clear intimation of how
much practical reason will come to dominate his thinking. Unlike
speculative reason, *ratio practica* is not an end unto itself; it rather exists
to serve the will and its end, the good. Up to a point, it follows from what
has just been explained, speculative reason ("its end is truth") and practical
reason ("its end is the good") might be said to move together, both fed by
the intellect in turn fueled by the impressions received by the senses. But
a crossroads is soon reached when speculative reason, having fulfilled itself
and yearning to enjoy truth, settles into a contemplative mode, the
reward for its intellectual efforts. Practical reason (or reason now become
practical), on the other hand, moves on, but since it too has gone as far as
knowledge intellectually derived will allow, it must change into a
different mode; not, however, into a contemplative one but into a
learning mode intimately bound to experience. In other words, to be
practically effective, reason (hitherto it has been neither speculative nor
practical, but both) has to become practical reason, because neither
prudence nor art will be attained unless intellectually-derived knowledge
is complemented by experience. *Scientia, ars, prudentia*: such is the
heritage of reason and the magical triad framework for Vives' scheme of
things. *Scientia*, although failing to fulfill the kind of destiny reserved for
it by Aristotle,[40] serves as platform for *ars* (the mainstay of the system),

---

[40] Science is the highest rung in Aristotle's ladder of knowledge. Sense-perception cannot
be regarded as wisdom, even though the senses give us the most accurate knowledge of
particulars; the reason is that they do not tell us the "why" of anything—why the fire is
hot—they only say "that" it is hot. "At first the inventor of any art which went further
than the ordinary sensations was admired by his fellow-men, not merely because some of
his inventions were useful but as being a wise and superior person. And as more and more
arts were discovered, some relating to the necessities and some to the pastime of life, the
inventions of the latter were always considered wiser than those of the former, because
their branches of knowledge did not aim at utility. Hence when all the discoveries of this
kind were fully developed the sciences which relate neither to pleasure nor yet to the
necessities of life were invented." *Metaphysics* I i 981b 14-17. It is in the "theoretical kinds
of knowledge," Aristotle points out, that we find most about the nature of wisdom,
knowledge about certain principles and causes. But these principles and causes must be,
respectively, first and universal; and so certain characteristics attach to "wisdom and the
wise" that derive from the knowledge associated with the latter. It is knowledge at its
most comprehensive; knowledge, moreover, whose objects, by reason of their very
highest universality, are also farthest removed from the senses and on the whole the
hardest for man to know; knowledge also which is the most precise because "the most
exact of the sciences are those which are most concerned with the first principles, for
those which are based on fewer principles are more exact than those which include
additional principles," and the most instructive, "for it is through these [first principles]
and from there that other things come to be known, and not these through the particulars

which itself fed by *scientia* in turn feeds *prudentia*—the ultimate goal. Any man aspiring to the status of *vir prudens* must rise through the cognitive hierarchy created by them; and for that reason much of what remains of this monograph is in a very real sense an exercise in unraveling their operational workings as understood by Vives. It is important, finally and before proceeding to our next topic, that we place what has been said so far within a framework capable of affording us the perspective needed to discover how Vives' work eventually issues into a scheme centered about the theme of prudence, itself the main mooring mast of his social and political thinking. To that end I will reiterate ideas that not only have already been explained but will again be revisited in chapters to come. Granted that thereby I may now, and later, incur the risk of being repetitious to the point of tediousness. Still, given Vives' own practice of grounding, invariably and in every individual instance, his approach to the different themes discussed in this monograph on those ideas, the risk is not only justifiable but unavoidable.

ii

Natural reason, which we have seen Vives divide into practical and speculative, was given to man by God in the beginning in order to enable him to reach the intrinsic goal that alone justifies his earthly existence; it was, in other words, the guide intended to point the way toward salvation. With its aid man, after penetrating to the most intimate recess of nature, would have been in a position to solve the riddle of his creation; and, of course, his divine nature. There was a time, then, when reason[41] might have opened man's path to God; a time, in short, when the *theologia gloriae* worked. But man's misconduct and malice forever thwarted the calculations implicit in this original master plan, and so his

---

which fall under them." *Metaphysics* I ii 982ab 5-7. This is the knowledge or science that Aristotle calls "supreme." This, "the first philosophy," the theology seeking after Being as being, desirable for its own sake, had its inception in early man's wonder about the world. And "he who wonders and is perplexed feels that he is ignorant . . . therefore if it was to escape ignorance that men studied philosophy, it is obvious that they pursued science for the sake of knowledge, and not for any practical utility . . . just as we call a man independent who exists for himself and not for another, so we call this the only independent science, since it alone exists for itself." *Metaphysics* I ii 982b 10-12 margin. Metaphysics, it follows, is wisdom, and its practitioner is the man who seeks knowledge, and for its own sake, of the ultimate nature of reality—"It is the most divine science, and although the least necessary, the most excellent." *Metaphysics* I ii 983a 14-15 margin.

[41] Or, more accurately, *ratio speculativa* in both its superior and inferior guises.

natural reason became hopelessly inadequate to the task.[42] Consequently, the *sapientia* or vision of the First Cause that once could be reached through *ratio* is today accessible by way of *pietas* alone;[43] in a sense Vives' own equivalent of Luther's *theologia crucis*. And with his ability to perceive (rationally) the First Cause gone, man next sought to go beyond nature, God's image, to an understanding[44] of the first causes that explain it. He hoped in this fashion at least to master a species of knowledge, *scientia*, located but one rung below *sapientia* in the hierarchy of knowledge. But that, too, soon proved to be beyond the powers of man, for it would seem that *ratio speculativa*, both superior and inferior, was damaged beyond repair by his rebellion. In short, in his fallen state, both knowledge of God and knowledge of first principles lie beyond the rational reach of man. By undermining the power of speculative reason to offer knowledge of the First Cause and of first causes (although *ratio speculativa inferior* does have an important role to play; one we shall presently have occasion to recall again), Vives has therefore placed both wisdom and science beyond man's rational ken. Unable to make either *scientia* or *sapientia* his, what is there left that man can effectively know? And, indeed, is that problematic knowledge that might truly be his, sufficient to illuminate his path toward *felicitas*? The answer to those two related questions must be found by returning to the *lumen* mentioned before and explaining its nature.

According to Vives, God had of course foreseen man's error and his subsequent failure to reach his ultimate objective directly, that is, through

---

[42] Man in the state of nature is man whose natural reason can accomplish everything he needs. But man in this state of nature perished with original sin. If we persist in considering, after the Fall, that man remains in a state of nature what we have is no longer man with a powerful natural reason but man with a flawed natural reason, which is no longer able to give him, by itself, what it could earlier. If man is to live in that new state of nature guided alone by his flawed natural reason, he will live like a beast. Man in the "new" state of nature, therefore, lives in a state of brutality. To climb out of it he needs the aid of his fellows and the creation of society.

[43] Man desires a participation in the divine nature. "Wherefore, since that is the perfection of man's nature, and the consummation of all its parts; and since piety is the only way of perfecting man, and accomplishing the end for which he was formed, therefore piety is of all things the only thing necessary." DTD I ii *Opera* VI 248; Watson 18. Compare this with Aristotle's definition of metaphysical knowledge cited earlier above.

[44] Man cannot understand nature. Descartes' premise is therefore false. But man, guided by the invisible secular hand of Providence (in the guise of *pietas* or religion—a natural creation of man) has created society. Society, therefore, can be known to man, as Vives demonstrates in *De disciplinis*.

ratio. And since it was not His intention to abandon His rebellious son, God now devised the means necessary to afford man a new opportunity (but following a more difficult and indirect path).[45] The first step taken by God was to endow him with an "intellectual light," which is in effect man's *ratio practica.* And Vives' fundamental argument, which radically separates him from St. Augustine and contemporary Protestants and in effect makes him into an optimist cloaked in gloomy pessimism, is precisely that man can reach eternal *felicitas*—his God-given inheritance—by way of an indirect path which, opened to him by practical reason, first leads to *bonitas.* In other words, it is only in the domain of *opinio* that man's faculties (or, more accurately, what under present conditions remains of them) function to perfection (they are, in other words, the mask of the *Fabula*) offering him, if not absolute certainty, at least *verisimilitudo.*[46] Reason, although in its present state very much removed from the original, is never seen by Vives as so depraved that it cannot generate the necessary norms to guide man in his search for the objective that fulfills his earthly existence. The loss has been great indeed but "the human mind has not become so dull and blunted as to be unable to discern the truth to the degree suitable to the needs of mankind."[47] In short, even though at the expense of considerable effort and toil on our part, God has nonetheless left us with the needed wherewithal to protect our lives and to bring to fruition the design the divine will has seen fit to project for humanity.[48] In fact, Vives additionally insists, there has never existed a nation so dull or obtuse, or an age so blind, as to have been ignorant of the moral principles which, if put into effect, would have led to happiness.[49] Considering all this Vives does not hesitate to conclude that in spite of all our numerous afflictions "we did not suffer the slightest setback in what concerns reaching that perfection which results from achieving the proposed end." Clearly, then, God's first provision obviously answers the question raised earlier relating to man's ability, after the Fall, to reach *felicitas.* Vives, however, cautions

---

[45] The heart of Vives' posture is to convince man that there is no reason to surrender to despair. However, what heretofore was easily and directly accessible must now be gained in an indirect way implying effort and the need to overcome numerous obstacles. How to travel that arduous road successfully is precisely what Vives wishes to show.

[46] See the *Fabula*, as Vives describes how well-suited the human "mask" is to its task.

[47] DPP I *Opera* III 185.

[48] Ibid. 190.

[49] Ibid

that this already toilsome path is made even more arduous by an additional difficulty, a difficulty, as we shall eventually see, largely responsible for the defilement of society. We know of course that practical reason is the instrument given to man in order to enable him, through *prudentia*, to reach that goal, *bonitas*, which once transmitted to the will and turned into *actio* is his ultimate goal in this existence. But it must be remembered that *ratio practica* is part of a larger whole, *ratio*, and that the latter, in addition to leading to that goal (via practical reason), also pretends (by means of *ratio speculativa* and despite the fact, plainly obvious but still stubbornly ignored by many men, that the Fall deprived it of its former keenness) to discriminate between what is true and what is false. And this important fact explains why man is eternally the victim of his own nature, a nature that compels him to follow, simultaneously, two mutually opposing paths: the *via activa* and the *via contemplativa*.[50] Vives, however, has already warned us against this peril inherent in man's rational nature, arguing that the indubitable knowledge of causes cannot be ours in this existence, but remains instead the reward inseparable from eternal life.[51] We therefore must, he additionally urges, avoid at all costs

---

[50] See DTD I ii *Opera* 248; Watson 18. Here Vives is using the example of Mary and Martha, precisely the same example used by Juan Ginés de Sepúlveda in his own discussion of the relative value of *actio* and *contemplatio*. But whereas the latter is using the example to prove the superiority of *contemplatio* over *actio* in a secular context, Vives uses it to buttress his contention that *felicitas* can only be used through *pietas*; hence the importance of religion. However, the following is worth noting. Sepúlveda indeed argues that *contemplatio* has greater *dignitas* than *actio*; but also that in terms of *necessitas*, *actio* has the edge. Similarly, Vives considers that happiness—the union with God—can only be reached through *pietas*; but before *pietas* can enter effectively into play, man must have reached the preparatory stage of *bonitas*, and the latter can only be attained by means of a whole lifetime of *actio*. This last thought is crucial. Man will not reach the happiness given by *pietas* through fideism alone. In other words, there seems to be a hint that religion alone, in the absence of a life committed to *actio*, cannot yield *pietas* and through it *felicitas*. The reason is perhaps that Vives, throughout, thinks of religion more in natural than in supernatural terms. And nature is a package deal, where religion and social action are inseparable. It would seem, then, that just as a life of intellectual contemplation is a thoroughly unsuitable preparation for the indispensable *bonitas* that alone paves the way to *felicitas*, so is the life of cloistered contemplation. In short, neither the ivory tower nor the monastery is worthwhile.

[51] Despite the mysterious compulsion that often drives man to scrutinize what lies beyond the world of nature, he ought to accept the inevitable: knowledge of the absolute and transcendental truths of nature lies beyond the ordinary reach of the human mind. This is then the second fundamental constraint imposed on man's acquisition of knowledge: he cannot have knowledge of causes and so his perception of nature must necessarily remain incomplete. As Vives puts it in the introduction to Book I of *De anima*, "only

the temptation of surrendering to the lure of *contemplatio*.[52]

---

through the effects they cause can we hope to have knowledge of things which are neither accidents—that is, ascertainable by the senses—nor involved in them." And the outstanding example, of course, is the soul itself. And what holds true for the soul applies to nature as well: its causes are not ours to know; only the effects, that is, nature itself. To inquire into why the planets are neither more nor less, or to ask for the reason behind the form given to living things by the Creator amounts to trespassing into the sphere of the divine. To understand what belongs to nature "as is sanctioned and established by its laws"—why fire consumes wood but not stone, why the days are longer in summer than in winter—is on the other hand proper to the mind. But Vives further hedges man's ability to know; even this modest knowledge is severely circumscribed because it does not equate with indubitable cognition; it does not, in fact, reach beyond conjecture. DPP I *Opera* III 187-88. And the fault does not rest with any imperfections inherent in nature; rather, it lies in our "darkened minds." Ibid. 190. Perfection or indubitable knowledge of causes cannot be ours in this life; it is instead the very reward that awaits us in the next.

[52] This interesting conclusion—delaying the quenching of that thirst—already gives us in advance an idea of how Vives will answer the most important question asked by contemporary political thought: what is the education best suited to the statesman? But it acquires even further significance if we move on to the seventeenth century and remember one of the themes that most interest the Spanish political thinkers of the Baroque. Already far removed from the political idealism characteristic of Christian humanism, these consistently pragmatic men endowed with a considerable streak of skepticism insist, as they seek solutions to the problems faced by a monarchy in serious difficulties, that nothing is more doleful for a commonwealth than a ruler totally immersed in the pursuit of that type of knowledge that Vives considers impossible to reach. Thus we encounter in the political treatises of the seventeenth century repeated references to Alfonso X of Castile as the erudite king whose obsessive thirst for knowledge led him to the loss of his kingdom, and to Fernando of Aragón as the experienced monarch, true model to any prince aspiring to be a sound ruler. Furthermore, and more to the point, the whole question of contemplation brings us to the debate between *otium* and *negotium,* and by that path to the political question whether the best regime is one in which only the prince participates in government or the one in which the learned citizens must also share in public affairs. To understand Vives better it might be interesting to quote Cicero. "To be drawn by study away from active life is contrary to moral duty. For the whole glory of virtue is in activity . . . all our thought and mental activity will be devoted either to planning for things that are morally right and that conduce to a good and happy life, or to the pursuit of science and learning." *De officiis* I vi 19. See also I ix 28; I xxvi 92; I xxxiv 124; I xliii 152, 155; I xliv 158. For a more extensive discussion of *actio* and *contemplatio* see *De finibus* V xx-xxi. Vives' world seems also to be divided into these two activities; and in fact, and contrary to what we would expect, the Christian faith does not seem to stand aside as a third, separate category; on the contrary, it seems to emerge out of the other two in the following way. Out of the first, the moral life, there emerges a naturalistic religion, which is really Christianity itself in its ethical, non-revelational aspects; out of the second, it would seem, should emerge the revelational side of Christianity, but in fact the process is reversed.

Rational knowledge of God is out of the question and so is any attempt to fathom the inner structure of nature. In a very real sense Vives' thought finds itself at the same crossroads as Greek culture in the fifth century. In the latter case the result was the advent of the Sophists and of Socrates' humanism. To find out how Vives may have been conscious of the parallel between his own dilemma and that of Socrates, we must briefly go to *De initiis, sectis et laudibus philosophiae* (1518). Before Socrates, Vives begins, man's interest was singlemindedly devoted to the investigation of nature. Socrates was the first to rescue philosophy from the study of the heavens and apply it to the investigation of the mores of man. In other words, Socrates transformed philosophy from natural to moral. He "was the first among philosophers to place philosophy at the service of cities and peoples."[53] Thanks to him, then, philosophy became incorporated into the realm of life. Socrates' goal was clear: to see to it that mortals would learn what was indispensable, "lest while dwelling on things certainly great and wonderful men would remain unknown to themselves . . . which is the first link in the chain of *sapientia*."[54] In other words, Socrates did not think it proper that great effort should be spent on things whose ignorance would have no great consequence while neglecting those whose absence would have the greatest consequences.[55] It is for this reason, explains Vives, that Socrates confessed his own ignorance of the workings of the natural world. He, a man wise beyond measure, did so to add the weight of his own prestige and authority and lead other men away from *naturae arcanorum scientia* and *ad morum compositionem*[56]—a task which although not so beautiful is indeed most necessary.

Little doubt should remain by now concerning Vives' epistemological position. Man is bereft of both rational knowledge of God and the opportunity to penetrate to nature's innermost recesses.[57]

Because inasmuch as man cannot attain to ultimate truth, his search for scientific knowledge cannot lead to the truths of Christianity; indeed, *pietas*, the revelational side of Christianity, leads, in another life, to what scientific knowledge seeks, ultimate truth.

[53] DISP *Opera* III 15.

[54] Ibid.

[55] Ibid.

[56] Ibid. 16.

[57] In connection with the second handicap and because of its importance I must reiterate that Vives blames, not any inherent imperfection on nature's part, but man's flawed judgment. Man, he says, as he seeks to apprehend the ultimate nature of reality, finds himself in the position of an observer who, ignorant of the principles of astronomy and

Only the path of *opinio* remains open to him. The time has come, then, (1) to show that there are strong Skeptical Academic elements present in Vives' thought, and (2) to understand how his position and conclusions compare with those of contemporaries and immediate successors who are consensually seen as sharply opposed to Renaissance intellectualism.

Vives and Renaissance Skepticism

i

There is no question that Renaissance doubt finds its origins in the classical Skeptical tradition founded by Pyrrho of Ellis.[58] Pyrrho taught

on the sole evidence of the senses, concludes that the sun is smaller than the earth. It is man's judgment that leads him to believe that his subjective conclusions are in fact objective. Vives underlines the significance of this point in the introduction to *De anima*'s Book Two, where he stresses how arduous a "task, sunk in the darkest pit, it is to search the operations of the soul's faculties. . . . Only a supreme intelligence, capable of assessing our own as the latter judges the senses and the vegetative part of the soul, could give us the right answers. . . . Still, the task of delving, insofar as our ability allows, into the quality of the intelligence, its powers, functions, and operations is indeed a worthwhile enterprise."

[58] Two things we know for certain concerning the sources of Renaissance skepticism. (1) Our main authority on Skepticism, Sextus Empiricus, did not become generally available to Renaissance thinkers until 1562, when Henri Estienne published a Latin version of the *Hypotyposes*. We also know that that Gian Francesco Pico used both the *Hypotyposes* and the *Adversus dogmaticos* in his *Examen vanitatis doctrina gentium* (1520). See R.H. Popkin, *The History of Scepticism from Eramus to Descartes*, revised edition (Assen, 1960). Estienne's edition was followed in 1569 by Gentian Hervet's translation of Sextus' works. (2) Cicero's *Academica*, whose importance as a source for the study of Skepticism is second only to Sextus' writings, had some diffusion before the sixteenth century, but it was only in the 1530s (shortly before Vives' death) that the philosophical aspects of the work began to attract the serious attention of students. See C. B. Schmitt, *Cicero scepticus* (The Hague, 1972). In addition to Sextus and Cicero (*De finibus, De natura deorum, Academica*) there are several additional sources dating from Antiquity that contain information about Skepticism: Plutarch, Eusebius, St. Augustine, and, especially, Diogenes Laertius. Sextus gives us the following account of the term. "Scepticism is an ability, or mental attitude, which opposes appearances to judgments in any way whatsoever, with the result that, owing to the equipollence of the objects and reasons thus opposed, we are brought firstly to a state of mental suspense and next to a stage of 'unperturbedness' or quietude. . . . By 'appearances' we now mean the objects of sense-perception, whence we contrast them with the objects of thought or 'judgments.'" *Hypotyposes* (Outlines of Pyrrhonism), trans. R.G. Bury, The Loeb Classical Library (4 vols., Cambridge, Mass., 1961) I 8-10. Although Skepticism as a system did not develop until the fourth century B.C., and then as a reaction to the dogmatism of post-Aristotelian philosophies such as Stoicism, its remote antecedents can be found among some representatives of the Ionian School (Xenophanes).

that neither sense-perception nor human reason is sufficient to penetrate
to the inner substance of things—their reality. We apprehend nothing but
appearances; namely, we do not know things as they really are but only
as they appear to us through the experience of the senses.[59] Pyrrhonism,
therefore, stands on a rejection of any form of philosophical speculation
leading to dogmatism: no theory about the nature of things is more
acceptable than any other because none is verifiable in experience.[60] The
Pyrrhonists, then, doubting the possibility of attaining to ultimate
knowledge, elected, as the cornerstone of their psychology, to avoid
commitment and suspend judgment on all questions pertaining to
knowledge. They therefore conformed to the existing social structure
without judging its laws and customs.[61] But Greek Skepticism did not

More recently, its roots are also present in the teachings of Socrates and the Socratics; and
especially in the thought of Democritus (d. ca. 350 B.C.), in whom we already observe,
in embryo, that Empiricism (the physician-philosopher Empedocles, d. ca. 430 B.C.;
Hippocrates, d. ca. 365 B.C.) that would in the end, as shown by the writings of Sextus
Empiricus (ca. 200 A.D.), also a physician and the last of the great Greek Skeptics, be the
final issue of Skepticism.

[59] The Pyrrhonist tradition denied that knowledge of the real world can be apprehended
at all. According to Pyrrho's doctrine, (1) sense-perception and belief yield that aspect of
the world that is phenomenal, (2) true knowledge is alone knowledge of that side of the
world that is real, and (3) knowledge can only originate with the data of the senses.
"Every intelligible thing derives its origin and source of confirmation from sensation."
Sextus Empiricus, *Adversus dogmaticos* (Against the Logicians), trans. R.G. Bury (vol. II)
II 356-57. The last premise, clearly vintage Aristotle, is best embodied in Sextus' own
empirical axiom: "Every conception, then, must be preceded by experience through sense,
and on this account if sensibles are abolished all conceptual thought is necessarily
abolished at the same time." Ibid. 60-61. Reason is evidently denied direct and
independent access to the world of reality. Since sense-perception gives us only knowledge
of the phenomenal or appearances, and the mind depends on the data of the senses, there
is no way for the mind to approach the real.

[60] "For every argument is judged to be either true or false according to its reference to the
thing concerning which it is brought forward; for if it is found to be in accord with the
thing concerning which it is brought forward, it is held to be true, but if at variance,
false." Ibid. 323-24. This condition of truth, that it be verifiable in experience, is what
Vives demands of his precepts foundation of the arts when he proposes the
verification/falsification of any hypothesis.

[61] Given the premises outlined earlier, Pyrrho's conclusions are not surprising: (1) we
know nothing as to the nature of things; and (2) we must practice *epochê*, i.e., suspend
judgment (the withholding of assent and dissent) on questions relating to
knowledge—"But with regard to the things about which our opponents argue so
positively, claiming to have definitely apprehended them, we suspend our judgment
because they are not certain, and confine knowledge to our impressions. For we admit

fully come into its own until Plato's Academy (the Middle Academy), now under the presidency of Arcesilaus (315-240 B.C., who drew a sharp distinction between opinion and knowledge reminiscent of Vives' own *opinio* vs. *scientia/sapientia*), reverted to the questioning attitude of Socrates and unleashed its attack on the *phantasiai kataleptikoi* of the Stoics, those irresistible or self-evident true representations that, apprehended by the Stoic wise man, unerringly lead him to the truth of things. Arcesilaus grants that whereas the wise man knows, the fool merely opines. "For that which they [the Stoics] call 'apprehension' and 'assent to an apprehensive representation' occurs either in a wise man or in a fool. But if it occurs in a wise man it is knowledge, and if in a fool, opinion."[62] He objects, however, that contrary to Stoic doctrine we have no certain criterion to distinguish between the perception of the sage and that of the fool.[63] Arcesilaus' conclusion is therefore that the "wise man in all cases suspends judgment."[64] But such a suspension of judgment, countered the Stoics, necessarily issues into a paralytic inactivity that in effect deprives man of all hope. The Academy could hardly countenance that, inasmuch as its members believed the highest goal to be virtue, called perfect action by Arcesilaus and rooted in knowledge. In answer to this criticism and difficulty, Arcesilaus developed the idea of the *eulogon*: no absolute certainty is needed before the will can act; that which is merely "reasonable" suffices.[65] Man's well-being depends neither on epistem-

---

that we see, and we recognize that we think this or that, but how we see and how we think we know not." Diogenes Laertius, *Lives of Eminent Philosophers*, trans. R.D. Hicks, The Loeb Classical Library (2 vols., Cambridge, Mass., 1958) IX 103-05—(3) the natural result of our suspension of judgment is *ataraxia* or tranquillity of soul, namely, peaceful living in accordance with the institutions of one's country.

[62] *Adversus dogmaticos* I 153-54. "Whereas the strongest point of the wise man, in the opinion of Arcesilaus, agreeing with Zeno, lies in avoiding being taken in and in seeing that he is not deceived—for nothing is more removed from the conception that we have of the dignity of the wise man than error, frivolity or rashness. What then shall I say about the wise man's firmness? Even you, Lucullus, allow that he never advances a mere opinion." Cicero, *Academica* (II), The Loeb Classical Library, trans. H. Rackham (Cambridge, Mass., 1972) XX 66.

[63] *Adversus dogmaticos* I 154-58.

[64] "'If the wise man ever assents to anything, he sometimes also forms an opinion; therefore he will not assent to anything.' This syllogism Arcesilas used to approve." Cicero, *Academica* (II) XXI 67.

[65] This is how Sextus Empiricus reports Arcesilaus' position. "But inasmuch as it was necessary, in the next place, to investigate also the conduct of life, which cannot, naturally, be directed without a criterion, upon which happiness—that is, the end of

ological theories nor on a criterion of knowledge, but only on the conduct of life. For the will to act, therefore, it is not necessary to be previously convinced of the truth of something. Action, then, is always possible, even when there is no criterion of truth. The only indispensable condition to be met before action becomes possible is that reason grant its approval to what is to be done.[66] Arcesilaus' "wisdom," which "consists in right actions" is of course practical wisdom, Vives' own *prudentia*. About one hundred years after the death of Arcesilaus, Carneades (sometimes said to have been the founder of the Third or New Academy) further strengthened the rigor of the Skeptical position in both its negative and positive aspects. On the constructive side, Carneades developed his doctrine of the probable—*pithanon*.[67] According to Carneades, there are two aspects to every "presentation" or notion: one, its relation to the subject represented; the other, its relation to the subject who has the notion. In the first aspect the notion may be true or false, but it is a relation lying beyond our powers of judgment to determine. "But in regard to its aspect in relation to the subject experiencing the presentation, the one kind of presentation is apparently true, the other apparently false; and of these the apparently true is termed by Academics

---

life—depends for its assurance, Arcesilaus asserts that he who suspends judgment about everything will regulate his inclinations and aversions, and his actions in general by the rule of 'the reasonable,' and by proceeding in accordance with this criterion he will act rightly; for happiness is attained by means of wisdom, and wisdom consists in right actions, and the right action is that which, when performed, possesses a reasonable justification. He, therefore, who attends to 'the reasonable' will act rightly and be happy." *Adversus dogmaticos* I 158-59.

[66] Ibid. I 158. This is precisely Arcesilaus' *eulogon* or ethical criterion: when the arguments for or against something are so balanced that knowledge becomes impossible, virtue consists in carrying out that which satisfies reason in the highest degree. Arcesilaus therefore teaches that in order to reach the desired well-being one must be guided by reason, although simultaneously we are fully aware of how uncertain all knowledge is. And this is also Vives' own underlying argument: reason gives us an imperfect form of knowledge, but since we have nothing better the alternative is an ignorance offensive to God. But Vives, once reason has been taken as premise, moves on to a judgment of probability as the immediate instrument that justifies action. In Vives' system Arcesilaus offers the mediate instrument, Carneades the immediate one.

[67] After explaining "the arguments which Carneades set forth in detail, in his controversy with the other philosophers, to prove the non-existence of the criterion," Sextus Empiricus goes on to point out that "he, too, himself requires a criterion for the conduct of life and for the attainment of happines, he is practically compelled on his own account to frame a theory about it, and to adopt both the probable representation and that which is at once probable and irreversible and tested." Ibid. 166-67.

'emphasis' and probability and probable representation."[68] For Carneades, in what concerns the conduct of life, that a given representation is true or false is irrelevant; in this instance what man must do is suspend judgment. What is in fact important is that the representation that seems probable be indeed accepted as such in practical relation to the art of living, because the structure of life itself depends on phenomena out of which emerge representations that seem probable.[69] In the end, therefore, the Academics, far from refraining from judging as counseled by Pyrrho, will in fact issue judgments (relative ones, to be sure, but judgments nonetheless) based on reasonableness and probability, and use them as a credible platform for action.[70]

On this fundamental question of judgment Vives, who found Phyrronism's empirical axiom congenial and accepted that reason cannot independently penetrate to the domain of the real (the real world cannot be known by the intellect), sides with the Academics. The Pyrrhonists believed that nothing is good or bad by nature; instead, things become so through custom or law, and we have no criterion that enables us to judge

---

[68] Ibid. 169-70. Of the above notions, only "that which appears true, and appears so vividly ['possesses this appearance of truth to an intense degree'] is the criterion of truth according to the School of Carneades." Having thus been turned into the criterion of truth, this presentation or notion must of necessity be comprehensive, including numerous varieties of notions, and so, when made comprehensive or "extended," "one presentation reveals itself as more probable and more vivid than another. Probability, in the present instance, is used in three senses: in the first, of that which both is and appears true; in the second, of that which is really false but appears true; in the third, of that which is at once true and false. Hence the criterion will be the apparently true presentation, which the Academics called 'probable.'" Ibid. 173-75.

[69] *Pithanon*, or concept of the probable, therefore, represents reality in our relation to life, but it is not knowledge. Therefore, the "art of living," which Carneades calls practical wisdom, rests on the indispensable foundation of probability. And just as the *ars vivendi* is *prudentia* is virtue, so also man's natural incentive toward that prudence is his *summum bonum*. And here again comes to mind the metaphor of the *Fabula*: man reaches to the gods and succeeds, but when he tries to reach God with the instrument of his mask (body/reason) alone he only succeeds in mimmicking him.

[70] It is unlikely, despite frequent reports in the literature to the contrary, that the Academics asserted that nothing can be known, True enough, they were often accused of dogmatism by the Pyrrhonists on that account (and conceivably they, notably Arcesilaus, were a little more willing to assert dogmatically that it is impossible to distinguish between opinion and knowledge). But Arcesilaus himself is said to have denied the charge, which suggests that at least during his lifetime the difference between the two approaches to Skepticism might well have been one of method—empirical for the Pyrrhonists (Sextus Empiricus), dialectical for the Academics.

values. On the whole Vives accepts these premises. He has already stated that only if there existed an agency outside of our mind (a "supreme intelligence" that could bridge the gap between the two sides of nature) capable of weighing its judgments, would the path to reality be opened; in other words, this is Arcesilaus' own argument that judgments cannot rise above opinion because a judgment cannot be a criterion of truth inasmuch as we have no criterion of judgment to prove that it cannot err.[71] In the absence of that supreme intelligence, however, Vives is content to make do with man's judgment (which, he agrees with Arcesilaus, leads not to knowledge of reality or true knowledge, but to knowledge of appearances or *opinio*, for judgments cannot rise above opinion), which, and here he parts company with the Pyrrhonists, is what endows things with their positive or negative qualities. His stand could hardly have been different. The Skeptics were both critics and inquirers (*skeptikoi*), and in the latter role they searched for that truth the Stoics claimed to have found. They had to provide, therefore, some kind of standard that, if not absolute, might nevertheless serve as a starting point for man's search for happiness. For Pyrrho, bound by his commitment to non-judgment, the standard was given by the laws and customs of society; Arcesilaus proposed reason; and Carneades stressed probability. For his part Vives, a social reformer yearning to turn each and every man into the quintessential *vir prudens* through education, could not possibly abide critically by law and custom as a means of achieving *ataraxia*; it would necessarily have barred the intellectual path to the goal that is the reason for being of his entire literary production: the reform of mores within the Christian commonwealth.

---

[71] There is a parallel between this yearned-for but non-existent superior intelligence of Vives and the *spiritus* of Marsiglio Ficino's natural magic tradition. In his *De vita triplici* (1489) Ficino claims that the *spiritus*, made of aether but enjoying also characteristics associated with the four elements that enter into the composition of the sublunar world, thereby making possible its affinity with the latter, connects the *anima mundi*, the domain of eternal reality, with the *corpus mundi*, or sublunar world realm of the phenomenal. By means of the *spiritus* and through the techniques of natural magic (talismans, astrological medicine, music), Ficino claimed to be able to capture the emanations from the *anima mundi*, which, when absorbed by the objects of the *corpus mundi*, can approximate those objects to their own archetypes; the archetypes (of which the objects of the sublunar world are but images), in other words, infused into the *anima mundi* out of the supreme realm of *mens* or intellect. By such and other similar methods the magical tradition—in the case of Ficino one with a pronounced Platonic and Neoplatonic flavor—of the Renaissance proposed to reach the kind of *sapientia* denied to be accessible to man by Vives.

ii

Having thus outlined in the briefest possible fashion the Pyrrhonic and Academic roots of Renaissance Skepticism, we are in a position to propose the following definition of the latter: in the absence of an infallible norm or criterion capable of verifying the validity of conclusions reached by reason, it is impossible to admit that the truths arrived at by the latter are indubitable. Although both early and tentative, this definition nevertheless already clearly suggests how important the practical results of a posture denying the possibility of knowing the truth of things will be. In the first place (and on this more later), just as in the case of its classical progenitor, the epistemological skepticism of the Renaissance necessarily culminates in a normative skepticism that forces man to reconsider his activity as a moral being. That is, and referring now specifically to how Vives himself understands the problem, man is offered two alternatives: to surrender to "ignorance" or to find a way of reaching the most probable or verisimilar truth, which in turn will enable him to act and to attain to virtue.[72] Second, because a stand that during the Renaissance asserts the impossibility of arriving at the truth clearly compels us to ask: what is its relation to religion? And it is precisely this question—which, it should be mentioned, lacks in classical precedent—what we are now interested in answering.

Consciously, I believe, the skepticism of the Renaissance is fundamentally "philosophical" both in intention and in method, and its posture does not imply hostile feelings toward religion. The skeptical preoccupation of the age, including that of Vives, centers on whether man, through the means of his natural reason, can arrive at a measure of knowledge worthy of trust. The antireligious side of skepticism will emerge later, and belongs to another age molded by different circumstances. From Lactantius to Gianfrancesco Pico skepticism moves hitched to religion. With Montaigne it begins to acquire that appearance, more its own and independent, that will accompany it until Pierre Bayle.

---

[72] In what concerns Vives the first alternative is inadmissible. The human being has no right to plunge into a way of life dominated by ignorance, because he was created to toil ceaselessly for the crumbs of knowledge to which he has access. The man who loses hope of reaching universal truths and decides to surrender himself to ignorance is guilty of rebellion against God, because it was by His will that man put into effect the powers that constitute his patrimony. Therefore, only the second alternative remains, which means that within the Renaissance skeptical tradition Vives is to be counted among those who are obligated to offer the age a method or system that, rooted in truths whose value can never extend beyond the probable, will allow the members of society to act both morally and effectively.

But it is only when we meet Hume that skepticism emerges as the ally of a critical current that aims directly at religious beliefs. And still in this context it is worth offering the testimony of Erasmus as he defends free will from Luther's attack: "So great is my dislike of assertions that I prefer the views of the sceptics whenever the inviolable authority of Scripture and the decisions of the Church permit."[73] Here Erasmus is merely reiterating what Renaissance skeptics have said and will say: doubt must be applied in the domain of philosophy, not theology. Erasmus is therefore here suggesting a point of view that in my opinion perfectly summarizes the intention of Renaissance skepticism. Truth carries within it two distinct facets: one, given by faith and indubitable, lies beyond the questioning powers of man *qua* rational being; the other, by contrast, is a field wide open to doubt, and as such it is also the very embodiment of the stimulus to endless inquiry.[74] But it is enough to remember the most elementary principles of Greek Skepticism to become aware that the problem created by attempting to graft classical doubting onto a trunk that, as is the case with the Renaissance itself, owes much to religion, is not solved merely by realizing that the Renaissance skeptic is a man given neither to interfering in the affairs of the faith nor to harboring anti-religious feelings. We have to find out (1) what the solution to the problem is, and (2) what are the consequences that result from this forced coexistence of skepticism and religion.

In the classical tradition *scientia* and *sapientia* were only differentiated in terms of degree, the former being a preliminary step culminating in the latter, the vision of God, the highest possible achievement of the human intellect.[75] The point to be underlined here is that among the Greeks both are but stages in the cognitive task carried out by *ratio*, alone because in fact there is nothing else. When the Skeptics doubt the possibility of knowing, therefore, they make no final distinction between knowledge of first causes and knowledge of the First Cause. The advent of Christianity, on the other hand, created an additional instrument for knowing: *pietas*, a criterion of truth unknown to the classical tradition but one that no Renaissance skeptic could ignore,

---

[73] *A Diatribe or Sermon Concerning Free Will*, trans and ed. E.F. Winter (New York, 1961) 6.

[74] In this context it is essential to remember Vives' aphorism: "man shall have truth, but not the whole truth."

[75] The fideist of the Reformation will in effect claim that such is precisely what Thomism, guided by Aristotle, issues into: knowledge of God, under Christianity the exclusive preserve of religion but now attainable through reason.

one whose existence must therefore always be reckoned with when drawing parallels between Skepticism and its Renaissance homonym.[76] For whereas Skepticism meant uncertainty both about the essence of nature and about God, the Renaissance skeptic never doubted (and in this he was no different from the fideist) man's ability to apprehend, eventually, the reality of his Creator; he merely argued that the apprehending instrument cannot be *ratio*.[77] To the Skeptic this claim obviously makes no sense at all; and to him the Renaissance skeptic remains an anomaly, a man who doubts the ability to Know while simultaneously admitting the apprehensibility of that same Knowledge, that he has denied to be rationally possible, provided that it is grasped by means of what Vives calls *pietas*—an instrument about which the Skeptic knows nothing. Here, then, lies the solution to the problem: the Renaissance created a formal, if implicit, distinction within the Skeptical tradition never contemplated by its founders and followers in Antiquity, a distinction between knowledge of nature/man and knowledge of God.[78]

---

[76] There is a measure of truth to the argument that the Renaissance skeptic was in fact no Skeptic at all, for whereas the former of necessity dealt with knowledge in a narrow and limited way, for the latter Knowledge continued to be the absolute concept defined by Aristotle. Only by abandoning all fideistic elements and reverting to the old idea of rational knowledge as Knowledge could the Renaissance skeptic have brought himself in line with his classical predecessors, an action that would have demanded automatically abandoning Christianity and implicitly lapsing into, to the age, some form of atheism. On the other hand, there is to my knowledge no reason to believe that Vives, or anyone else in the Renaissance for that matter, felt compelled to tread the Skeptical path *in toto*. Instead, true to the eclectic mood of the age, he was simply looting the past and enlisting some of the spoils in the service of his present.

[77] To anticipate here what will be argued at length in the next section, the skeptic and the fideist are as one in this: they both reject what they see as the boundless intellectualism that to all appearances aspires to become the criterion of religious truth—this fideistic element the Renaissance skeptic will not, and cannot, ever shed. Luther will accuse Thomism of embodying that rationalist ambition; Vives, perhaps more prudent and certainly less revolutionary, contents himself with denying Aristotelian dogmatism and attacking the later, decadent "schoolmen." What follows, however, is even more significant. From this common platform a skeptic of Vives' stripe moves on to argue that although unrestrained intellectualism is a blind alley, reason (*ratio practica* leading to *prudentia* [virtue]) does have some input in determining man's ultimate spiritual fate. A revolutionary like Luther, on the other hand—and such is the essence of fideism— launches himself into a path that leads to the prompt abandonment of any skeptical stance and the adoption of a dogmatic posture that unconditionally asserts that neither a depraved reason nor an impotent will can contribute anything to salvation.

[78] The Renaissance dogmatist believes that man can rationally penetrate to the most intimate essence of nature (although not necessarily to the First Cause itself), while the

When the Renaissance skeptic, therefore, doubts/denies that we can know, he doubts/denies that we can know nature, not that we can Know God.[79] He is prepared to question the range and possibilities of human reason while retaining intact the potential for spiritual cognition inherent in man. But what consequences does this posture have? We will find the answer if we succeed in understanding how all this affects Vives.

Understood in terms of what has been sketched above, the epistemological problem faced by Vives is more limited and manageable—meaning far less potentially destructive in its consequences, although, we shall see below, it creates a serious problem of its own—than that of the Skeptics. His faith leaves him no room for doubting that knowledge is ultimately available— fideistically. The question for Vives, then, narrows down to this: is knowledge of first causes (a realm presumably open to reason) reachable? And here again faith points the way, for in a very Augustinian sense Vives "knows" that all knowledge about nature's truths is, by cause of original sin, beyond the ken of man's reason. Vives is here evidently adopting that Pyrrhonic stance that denied reason independent access to the world of reality. But the problem mentioned earlier now intrudes, for Vives' faith gives him, insofar as knowledge of God and man's uncertain apprehension of nature are concerned, the kind of certitude born of dogmatic premises that no Skeptic, least of all one who has just, like Vives, made his own a claim fundamental to Pyrrhonism, could possibly accept. In other words, Vives the skeptic does after all have a criterion of truth. Sextus Empiricus' objection that "in order to decide the dispute which has arisen about the criterion, we must possess an accepted criterion by which we shall be able to judge the dispute; and in

---

skeptic doubts/denies his ability to do so. The Renaissance *magus* is a peculiar breed of dogmatist in that he will use an amorphous mixture of *ratio* (issuing into Ficino's *magia naturalis*, with the elements of practical Cabala later added by Giovanni Pico) and *pietas* (resulting in Agrippa's religious magic; his contribution explaining the ease with which, in *De incertitudine*, he launches into a fideistic tirade against rational knowledge) to achieve Knowledge in the classical sense. The activities of the traditional (meaning that Paracelsus should be at least partially excepted) alchemist are particularly noteworthy in this context. He sought, in his laboratory, to reproduce the most basic process he believed took place in nature—the transmutation of metals—but ultimately only as a metaphor of what was his real goal: the purification of the human soul.

[79] Vives' own skepticism, although more systematically developed, accurately mirrors Erasmus' posture on at least one occasion. In fact, at least in the treatise where he confronts Luther, the dogmatist *par excellence*, Erasmus' Skeptical credentials are unimpeachable: "Therefore, I merely want to analyze and not to judge, to inquire and not to dogmatize." *Discourse on Free Will*, 6.

order to possess an accepted criterion, the dispute about the criterion must first be decided"[80] is thus circumvented by appealing to a higher authority that cannot be known rationally, a claim patently absurd in Sextus' eyes but an eminently sensible, indeed unavoidable, one for a Christian.[81] The entire affair, then, comes down to this: a Skeptic cannot justify his doubt on the basis of dogmatic premises. A Renaissance skeptic like Vives starts his journey toward skepticism out of a fideistic, hence dogmatic, assumption.[82] But once this most un-Skeptical step has been taken and noticed, the decks are fully clear, and what remains open to the doubting inquirer is a field of action encompassed solely and exclusively by reason. In it Vives, the erstwhile Renaissance skeptic, now functions

---

[80] Sextus Empiricus, *Hypotyposes* II 20-21.

[81] Vives is indeed a Renaissance skeptic, but one who has embraced that posture toward knowledge out of theological, not philosophical, premises. In this sense he differs from Montaigne, for whereas the Frenchman's skepticism appears to be the result of a systematic appraisal of all facets of human activity, which gradually but inexorably builds in man the irrefutable conclusion that he knows nothing (this interpretation, it must be emphasized, holds true so long as we are willing to take the narrative of the *Essays* at face value, a somewhat risky commitment when dealing with Montaigne), with Vives the process is to all appearances reversed: he starts out of a fideistic assumption—man *can* know nothing—about knowledge, which he then sees validated by the course of human affairs. It would seem, moreover, that on the basis of what has just transpired a strong case could be made for Vives' fideism. What rescues him from such a fate is his conviction that God did not intend man to be His slave and therefore (1) *ratio practica* was not crippled by original sin, and (2) the human will is free.

[82] Vives' Christian *knowing* that man's knowledge is of necessity limited and imperfect also contributes to explaining why it will be possible for him to adopt a position that often and simultaneously borrows from both Skeptic and Stoic. The two ancient schools had clashed over the latter's criterion of truth. Reality, in the Stoic scheme of things, does not lie beyond the phenomena but includes them; what distinguishes a true from a false idea is that the former embodies the real. And we know that the object of the idea is in fact real by virtue of the compelling intensity with which the idea impresses itself upon the mind. The judgment tests the idea, and if the latter is true the former assents to it. In Vives' attitude toward knowledge it is implicitly underlined that the faith of an ordinary Christian man allows him to apprehend the sort of impression that in the Stoic view is open to the sage alone. Zeno had been forced, to support his ethical doctrine, to create the weak metaphysical foundation that Academic Skepticism had so successfully undermined. Vives removes the millstone weighing Zeno's system down by having recourse to Christian providentialism and thus consigning to the realm of divine revelation the uncertain metaphysical elements that had been the weak link in the Stoic chain. The Stoic criterion of truth is in this fashion both withdrawn from the realm of reason and incorporated into a body of faith, by definition indubitable, thereby making it inaccessible to Skeptical doubt.

as a full-fledged Skeptic, and faces the same seemingly insoluble dilemma which confronted both Arcesilaus and Carneades: to reconcile the need for action with the impossibility of ascertaining the rational criterion of truth indispensable to it. One possible course of action, paralleling that followed by the Academics, remains open to Vives: all the rational instruments for knowing available to man must be marshaled to the end of enhancing the likelihood of that imperfect knowledge available to him. In short, probability is Vives' criterion of truth.

On the basis of the statement of Erasmus and of everything else mentioned until now, we are in a position to propose the following conclusion concerning Renaissance skepticism: given, on the one hand, the conditions within which the age's spirituality compels the skeptic to act and, on the other, the very definition of Skepticism inflexibly ruled by classical premises, Renaissance skepticism, as it seeks to counteract contemporary dogmatic positions, is as different from Greek Skepticism in both its origin and inspiration, as Renaissance dogmatism is different from the Aristotelianism that supports and sustains it. Now, although this proposition suggests that we question the wisdom of describing Renaissance doubting as Skeptical, it is not my intention, once agreed that we cannot call the latter Skepticism (because between the two stands the obstacle represented by the Christian faith) to carry this terminological problem any further. But we are indeed interested in understanding the effects of the second consequence; namely, to know whether (as both the conclusion just proposed and what I have said concerning the dogmatic premises born out of the Christian faith that guide Vives seem to suggest) what we have called Vives' skepticism is but another manifestation of Renaissance fideism, the second watershed of the age's antirationalist tradition.

iii

What is fideism? Here is the answer given by one of its most remarkable spokesmen, Cornelius Agrippa. Learning, according to Agrippa, makes the wicked more dangerous and the fool bolder, but it adds nothing to the good man.[83] It certainly makes him no happier, "for the true felicity consists not in the knowledge of goodness, but in a good life; not in understanding, but in living with understanding."[84] So far, there is scant difference between Agrippa and the Academics or Vives

---

[83] Cornelius Agrippa, *Of the Vanitie and Uncertaintie of the Artes and Sciences*, trans. J. Stanford (1569), ed. C.M Dunn (Northridge Ca., 1974) 13-14.

[84] Ibid. 387-88.

himself, because the truth of the matter is that Agrippa is here returning to the old conflict between Socrates and Aristotle, the paradigm also for much that is polemical in the Renaissance.[85] But what had perplexed Aristotle need not unduly disturb a Christian, particularly one who like Agrippa, and here he moves away from both Skeptics and Vives, professes boundless respect for Holy Writ.[86] "For it is better and more profitable to be idiots and know nothing, to believe by faith and charity, and to become next unto God, than being lofty and proud through the subtleties of sciences to fall into the possession of the Serpent."[87] Not for Agrippa, then, the Aristotelian notion that man can behold God through knowledge of the sciences ("The which act of contemplation, being so easy and common to all men, is not made perfect with syllogisms and demonstrations, but with belief and worship")[88] or the Academic axiom that man must forever be *skeptikoi* ("the sciences . . . show not the true whereby we may be made altogether happy");[89] only the belief that "all things are contained and taught in the one volume of the Holy Bible" is what man needs for *felicitas*.[90] Finally, and as if conspiring with Luther to dash the high hopes placed by Vives on a *prudentia* brought into being by the collaboration of man's right reason and will, Agrippa is of the "opinion that there can chance to the life and salvation of our souls nothing more hurtful and pestilential than the arts and the sciences."[91] Evidently Agrippa's radically hostile attitude toward knowledge has little to do with Vives' intention to use that knowledge/*opinio* as the

---

[85] Socrates maintained that practicing the good is what matters. For his part Aristotle asked: how can one practice what one does not know? Socrates is often claimed as their own by skeptic and fideist alike, while Aristotle remains of course the patron saint of the stalwart seekers after wisdom. Although broad generalizations have an unsettling tendency to return and haunt their maker, it is, I think, not too risky in this instance to say that the fideist will harp on Socrates' famous confession of ignorance while damning Aristotle altogether. The skeptic, on the other hand, goes to Socrates not to reject the value of human knowledge but, in the tradition of Skepticism, to find a foil to dogmatism. In the case of Vives the source of that dogmatism is not Zeno but Aristotle; the Philosopher is not disowned, but his value as infallible authority is questioned and toned down.

[86] Ibid. 381.

[87] Ibid. 389

[88] Ibid. 15.

[89] Ibid. 14

[90] Ibid. 11, 389

[91] Ibid. 11.

foundation of a virtuous life. We may therefore conclude at this point that the Spanish humanist cannot possibly be a fideist if the latter is defined according to Agrippa's norms.

But the truth of the matter is that sixteenth-century fideism does not always emerge out of conditions like those outlined for Agrippa's case. In other words, the consummate representative of Renaissance magic who at a given moment in his career bitterly rebels against that insatiable hungering after knowledge that had been and would again be the guiding passion of his life represents only one facet, and not necessarily the most significant one, of the attack unleashed toward the middle of the century against man's *ratio* and *voluntas*. For out of the bosom of the Protestant Reformation there emerges a fideism that denying both free will and reason, withholds from man the ability to apprehend moral knowledge in as categorical a fashion as Vives' skepticism denies him access to intellectual knowledge. In this its more extreme format fideism represents an unqualified repudiation of that form of moral life, rooted since Antiquity in reason, that both embodied norms trustworthy as guides toward the right ordering of human life, and represented a means to beatitude. It constitutes, in other words, a rejection of everything that Vives stands for. But there is something in this second facet of fideism that prevents us from bringing our comments to a close here and concluding, as we did in Agrippa's case, that Vives' skepticism has nothing to do with Protestant fideism. It must be admitted that fideism is also predicated on an assumption seemingly identical to that which justifies Vives'own depreciation of rational knowledge: the corruption of human reason through original sin, something, we have already noted, that might logically lead us to conclude that Vives is a partisan of fideism. Given that our aim here is precisely the opposite, it is imperative that we now explicitly demonstrate that such assumption is false.

To begin with, it must be noted that the resemblance as to origins is more superficial than substantial, for in Vives reason suffered only in its two speculative manifestations, while *ratio practica* and the will emerged comparatively unscathed from the crisis; or, speaking with greater rigor, they were the result of that very crisis: the very act of God that deprived man of the full value of speculative reason simultaneously endowed him with practical reason and will. Man, therefore, may be sunk in profound, if partial, darkness, but he is not mired in hopeless depravity.[92] In fact, and given these premises, what at first sight appears

---

[92] This is also the key source of disagreement between Erasmus and Luther in their debate over the nature of the will. As the former points out, "our power of judgment—whether

to be a common bond turns out to be a source of discord between fideism and Vivesian skepticism. And predicating our next step on the assumption that to understand the respective positions of fideism and skepticism we must equally understand their outlook toward will and reason, let us begin with the former. Vives claims that reason, although impotent in the realm of faith and crippled in what pertains to knowledge of first principles, is eminently suited to plan and to execute the moral life of man. But everything hinges on the will. The basic question, therefore, is obviously whether the will can indeed "turn away or pursue," namely, whether "the will is free and to what extent it is free." We already know Vives' answer. Both Luther and his followers deny that the will is free. And since the will has no freedom it matters not in the least how much cognitive grist reason, practical or otherwise, may feed the former's mill: the will has in effect no power to act upon it, unless it be at the very superficial level of external acts. This and only this, that there is in the human will "a certain freedom in outward works," is what Protestantism is willing to grant. But such works are worthless and irrelevant to the end of beatitude, for what is in truth solely indispensable to that end, the "purity of heart" that alone impresses God, only His grace can grant. In the absence of certain knowledge the Skeptics argued that action remains possible (Arcesilaus) but the outcome uncertain and at best but probable (Carneades). For Vives that probability was strong enough to warrant man's moral life. In the Christian context proposed by Protestant fideism the certitude absent from the Skeptic exists, but only when executed by God. Outside of His purview everything remains a probability insufficient to justify, or even carry out, meaningful action. Vives always asks: does reason give man what he truly needs, the wherewithal to prepare himself for salvation? For the Protestant fideist the question is merely academic; it matters not whether reason can identify the good, since the will is impotent to act upon it.

And now the question of reason. Luther, besides insisting on the slave nature of the will, damns the *ratio speculativa* of the schoolmen for claiming that it affords knowledge of the divine mysteries, and rejects the *recta ratio* of the Christian humanists as responsible for deluding the faithful into thinking that their banal acts of charity have the power to unlock the gates of heaven. Knowledge of God lies beyond man's rational search: in this divorcing of faith from reason Vives disagrees with mainstream Reformation thought in neither form nor substance. But on

---

we call it *nous*, i.e., mind or intellect, or rather *logos*, i.e., reason—has only been obscured by sin, and not extinguished." *Discourse on Free Will* 22.

the issue of attaining salvation Luther's characterization of reason's
contribution as "darkness and deception" becomes "understanding of the
necessary actions conducive to the moderation of our mores, in order that
rejecting vice we may follow the path of virtue" in Vives. The reformer,
we have seen, is concerned with what he perceives to be the intrusion of
an instrument—"the devil's harlot"—designed (and not very well, at that)
for use in man's earthly existence into matters clearly the preserve of
faith. Vives, on the other hand, having agreed that reason has no business
in the realm reserved for *pietas*, understands the former, in the classical
tradition from Plato to Aquinas, as a faculty unique to man and fit to
discharge two functions. In the first, the directing of man's thought (in
the guise of *ratio speculativa inferior*), it meets with only indifferent
success—witness its failure to uncover first principles. In pursuit of the
second, the regulating of human behavior, it carries, as *recta ratio*, the day
splendidly, because it is precisely on that account that God chose to leave
man's right reason or *ratio practica* intact. For Vives, then, reason has
moral value; it can point the way to the good and thus issue into that very
natural morality so despised by Luther. His own skeptical posture, to be
sure, bars the direct rational path to God, negates the value of the higher
form of speculative knowledge (and to that extent alone he is at one with
the fideists), and even questions the ultimate effectiveness of lesser
speculation. But where Luther implacably assails the very notion of
natural morality, Vives views it as something not only possible but in fact
mandated by God. In the eyes of the Reformation, the Fall plunged
speculative *and* practical reason into such an abyss of depravity that
neither man's learning nor his morality is worth anything in the sight of
God. By contrast, for Vives practical or right reason, by express divine
design, survived the shipwreck, enabling man to retain the efficacy of his
moral acts and so leaving the door open for man to reap salvation as
reward for his effort—with the aid of the will, "free and a gift of God,
whereby He made us His sons instead of His slaves and placed in our
hands the means of molding ourselves with the aid of His favor and
grace."[93] In fact, the moral value of reason is so important a cog in Vives'
system that it brings him into conflict with contemporary skeptics who
cast a vote of confidence for ignorance, thus implicitly advocating
non-action and by so doing breaking with the guidelines established by

---

[93] The need for right living is of course of overwhelming importance for Erasmus. "Other
things He wanted us to know with the utmost clarity, as for example, the precepts for a
morally good life. . . . This indeed must be learned well by all. The remaining is better
committed to God." *Discourse on Free Will* 9-10.

Academic Skepticism, as the best treatment for man's incurable epistemological ills. Moral life, for Vives, rests on a foundation of prudence that only the accumulated knowledge of the arts (itself resting on the contribution of *ratio speculativa inferior*, the endlessly investigative and creative travail of man) can possibly lay down.

With these arguments, which confirm that in fact Vives cannot possibly be a follower of Renaissance fideism, we have accomplished the last part of what we set out to do in this chapter. Let us therefore propose the following definitions. Renaissance skepticism represents an approximation to the problem of knowledge that (1) moves within a jurisdiction whose boundaries are given by philosophical doubting, (2) has as its goal to fulfill the commitment of an antirationalism opposed to dogmatic approximation to the problem of knowledge, and (3) fulfills that commitment starting from and by means of premises that clearly go back to the Skeptical tradition. Anyone who during the Renaissance moves within a domain limited by those premises, and, regardless of whether the center of gravity of his thought rests on Pyrrhonic or Academic premises, is a Renaissance skeptic; for example, men like Erasmus, Vives, Brués, Agrippa, Francisco Sánchez, Huarte de San Juan, Montaigne, and Charron. On the other hand, whoever resolves that neither the senses nor reason can provide man with both certain and useful knowledge, insisting on the contrary that only faith can point the way to *felicitas*, belongs within the ranks of Renaissance fideism. If we remember what was said earlier about Agrippa it is clear that this Renaissance *magus* is a worthy representative of fideism; and the same argument applies to Montaigne. It is true that modern scholarly opinion has given the French thinker, on the basis that he is the first to integrate methodically the premises of Pyrrhonism into the context of the Renaissance anti-dogmatic tradition, the distinction of being the epitome of Renaissance skepticism. But as I understand the reasoning of the *Apologie de Raimond Sebond*, it is equally plain that the ultimate result of Montaigne's posture might very well be total passivity and fideism; and this in my view is precisely what the author hints at as he summarizes what makes Pyrrhonism valuable. "There is nothing in man's invention that has so much verisimilitude and usefulness. It presents man naked and empty, acknowledging his natural weakness, fit to receive from above some outside power; stripped of human knowledge, and all the more apt to lodge divine knowledge in himself, annihilating his judgment to make more room for faith. . . . He is a blank tablet prepared to take from the finger of God such forms as he shall be pleased to engrave on it. The more we cast ourselves on God and

commit ourselves to him, and renounce ourselves, the better we are."[94]
And fideist as well is he who, doubting not only the value of reason but
the autonomy of the will also, concludes that (1) we are incapable of
knowing, and (2) we cannot reach any kind of knowledge endowed with
moral worth; further adding that even if indeed we could know it would
still be a meaningless accomplishment, because our will, flawed and
unable to act at all save at the most elementary level, would not be able
to translate that hypothetical knowledge into an *actio* morally valuable
(Luther, Melanchthon, Calvin). Now, if in addition to defining
Renaissance skepticism in the manner just outlined and demanding that
it meet the above conditions, we also insist that it face the normative
consequences of epistemological doubting (or, to put it differently, if we
prescribe that the skeptic, rejecting dogmatism and denying that man can
attain to the whole truth, should in addition put forth a social and
political program), then only Vives is fully up to the task during the first
half of the sixteenth century. In other words, in Vives we meet a skeptic
who undertakes to raise (on the foundation, it must be remembered, of
criteria of doubt and action formulated by Antiquity) a structure in which
recta ratio and a verisimilitude (*opinio*) reinforced by an argument of
probability together offer man a criterion of moral judgment (*prudentia*)
which, if certainly not indubitable, is at least sufficiently trustworthy to
yield the tranquillity and virtue that are in turn the indispensable
conditions to achieve *felicitas*. This very theme— what epistemological
doubting implies, its consequences for man's society, and how Vives
understands man ought to behave within a society thus molded—is
precisely what we wish to study next in this monograph.

iv

But before undertaking that task we should, by way of conclusion,
bring up the following considerations. Vives' approach to knowledge and
his concomitant understanding of the nature and end of philosophy are
indisputably the product of a fundamentally eclectic temperament
determined, without regard for authority, to take from traditional
wisdom only that which passes the muster of its uncompromisingly
critical bent. To be sure, Vives is Aristotelian in that he will find in the
hoary oracle of Antiquity the essential wherewithal to lay the foundations
of his own epistemology. From St. Augustine, on the other hand, he
inherits both the Fall and the unrelenting emphasis on its consequences
for the future of man. And he enthusiastically shares St. Thomas' faith in

---

[94] *The Complete Essays of Montaigne*, trans. D.M. Frame (Stanford, 1965) 375.

the power and freedom of the human will. All this notwithstanding, we must note that Vives still remains most definitely his own man. Just as those who came before Aristotle were called to account for their errors by him, so Vives claims as his own the right to disagree with the master and to expect that his arguments will be judged on their own merits, and not rejected merely on the grounds of authority. And in the concrete case of knowledge Vives does not hesitate to take issue with both Aristotle's *episteme* and its medieval adumbrations. Theoretical speculation rooted in axiomatic propositions and governed by formal rules of validity to be applied mechanically might conceivably lead to reality—provided that the seeker shared in the perspective and yearnings of the schoolmen. But to Vives it was a disembodied reality that could not possibly have anything to do with man's own earthly reality, what elsewhere I have dubbed his theatrical persona or make-believe. And for Vives, given the limitations imposed on man by sin, rationally searching for a reality other than man's make-believe is of course criminally indulging in a fool's errand. Knowing, in other words, cannot be an end unto itself or serve a reality not demonstrably man's, for otherwise it becomes but an artificial construct devoid of meaning in that world defined by man's stage persona. Knowledge, then, has to be a tool, a practical means exclusively aimed at furthering the cause of man in this existence. Man carries a moral seed planted in him by nature and the concomitant obligation to nurture it. To ease the burden thus imposed on him man was endowed with reason and the will. With the former (clearly *ratio practica*), man creates the knowledge that the latter will apply to the task of making the seed germinate into moral life, the only reality truly accessible to him. Constrained to move within such boundaries, Vives has no choice but to reject the theoretical rationality of the Peripatetics. Fortunately, a suitable alternative is ready at hand in the form of the Academy's reaction against the Hellenistic version of Aristotelian dogmatism embodied in Stoicism. The skeptical epistemology of Arcesilaus and Carneades gives Vives the criterion for action firmly congruent with man's make-believe. Probable knowledge is therefore the ideal instrument, now in the hands of the will, to translate thought into *actio* after the fashion of moralizing Roman Stoicism. The principal—nay, the sole—end of all of man's cognitive activities must be his moral life; nothing else really matters, and so Vives will summarily excise any pursuit or form of knowledge that cannot be justified in terms of that end. Man's *ars vivendi* is the keystone of Vives' entire system, a crucial fact that automatically sets the Spanish humanist at odds with Luther's own uncompromising devaluation of both *recta ratio* and *voluntas*. But there is more, because the sequence reason, knowledge, will, moral life is incomplete as it stands. The transcendental element, what on another occasion I called man's divine essence, that true reality from which he was sundered by the Fall, is missing. And here again Vives departs from learned tradition. His is not the rational theology of St. Thomas, nor is it the revelational vision of St. Augustine. Instead, he adopts a mystical transcendentalism reminiscent of the Neoplatonic philosophizing of the early Fathers as well as German and Spanish mysticism, and centered upon the idea of love. After the earthly preparation issuing in *bonitas* love—symbolized in this life by *caritas*, a reflection of the love divine—alone can elevate man to the otherworldly realm of *sapientia*, there at last, having left behind the mask of make-believe, to fathom his own reality and to unravel the mystery of his own nature. Needless to say, at this point religion, which throughout the discourse involving man's make-believe had remained confined to its most natural level, becomes Christianity and therefore acquires, at least by association, a decidedly revelational character. Of course, how this transition takes place in practice can be properly understood only after we have followed Vives as he explains the genesis and evolution of society and the creation of the foundation on which it stands, the arts. Finally, the issue of ignorance. Like Agrippa, Vives believes that knowledge of God cannot be had "with syllogisms and demonstrations." But unlike Agrippa he cannot accept that "belief and worship" are enough. The latter cannot, willy-nilly, elevate man to the divinity from a dead start of ignorance. In full, if perhaps unconscious, agreement with the medieval Church's teaching concerning man's ability to contribute to his own salvation, Vives holds that God intended man to lift himself, by his own bootstraps, out of the muck of ignorance and into a moral life. Then and only then will Agrippa's "belief and worship" work.

*C*hapter Three: The Making of Society

Instinct and Necessity

i

THOUGH THE NEED TO AVOID SURRENDERING to the lure of *contemplatio* is self-evident, Vives laments (as we noted in Chapter Two but reiterate for reasons soon to be clear) that it is often ignored by men who, seduced by the mirage of boundless knowledge, "scrutinize the why and how of everything" and move away from the cultivation of virtue (which, as Vives himself will in the end reveal, is nothing more than prudence). Absorbed in excessive devotion to their studies, these men have no time left to govern their people, manage their households, or control their own mores (meaning that they will have little time left to devote to self-knowledge); no time at all, that is, to spend on the branches of philosophy that Vives clearly associates with prudence: politics, economics, and ethics. He further insists that the proper order of things is the "cultivation of virtue"—meaning man's obligation to fulfill his duties to commonwealth, family, and self—in this life, relegating to eternity the pleasure of seeking and enjoying knowledge of ultimate causes (the "quenching of that all-consuming thirst").[1] Practical reason, then, offers man the only kind of knowledge truly available to him, a knowledge with which to travel the arduous and uncertain road leading to *felicitas*. Such is obviously the first provision made by God on behalf of his fallen creature. But the very reproaches that Vives hurls at those who still insist on pursuing the elusive goal of contemplation at the expense of the active life, which remains the one and only hope for man, clearly suggest (the entire course of Western civilization as it unfolds in *De disciplinis* [1531] unerringly points to it) that the *lumen* that is (a) God's first provision in His new plan for man, and (b) the beacon by whose tremulous light he must learn the art of living, cannot fulfill its promise in a vacuum. *Ratio practica*, in other words, needs a specific and well-defined context. The Divine Providence must therefore have devised a second and further means to help His rebellious son. During mankind's pre-lapsarian stage and with humanity in complete control of all its intellectual faculties, men were able to fulfill their own respective destinies individually and by themselves. After the Fall, with those powers dramatically diminished and a new, indirect way laid open to man as the only alternative, his former self-sufficiency waned. "As a result of this wicked act man lost dominion

---

[1] DPP I *Opera* III 190-91.

over the world."[2] Under the circumstances, God once more came to the rescue by further endowing man with the indispensable milieu wherein to follow the new path. As a consequence of what in this fashion God decreed and man executed, the latter became a social being meant to live in the organized company of his peers. It is therefore from within the context of society, the second fundamental provision of God's alternate plan, that man will wield and manage those faculties that enable him to arrive at an *opinio* governed by *verisimilitudo*.[3]

In conclusion, man is indeed a social animal in the full Aristotelian and Thomist sense. But two limiting conditions must be attached to that statement. First, and despite occasional testimonies to the contrary,[4] man was not originally created by God as a social being. Heir to the angels and fated to do again what the rebels among them had undone, man once enjoyed a self- sufficiency and independence that clearly made sociability unnecessary; indeed, irrelevant, for the concept has only meaning in terms of post-Fall events. But man's willful decision to transgress against his Creator derailed the original divine plan. God, however, had scripted an

---

[2] Ibid. 191.

[3] But before we begin our study of that context we should attempt to answer the following preliminary question: is society truly and uniquely a human creation? The answer is yes, but with the usual word to the wise attached. Society, to be sure, is a creation of nature, and there was a time when man was indeed the master of the latter. But the two instances are not synchronous, for separating them stands the Fall. They belong instead to two distinct epochs in the existence of mankind. Before the Fall (1) man, in control of nature, was not a social being (this statement, proposed now with little proof, will in pages to come be given a suitable foundation) and (2) nature was presumably a direct bridge between man and God. These two premises, critical components of God's original plan, ceased to apply when the latter was invalidated by human disobedience; and in the new script drafted by the Creator the role of nature changed from servant to master. We have already noted how man forfeited the lordship of nature. He was unquestionably deprived of his right to rule the rest of creation. Branded with the stigma of the first rebellion his body, meaning the passions, no longer obeyed the mind. And with the waning of both bodily strength and intellectual clarity man forsook the obedience of his inferiors and his kingdom. Nature now became an autonomous instrument, the image of God, imprinted with the instructions that the Divine will wished man to follow. In this new arrangement society (or, in the vein of the metaphor introduced in Chapter Two, the soil designed to offer the moral seed the maximum opportunity for growth), the environment within which man must abide by those instructions, is then of nature and therefore invented by man as he obeys his own natural instinct. Still, his is only an immediate invention; mediately, society remains of God. Precisely what this means will, it is hoped, become clear as we follow Vives' version of how society came into being.

[4] "Daily reality confirms that man was created by God for society in this life." *De disciplinis* VII i Opera VI 222.

alternate plan that was automatically put in place after the Fall; a plan centered about a faculty, practical reason, and an institution, society, that would still enable man, no longer self-sufficient, to reach the end for which he was created in community with his peers. To the important question: was there a stage in the evolution of mankind when society did not exist and men indeed lived in solitude? Vives obviously gives an affirmative answer.[5] True, he never, to my knowledge, explicitly says so; but the internal logic of his argument makes the conclusion inescapable. His position, moreover, places him clearly at odds with the architect of the most influential and enduring vision of Christianity as theology and religion: St. Augustine.

For the illustrious bishop of Hippo man's sociability was already a fact in the very beginning of his history, before the Fall. For while still in Paradise and living in a "state of innocence"—meaning that Adam was endowed with a pristine will in full and total control of the passions, knowledge of what was good, and the unique ability to shape his own destiny—man was presented with a companion, Eve. Several important consequences followed from the divine decision. To begin with, a natural bond was created between the two creatures; a bond that, moreover, was automatically passed on, through heredity and the power of friendship respectively, to the children of the union and to mankind at large. Additionally, all men are (1) descended from one original family and therefore kin, and (2) endowed with reason. With mankind's sociability thus firmly grounded, St. Augustine next axiomatically proposes the existence of a "natural" law, separate and distinct from both positive and divine law, embodying a basic precept: "do not do unto others what you would not have others do unto you," a maxim St. Augustine sees as the foundation for all the moral rules and norms guiding and regulating the conduct of man toward his fellows. In short, having made clear that nature leaves man no choice but to live in friendship and fellowship with his own kind, St. Augustine reveals the instrument placed by that selfsame nature at the disposal of man to achieve what he must. But all this, it must be remembered, took place when man lived in a state of innocence. What happened to both natural law and human sociability once man decided to disobey his Creator? Man's turning away from God generated the sin and unrighteousness that in turn caused natural law to be nearly wiped out from his being. The attendant consequences were disastrous: (1) man can no longer live a good social life merely by fulfilling the obligations imposed upon him by the law of nature; and (2) he is no longer

---

[5] In fact, we shall soon note, twice did man live in solitude. First, in the pre-lapsarian epoch—although he might have also lived organized in families. Second, in the very early stages of the post-lapsarian age, when he lived like a beast.

automatically deserving of everlasting salvation. He now needs the grace of God, which He has made available to him through the sacrifice of His Son. But God's grace guarantees neither the uplifting of all men nor the redemption of a society whose underpinnings have been fatally compromised by the subversion of natural law. In fact, the vast majority of humankind remains unredeemed, so their community is prone to strife and disorder. God, however, did not leave the City of Man entirely to its own devices. Instead, to insure a measure of peace and stability in that earthly society, God introduced coercive law and political authority. Clearly, they serve to bring into the post-Fall world the stern discipline that alone can restrain, through repression and coercion, the unruly passions of men. The law and the state are therefore simultaneously the remedy for man's present disorder of soul, and the punishment meted out by God to the godless, whose flawed reason can no longer fathom the precepts of natural law and whose bodies refuse to obey the will. And because both law and the state are of God they must be obeyed. True, some laws will be just and others unjust; some rulers will be fair and some will be foul criminals dealing harshly with those entrusted to their care.[6] No matter, for all—good and bad laws, saintly and vicious rulers—are part and parcel of God's decree; to rebel against them is to rebel against God.[7] But the bishop of Hippo is not the only venerable authority whose premises concerning society are implicitly challenged by Vives. One of the most cherished assumptions of contemporary Thomism was the natural and spontaneous existence/rise of society. Indeed, the question whether man had at any time existed in solitude does not seem to have occurred to St. Thomas. The closest he ever comes to identifying a possible pre-social stage in the evolution of man is the state of innocence, when "the first man had absolute rule and command over the animate creatures of the earth."[8] But although at this stage "man could not have been master of other men in the sense of holding them in thrall or slavery,"[9] even in the state of innocence "there would still have been need of social order, there would have been rulers and subjects. Parents, too, would have ruled and guided their children. But there would have been no harshness of rule, no injustice, no resentment in those ruled against their rulers."[10] In contrast with what I interpret to be Vives' position,

---

[6] *Civitas Dei* Book V Chapter xxi.

[7] Ibid. Book XIX Chapter xv. For all this see H.A. Deane, *The Political and Social Ideas of St. Augustine* (New York, 1963).

[8] *Summa theologiae* Ia q.96 a.1.

[9] Ibid. a.4. Slavery—and political obedience, according to Alonso de Castrillo—of course would appear later, one of the consequences suffered by man as he broke faith with God.

[10] Ibid.

Aquinas sees society (and government) as parts of God's original plan, namely, they were both divinely willed simultaneously with the creation of man; both, in short, are of divine origin, antedate (and here St. Thomas, on the matter of the state, sharply departs from St. Augustine's own stand) the Fall, and cannot be said to be a creation wrought as a result of and to control sin. The second caveat above also separates Vives from both St. Augustine and St. Thomas. For the last two see, at least implicitly, society like Athena emerging fully formed from Zeus' head, whereas for Vives it owes its existence to an evolutionary process sustained, in turn, by three distinct but mutually complementary operating agencies "imprinted in man's nature by the Supreme Maker of all things": two constructive, instinctive love of self and reason (*ratio practica*, of course), and one, *commoditas*, destructive. It is precisely the rise of society under the influence of these agencies that interests us here.

ii

God, foreseeing the needs and wants of man after the Fall, "created the necessary wherewithal."[11] He caused the earth to yield some foods in the shape of trees, bushes, herbs, roots. Cattle on the land, fishes in the water, and birds in the air also became sources of nourishment for man, while the fur and hides of animals supplied a means of protecting his body and keeping it warm.[12] The following question obviously comes to mind: how did man become aware that all this bounty had been fashioned to satisfy needs indispensable to his survival? Instinct is the answer. Endowed by nature with a sure instinct for self-preservation (*amor tuendi sui*)[13] primitive man soon discovered and learned to use what the Creator had left for his sustenance and warmth.[14]

It would seem that instinct went a long way indeed. It enabled man to discern the need for bodily subsistence; it further made him aware of the frailty of that body and how prone it is to illness, thus leading him to search for the means to ward off sickness and to protect himself from harshness of climate with coverings of hides and shelter from wild beasts, piling up the rocks and timber also provided by nature to fashion a rough

---

[11] DSP I ii *Opera* IV 423.

[12] Ibid.

[13] DTD I i *Opera* VI 243. Besides the natural law St. Augustine had proposed the existence of another "law of nature which men share with the beasts: self-preservation or self-love, both instinctual and innate which does not require reason for its application." Deane, op. cit. 87-88. "For love of self is inherent in every species; since what species exists that ever abandons itself or any part of itself, or any habit or faculty of any such part, or any of the things, whether processes or states, that are in accordance with its nature?" Cicero, *De finibus* IV xiii.

[14] DTD I i *Opera* VI 243. Aristotle, *Politics*.

abode.[15] A hunter and a gatherer, man, now supported by a nature, the immediate cause of instinct, whose role had been redefined in God's new plan, entered into the first and most savage stage in his evolution.[16] This is clearly a stage with no Aristotelian precedent. Aristotle saw the phenomenon of human association as an organic process evolving in stages, each of which springs out of desires and needs whose fulfillment defines the degree of evolutionary success attached to each stage: sexual and parental instinct, the primitive wants of the family and its extension, the clan; the imperatives created by the coming together of those distinguished by natural selection as fit to command or to obey; the more complex needs associated with the search for the good life. "If accordingly, we begin at the beginning, and consider things in the process of their growth, we shall best be able . . . to attain scientific conclusions . . . . First of all, there must necessarily be a union or pairing of those who cannot exist without one another. Male and female must unite for the reproduction of the species."[17] Aristotle obviously assumes that such union must necessarily issue into a family. And although Vives does not explicitly answer Aristotle's implicit objection—how can man live in solitude without the species ultimately becoming extinct?—there is at least one precedent in classical literature that resolves the impasse by admitting

---

[15] DTD I i *Opera* VI 244. The early evolution of mankind, from man the wanderer to the rise of the family, is also discussed in *De subventione*, a treatise where Vives discourses on mendicity, proposing solutions to one of the most pressing social problems facing sixteenth-century cities. Here again, but far more explicitly, instinct-driven *necessitas* plays a pivotal role. Primitive man soon realized the need to sustain his body—the instinct of self-preservation instilled in him by nature told him as much. At this the earliest stage in his evolution, therefore, man acted moved by *necessitas*. He learned everything pertaining to food and drink, what was good for him and what was not, and how to procure and preserve the needed things. Furthermore, inasmuch as the body is easy prey to diverse illnesses, man sought the means to prevent or to cure them. He next found a way of protecting the body from inclement weather, first with clothing and, later, by building shelters which afforded additional protection against predators. DSP II ii *Opera* IV 423.

[16] "Men dragged out life like forest-ranging beasts. Then no hardy farmer guided the curved plow or knew how to till the soil with the hoe, to set new cuttings in the earth. . . .Whatever gifts the sun and rain had given and the earth created of its own will sufficiently pleased their hearts. . . .Then the earth's burgeoning youth produced much provender, harsh but ample for wretched men. . . .Not yet did they know how to employ skins and to clothe their bodies with the spoils of wild beasts; they lived in groves and in mountain caves and forests. . . .They could not have regard for the common good, nor did they know how to observe any customs or laws among themselves. Whatever booty Fortune offered to a man he carried off, taught by its own nature to seek strength and to live by himself alone." Lucretius, *On Nature*, trans. R.M. Geer (Indianapolis, 1965) Book V 930-60. See also Cicero, *The Speeches* Pro Sestio XLII.

[17] Aristotle, *Politics* 1252a. The Baker translation.

the existence of a time when pairing was both occasional and for purely sexual purposes: "Venus joined the bodies of lovers in the forests; for one woman yielded to natural love, another to the violent force and uncontrollable passion of the man, another to a bribe."[18] A time when, all told, man was but a beast, motivated only by the threefold drive common to all animals: hunger, fear, and procreation. Soon enough, however, self-love caused this solitary wanderer to perceive one fundamental fact: so great is man's frailty and his need for many and diverse things that no one is self-sufficient.[19] What happened next is not completely clear, although there is no question as to the outcome: the creation of the family. In *De tradendis disciplinis* (1531) Vives suggests that once aware of his need for company man sought out his fellows and "many men gathered together in a cave,"[20] thus to all appearances bringing to an end mankind's first, and pre-social stage. "Bound by the strength of love [*caritas, not amor*], husband, wife, and children soon abandoned the communal cave"[21] and built their own shelter, a hut, "with pieces of loose timber and a thatched roof."[22] *De subventione*, on the other hand, chronicles the rise of the family in more conventional terms. *Necessitas* continued to propel man forward, and soon he became aware that "no man is endowed with a body so strong and a mind so penetrating that, if he is to live as a human being ought to, he can be totally self-sufficient."[23]

---

[18] Lucretius, op. cit. Book V 960-70. This stage of primeval savagery was eventually replaced by a second one heralded by the creation of the family. "After the woman joined to the man had come into a lasting (union. . .and the laws of the family were known)." Book V 1010-20.

[19] In Vives' scheme of things, therefore, instinct accomplishes for man what reason does in St. Thomas'. Frailty and need for the things indispensable for human life: this is a theme common to all Spanish writers, and one clearly spelled out by Aquinas.

[20] DTD I i *Opera* VI 244.

[21] Ibid.

[22] Ibid. "For since the reproductive instinct is by Nature's gift the common possession of all living creatures, the first bond of union is that between husband and wife." Cicero, *De officiis* I xvii. "In the first place there must be a union of those who cannot exist without each other, namely, of male and female, that the race may continue." Aristotle, op. cit. 1252a 25-30. There is no consideration on the part of Aristotle of the pre-family state. In Aristotle, then, the social sequence begins as a result of (a) a sexual and paternal instinct common to all humans, (b) the coming together of those whom nature meant to rule and to be ruled. Ibid. 1252b 5-10.

[23] DSP I ii *Opera* VI 423. At this point Vives, who has wholeheartedly agreed with Cicero on the issue of the importance of activity over contemplation, fundamentally parts company with him. For Vives *necessitas* is the major motor force behind every aspect of society, from its creation to its preservation. But Cicero in the same passage where he exhorts men to follow an active life also points out that "it is a very false notion that hath

Unquestionably, at this point man has taken the first step down the road leading away from the beast and toward the discovery of his own humanity. And upon taking that fateful first step man simultaneously caused the first suggestion of a social organization to be brought into being.

He realized, in other words, that he needed a companion, a wife to give him children and to help in the all-important task of preserving whatever he was able to acquire in the way of material goods—"women, although timorous, are tenacious preservers."[24] In addition he sought the fellowship of other men, presumably similarly organized in family units,[25] "men whom he liked and whom he wished to help." The evolutionary pattern outlined in both pieces is roughly the same, but with one significant difference. In *De tradendis* Vives implicitly suggests that the family emerged out of a tentative and embryonic, but decidedly communal, form of association. In *De subventione*, by contrast, the family is said to predate any species, however primitive, of community; in other words, the institution of the family had its genesis during man's pre-social existence. But regardless of which version reflects more accurately Vives' true intentions, the important fact is that for a long time afterward

---

been advanced by some people, that necessity alone was the motive to this society, which we have often mentioned; and that men would never have associated together, but that they were not able, in a solitary life, to furnish themselves with the necessaries of nature; and that every great and exalted genius, would Providence supply him with food and the other conveniences of life, would withdraw from all business and intercourse with mankind, and give himself wholly to study and contemplation. This is not so; for he would avoid solitude, endeavour to find a companion in his studies, and always be desirous of teaching and learning, of hearing and speaking: from all which things it is abundantly evident that the duties belonging to human society should in reason take place before those which relate to inactive knowledge." *De officiis* Book I Chapter xliv pp. 69-70.

[24] DSP I ii *Opera* IV 424.

[25] Ibid. "They came out of the caves, and built for themselves huts. . . .At first these huts were built here and there in spots widely spread over the open plain." DTD I i *Opera* VI 243-44. Watson 12. "Nature likewise by the power of reason associates man with man in the common bonds of speech and life; she implants in him above all, I may say, a strangely tender love for his offspring. She also prompts men to meet in companies, to form public assemblies. . .and she further dictates. . .the effort on man's part to provide a store of things that minister to his comforts and wants—and not for himself alone, but for his wife and children and the others whom he holds dear and for whom he ought to provide." Cicero, *De officiis* I iv. "After they had prepared huts and skins and fire, after the woman joined to the man had come into a lasting union. . .and the laws of the family were known, and after they saw children sprung from themselves. . . .Then, too, neighbors, desiring neither to injure nor to be injured, began to join in bonds of friendship." Lucretius, op. cit. V 1010-20.

mankind remained divided into family units existing in isolation, and presumably still living off the bounty provided by nature. Eventually, and Vives makes it "much later" in *De tradendis*, the imperative of instinct once more made itself felt through *necessitas*, and "families built their huts in close proximity to each other, hence creating neighborhoods [*vici*]."[26] This is clearly Aristotle's second stage. But when several families unite, "and the association aims at something more than the supply of daily needs, the first society to be formed is the village. And the most natural form of the village appears to be that of a colony from the family, composed of the children and grandchildren, who are said to be suckled with the same milk."[27] This is perhaps what Vives refers to as a "nucleus of society" when explaining how men sought the company of other men already associated in family units.[28] Although in *De tradendis* need remains the compelling force behind the rise of the village, "affection" also plays a role, a fact that Vives does not lose sight of in *De subventione.*[29] He therefore reprises the story of the man who for the sake of friendship/need sought the company of other men. *Gliscit amor et societas paulatim* developed, which expanded outward to the point that it could no longer be contained within the boundaries of one hearth.[30] In such wise the original human nucleus evolved into a larger community, a process, Vives takes pains to emphasize, that took place in the spirit of "the most marvelous concord."[31] And because nature gifted men, as it did

---

[26] DTD I i Opera VI 244.

[27] Aristotle, op. cit. 1252b 10-17.

[28] DSP I ii Opera IV 423.

[29] The time lapse between the rise of the family and that of the community, which Vives emphasizes in *De tradendis disciplinis*, is missing from *De subventione pauperum*.

[30] DSP I ii *Opera* IV 423-24. "But soon, because affection exhorted those who wished each other well not to go farther away, and because need of mutual help urged them, certain persons brought their own huts together into a kind of village." DTD I i Opera VI 243-44. Watson 13. Fellowship, love, mutual need: the points outlined here and immediately before are worth emphasizing now, because Vives is setting in motion a trend of thought that in the end will lead to the conclusion that the ultimate responsibility of the state and the ruler who embodies it is the protection of society, inasmuch as the latter in turn will protect the individual. There is, however, a price to be paid for this protection; a price Vives is willing to pay—a willingness which in turn is in my view one of the constants of Vives' political thought. Because in exchange for the protection offered immediately by the state and mediately by society, the individual must subordinate much of his independence to the group. "But of all the bonds of fellowship, there is none more noble, none more powerful than when good men of congenial character are joined in intimate friendship." Cicero, *De officiis* I xvii.

[31] DSP Opera IV 423.

all other animals, with an instinctive sense of gratitude, the inhabitants of these early communities felt that the best way to reciprocate the favors they received from each other was to specialize their contributions to the community. Gratitude, then, caused the creation of different occupations. In each community men henceforth devoted their whole attention to whatever form of endeavor best suited their natural temperaments. In this fashion a growing process of division of labor led some men to become fishermen; others chose to be hunters, while still others took to weaving and similar occupations, and many selected to tend the flocks or preferred to work the land, all of them occupations eminently useful to life in common.[32]

Natural instinct obviously served man well as he progressed along the evolutionary path. It taught him to understand his body and how to provide for its needs, form a family, structure a community, and develop the arts that made the latter functional. But man is "an animal exposed to and suspicious of injury." And despite the simplicity, good will, and concord attendant to life in those early human gatherings, differences inevitably arose among their inhabitants. Instinct once more came to the rescue and it was deemed but natural, under the circumstances, to submit those differences to the arbitration of the settlement's elder, much as children bring their disagreements to their father for resolution. Such a man, in an age "far less corrupt than our own," had authority (*imperium*) over the rest because it was then believed that the years had adorned him with the necessary experience and prudence.[33] And inasmuch as respect for *ius* and *aequitas* ran deep and strong among these early men, once the patriarch had issued his judgment, the hands and will of the entire community were tied into obedience.[34] And indeed, up to this point men behaved toward one another in "absolute concord,"[35] the single social commodity most highly prized by Vives, and so benevolence (engraved

---

[32] Ibid. 424.

[33] DTD I i *Opera* VI 244. "Every family is run by the eldest and therefore in the colonies the kingly form of government prevailed because they were of the same blood." Op. cit. 1252b 20ff. Of course, in Aristotle the state, albeit in an embryonic fashion, has already arisen with the family. Not so with Vives. Toward the end of the second or primitive social stage, a leader of unusual talent arises and ushers mankind into its third stage. "From day to day those who were outstanding in talent and vigorous of mind showed men how to change their earlier manner of life by new discoveries and, in particular, by the use of fire. These men, becoming kings, began to found cities and to construct citadels as places of refuge for themselves; they divided herds and fields and distributed them to their followers." Lucretius op. cit. V 1100-10. Despite the similar terminology, this is not the age equivalent to Vives' *civitas*. Lucretius' kings are closer to Vives' clan elders.

[34] DTD I i *Opera* VI 245.

[35] DSP I ii *Opera* IV 424.

by God in every man to serve as the glue that keeps society together) reigned supreme among them.[36] What is absolutely clear so far, despite the author's maddening nonchalance in this matter, is that (a) the developments that are about to overtake and bring to an end mankind's pre-political condition constitute social humanity's most profound and telling revolution, the rise of the state; (b) reason is about to enter the stage.

To begin with, as the society-making process outlined above moved forward, an unavoidable internal conflict broke out, pitting the interest of the individual against the group's. The *benevolentia* that in the society-forming stage had served to channel, and curb, self-love in the direction of sociability, returned, once its purpose had been accomplished, to a "state of quiescence." Given the swiftly evolving conditions to which man's pre-political society was now subjected, uncontrolled self-love threatened to engulf *iustitia/aequitas*, the successor to benevolence in the new and unfolding order of things, and the guardian of the community's interest. Left unchecked, this state of affairs would have had fatal consequences, for in the absence of *iustitia/aequitas* society cannot exist, let alone be preserved.[37] In other words, individual self-love (*amor*, instinct), the force behind the *necessitas* that, impelling men forward, had been heretofore so useful to mankind, now promised to overwhelm the collective *necessitas*—in the guise of *iustitia/aequitas*—of society. A new institutional framework was needed to arrest the disastrous trend. Man soon found out that the most suitable resolution to this conflict between individual and collective interest lay in strengthening the principle of *iustitia/aequitas*—on which, it must be reiterated, the well-being of society rested—with the power of *potestas*.[38] Clearly, Vives' approach to man's individuality is twofold. Throughout its early history mankind was well served by the distinctive personality, instinctive self-love, with which nature had endowed its members. In his pre-social state man survived by virtue of the very ensemble of unique characteristics that defined him as an entity distinct and separate from every other member of the species; indeed, he had nothing else but his own individuality. And man did far more than just survive. Unknowingly following the divine plan drawn for him by God, true, but propelled by his own individuality, he was carried forward and upward by the evolutionary current toward a prearranged goal. Once the latter, society, was reached, however, the mechanism that had taken him so far became obsolete—nay, more, it became a threat. Comfortably living in community with his peers, man failed to realize that what had formerly lifted him out of the slime now presented a clear

---

[36] *De disciplinis* VII i *Opera* VI 222.

[37] Ibid. 223. "We are born for Justice, and that right is based, not upon men's opinions, but upon Nature." Cicero, *De legibus* I x 29

[38] *De disciplinis* VII i *Opera* VI 223.

danger to the very thing it had achieved. And so man's individuality, the focal point of the unruly passions unleashed by the Fall, continued to assert itself, relentlessly pursuing its own self-interest without regard for the welfare of the whole within which it now existed. To arrest the unbridled egoism of man's individuality and to forestall its consequences political society was created. What contemporary Scholastics often accounted for by simply stating that political authority had to exist, for it could not be otherwise if what nature decreed (society) was to endure, Vives explains as an act of self-defense by the community trying to protect itself from the self-centered unruliness of its individual members. Far more explicitly than any schoolman, then, Vives sees the rise of the state as the visible outcome of the community's efforts at internal prophylaxis.

It would be, however, untimely at this point to call this newly arisen form of authority political, for only after some equally influential developments are fully accounted for can we truly say that we are in the presence of what Vives would call the state. And indeed, while on the one hand tensions were rising due to the conflictive clash of individual and community interests, contumacy within the commonwealth, on the other, gradually swelled to such proportions that mere prohibition, although backed by the personal *imperium* of the clan's patriarch, no longer sufficed to deter or control anti-social behavior. Laws had therefore to be proclaimed which carried with them penalties designed to dissuade the potential malefactor from transgressing against his fellows.[39] In *De subventione* the author puts the matter in even harsher terms. The spirit of harmony reigning among early men did not last long. Man's doleful obverse nature[40] soon made itself felt, and there appeared in the midst of humanity those who, unlawfully wishing to enjoy the fruits of the work of others, imposed through astuteness and terror their tyranny over them.[41] Deeply concerned in this work with the problem of indigence, Vives now adds an economic element missing from the other treatises. Forced by the depredations of evil men to surround their cities with walls, honest citizens were further moved to deal with the problem of "human laziness, arrogance, and indigence," the scourges, it would seem, of urban life. To solve it several measures were taken. To begin with, the land was divided among the citizens and laws were further enacted to enforce respect for the boundaries thus established. But the

---

[39] DTD I i *Opera* VI 245 Despite the coercion of the law, however, ill will grew and "public hatred" eventually led to the breakup of the unity that had hitherto characterized mankind. "Those sharing a community of interests surrounded themselves with walls and wielded weapons to repel aggression." Ibid.

[40] DSP I ii *Opera* IV 424.

[41] Ibid.

reformers did not stop there. At first bartering had been enough to satisfy
the economic needs of a fledgling society, but soon the latter's growing
complexity forced man to abandon that primitive method of exchange
and to replace it with a more sophisticated instrument rooted in the
invention of money. In the beginning money was minted in huge
quantities and distributed among the citizens in order to: (1) enable
members of the community to transact business more efficiently; and (2)
provide them with a means of exchange to pay for the goods and services
offered by other citizens. The function of money at this point was to
maintain an economic balance itself rooted in equity: "That each man
should have what was his." But the economic stability brought about by
this equitable distribution of money was soon shattered by the impact of
several factors: (1) in some cases illness compels a man to spend money
that he, unable to work, cannot replace, thus sinking him into an abyss
of poverty; (2) other men lose their goods in the course of wars and other
calamities beyond their control; (3) still others stupidly squander their
wealth; (4) many whose trade or profession suddenly loses favor with
fashion find themselves unemployed, in misery and want.[42] But regardless
of whether the medium is an educational treatise or a blueprint for the
eradication of beggary, the message remains the same in both pieces: the
growing violence was responsible for the introduction of coercive law.[43]

---

[42] Ibid. 425.

[43] The end of man's primitive society came, according to Lucretius, as a result of the
introduction of wealth. It issued mankind into a further stage in its evolution,
characterized by ambition, greed, and unbridled violence. Finally, tired of anarchy, some
men "taught how to elect magistrates, and they set up courts so that they might consent
to abide by the laws. For the human race, weary of protecting its life by means of
violence, was growing weak as a result of its hatreds. Therefore the more willingly did it
submit to laws and to the strict administration of justice." Lucretius, op. cit. V 1140-50.
Undoubtedly this is the stage equivalent to Vives' *civitas*. What Vives and Lucretius
laboriously explain in terms of stages, Cicero—no doubt summarizing Lucretius—
ondenses into a single paragraph. "For which of us, gentlemen, does not know the natural
course of human history—how there was once a time, before either natural or civil law
[*neque naturali neque civili iure*] had been formulated, when men roamed, scattered and
dispersed over the country, and had no other possessions than just so much as they had
been able either to seize by strength and violence, or keep at the cost of slaughter and
wounds? So then those who at first showed themselves to be most eminent for merit and
wisdom having perceived the essential teacheableness of human nature, gathered together
into one place those who had been scattered abroad, and brought them from that state of
savagery to one of justice and humanity. Then things serving for common use, which we
call public, associations of men, which were afterwards called states, then continuous
series of dwelling-places which we call cities, they enclosed with walls, after divine and
human law had been introduced. Now, between life thus refined and humanized, and that
life of savagery, nothing marks the difference so clearly as law and violence." *Speeches* Pro

Still, cautions Vives, it will not do to exaggerate the gravity of the crisis. For the most part extreme violence was exceptional during this transitional period. Far more commonplace was the opposite trend: to cement further already existing human relations and to establish new ones conducive to the preservation and continuity of society. Out of the needs created by this ongoing sense of fellowship there emerged language, one of the most powerful of social instruments. One after another and under the stimulus of friendly social intercourse, words were born, followed by entire phrases whose meaning was then fixed by common agreement.[44] And so *sermo* came into being, so important to maintain "social relations" that in *De disciplinis* Vives does not hesitate to call it "a rudder governing the course of human fellowship."[45]

The Rise of Political Society

The individual-community conflict, increased violence, continuing sociability: such are the central factors that both dominated the scene and guided pre-political society into the next, or political, stage. In turn, their impact upon the body social was responsible for the rise of *iustitia, lex,* and *sermo*. What is truly fundamental about the whole process, however, is that at its very foundation lies a profound and revolution-making shift in the essence of necessity away from a *necessitas* fueled by nature through love of self and toward a *necessitas* stoked by nature through *ratio*. Not unexpectedly, therefore, it is *ratio* that will bring *iustitia, lex,* and *sermo* together into a new institution, the state. Let us now see how, in practice, the laws were created, and in whose hands was entrusted the *potestas*

Sestio XLII 91-92.

[44] DTD I i *Opera* VI 245. In Lucretius' scheme, family and associations of families—society—begin at the very end of the first, savage, state of mankind. The second period, with very tentative social forms already in place, begins with the invention of fire and the appearance of speech. "Nature forced men to emit various sounds of the tongue, and utility molded the names of things." Lucretius, op. cit. V 1030. This second stage, when man lived in primitive society, is the closest that Lucretius comes to formulating a Golden Age.

[45] *De disciplinis* IV i *Opera* VI 152. Human society, invariably and in all cases, is kept together by means of two bonds, *iustitia et sermo*. The absence of either of those two "rudders"—which guide man's ability to live together in an orderly manner—makes any form of human association, be it public or private, unstable and ephemeral. The former, in a deliberate and quiet fashion embodies *ratio et consilium*, while the latter upholds the strength of justice more lively and actively through its ability to awaken the "movements of the soul." "The first principle is that which is found in the connection subsisting between all members of the human race, and the bond of connection is reason and speech which . . . associate men together." Cicero, *De officiis* I xvi.

inhering in the new institution.

i

All things, we already know, testify that man was created by God for life in common. He also infused him with benevolence, the cement needed to keep together the society that he must create. But mere *benevolentia* can easily be smothered once the conflict between individual and community begins, and so it has to give way to *iustitia*, which banishes injury from among men.[46] Justice itself, however, would in turn have foundered in the stormy seas of ignorance and passion were it not for the strength lent to it by the power of authority (*potestas*)—this, then, is how Vives explains the Scholastic commonplace that made the state a logical outcome of society: the latter cannot exist without some form of authority. And this in turn logically sets the stage for the entrance of the lawgiver. Everything that pertained to all in the community and was necessary to their good life[47] now, "by the general consensus and permission," became delegated into the hands of some men thought to be wise, of judicious temper, and controlled affections.[48] The intention guiding the choice made by the community through a general election was that those men, after having determined by the light of their reason[49] where equity lies, should make their findings public in the interest of the common weal. Upon examination of those findings by the assembly of all men they were, if approved, confirmed and firmly established with the weight of authority, fear, and punishment.[50] But we may ask: are those lawgivers also the men who hold and wield the *magna potestas* to apply the coercive force with which the laws are endowed? In the dawn of mankind, it will be useful to recall, the patriarch exercised *imperium*, a form of authority that gave him the right to interpret the unwritten custom that had its origin in the community itself, and to apply it in the resolution of whatever differences might arise among his fellow clansmen, a custom, however, devoid of coercive power. He was, then, the clan's leader, but not its lawgiver. Precisely the opposite seems to be the case now, for what we have in the present instance is wise men who formulate

---

[46] "Atque ab hominum convictu iniuriam omnem arceret." *De disciplinis* VII i *Opera* VI 223.

[47] "Ergo quod ex usu erat omnium, ad quiete et iucunde vivendum. " Ibid.

[48] Vives admits that in some cases men, on their own initiative, undertook to carry out the task, presumably without the express consent of the community.

[49] We shall soon see, in conformity with Vives' crucial argument concerning the fallibility of human judgment, that even that of wise men—let alone that of the community at large—can be vitiated by "ignorance and passion."

[50] "Confirmaretque, et constabiliret magna potestate, poenis, metu." Ibid.

coercive standards subject to the community's approval and which they
are not given the authority to enforce. Who, then, wields that power? In
the beginning, Vives answers, and presumably after the lawgiving process
had been set in motion, "just as the human mass was starting to coalesce
into an organized community, the need for leadership made itself felt."[51]
Out of that "monstrous body," a leader (*rector*) was chosen (*eligebatur*) of
great prudence and wisdom whom all agreed to obey to the end that he,
with the support of universal consensus, on which basis strength and
power rest their fullness,[52] would restrain evildoers, protect the righteous,
consecrate justice (*ius diceret*), and give all their due. This man's decrees
and commands, validated by right, were called laws.[53] So far we have a
body of laws, an elected leader to apply and enforce them, and a form of
authority, *potestas*, sanctioned by the community and entrusted to the
hands of the leader. In other words, the *civitas* (undoubtedly Vives'
favorite form of political society) is now in possession of everything it
needs to function as a political community;[54] it is, in other words, a

---

[51] *A principio enim, coalita hominum congregatione, quum, velut moles quaedam, rectore
indigeret.* Ibid. 224.

[52] *Ut ille fultus consensu universorum, quae amplissimae sunt opes ac potentia.* Ibid. 225.

[53] *Cuius decreta, ac iussa, essent ius ratum, ac leges dicerentur.* Ibid.

[54] *Ex eo in civitatem deduxerunt quantum quidem videbatur illi congregationi opus esse,
easque leges nominarunt.* Which must constantly be infused with equity, for the latter is
the soul, strength, and vigor of the former. *Aequitas universalitas est quaedam; lex, deductio
et species.* Nothing is more iniquitous than laws not moved by equity; and for that reason
ius is defined as the art of the good and the equitable. *Ius finitur ars boni et aequi.* Ibid.
223-24. Still, and despite the laws restraining power, ill will continued to spread
throughout the human race; and to ward off the calamities promised by the resulting
confrontation among people, those bound by common interests armed and surrounded
themselves with walls to ward off external attacks. DTD I i *Opera* VI 245; DSP I ii *Opera*
IV 424-25. "When several villages are united into a single complete community large
enough to be nearly or quite self-sufficient, the state comes into existence, originating in
the bare needs of life, and continuing in existence for the sake of a good life." Aristotle,
op. cit. 27-30. This is how Cicero puts it while discussing the nature of kinship. "For since
the reproductive instinct is by Nature's gift the common possession of all creatures, the
first bond of union is that between husband and wife; the next, that between parents and
children, then we find one home, with everything in common. And this is the foundation
of civil government, the nursery, as it were, of the state. Then follow the bonds between
brothers and sisters, and next those of first and then of second cousins; and when they can
no longer be sheltered under one roof, they go out into other homes, as into colonies.

Then follow between these, in turn, marriages and connections by marriage, and from
these again a new stock of relations; and from this propagation and after-growth states
have their beginnings." *De officiis* I xvii.

communitas perfecta, arrived at by man's autonomous will and reason. But there is more, because having assured the survival of justice through coercive laws and a ruler to wield the *potestas* needed to enforce them, *necessitas*, in its continuing guise as *ratio*, maintained its relentless forward momentum. Out of the favorable setting created by the application of reason to public life there issued *prudentia*, a species of practical wisdom which "is to life what the rudder is to a ship." Prudence must therefore be constantly applied to all facets of organized life in common, be it in what pertains to individuals, the family, or public life itself; if, of course, we would lead an existence suitable to human beings. We have reached, in fact, what in Vives' scheme of things is the climax of human evolution. It is also a pattern akin to the one suggested by Aristotle (the earliest stage excepted): a solitary hunter–gatherer, the family and its extension, the clan, the *civitas*. A society that develops along normal lines embodies the gradual realization, first through instinct and then reason, by mankind of its God-given potential. Such potential is said to be realized in its fullness when man "invents" political society, the *civitas*, governed by prudence, the creator, in turn, of a supreme trilogy (ethics, economics, politics) to rule and guide in justice the three elements that in themselves subsume the story of mankind's evolutionary progress: the individual, the family, the state. It is worth reiterating that for Vives this achievement is both the consummation of and the justification for human evolution; a development surely mandated by man's own fallen nature and made possible in practice by the "stimuli imprinted in it by the Supreme Maker of all things."[55]

ii

Man has now been provided with the environment suitable to afford him the opportunity to live like a human being among his fellows: (1) a community that is manageable (i.e., one of many grown out of the single original association of men broken up by discord); (2) organized as a *civitas* under the tight control of community-legislated coercive and equitable norms designed to administer and preserve *iustitia/aequitas*; (3) led by a ruler chosen by the assembly of all men and given the *potestas* to apply and enforce those norms; and (4) guided by practical wisdom (*prudentia*).[56] But there is more; indeed, there has to be more, because

[55] DTD I i *Opera* VI 245-46.

[56] It must be further added that Vives' vision of society is fundamentally Aristotelian in another important respect. Man's social evolution is but an outward manifestation of his gradual realization of what the good life is. The earliest forms of sociability are the most primitive and least desirable because they cater to man's simplest needs. The *civitas* or *polis* is by contrast the most excellent because it affords man the good life. Only as a member of the *civitas* can man actualize his full potential *qua* man. And the *civitas* is by definition a politically organized society. In this sense can we say, both in the Vivesian

Vives has so far chronicled the evolution of mankind from the uncouthness of solitary savagery to the sophistication of well-organized *civitas* in what amounts to a spiritual vacuum. In other words, as conceived by Vives the *civitas* is an Aristotelian *polis* with neither room for nor need of knowledge of God. And yet, Vives never tires of repeating that fallen man structured society as a means to achieve the *bonitas* that is in turn the indispensable springboard to that everlasting salvation man's sinfulness seemingly lost for him. The *bonitas, summum bonum*, or good life, therefore, which in Aristotle is the ultimate and sole justification for the existence of the *polis*, is (indeed, must be) for Vives but a means to a still higher end. The internal logic of the humanist's entire system consequently demands that a society bereft of knowledge of God be but a contradiction in terms. Vives resolves the impasse in a surprisingly Toynbeean fashion: civilization (*civitas*) is not the supreme accomplishment of man; rather, it serves as chrysalis to nurture a still higher achievement, religion. But for the latter to emerge the former must die. We therefore ask of Vives: what happens to society after reaching the stage of *civitas*? The humanist, optimistic heretofore concerning man's potential, now reverts to a pessimistic and thoroughly Augustinian mood: haunted by his first transgression, man will inevitably pervert what he has created. Three things transpired: (1) the laws were defiled; (2) the ruler became a despot; (3) *commoditas* took the place of *necessitas* as the agency maintaining society's evolutionary momentum. Let us look at each in turn.

The earliest disorder suffered by the laws was at the hands of those from whom they derived, because the men upon whose shoulders rested the responsibility for modification or sanction were either the victims of incompetence or ignorance or the plaything of the passions. Ignorance is at fault when laws are dictated without regard for the nature of the place and their impact on those who dwell in it. When the passions are involved, several scenarios are possible. There were cases, for instance, of legislators who, becoming prey to their own self-importance, twisted the laws into serving their own interests instead of those of the community, the "Greek tyrants" being a case in point. Other lawgivers, moved by their own special hatred of certain vices, made laws harsh to the point of brutality (Draco, for example). In still other cases laws were legislated suitable to the inhabitants of the *civitas* but inimical to outsiders; or were influenced by social antagonisms—plebeians and patricians in Rome—or

---

and Aristotelian scheme of things, that man is by nature a political animal. "And therefore, if the earlier forms of society are natural, so is the state. . . .Hence it is evident that the state is a creation of nature, and that man is by nature a political animal." Aristotle, op. cit. I. 2. 1252b30-1253a. The Jowett translation.

greed or fear.[57] This last variation on the theme of the perversion of the laws, the enactment of legislation by men who out of fear slavishly prostrated themselves before *de immodica Principum potentia*, serves Vives as a natural platform from which to consider explicitly the fate of the man elected by the community to lead it. Since such a man was, in the first place, elected to his office, the community automatically felt that it would be wrong for him, prudent and honest as he was, to be bound by the same laws that constrained the rest of the polity. After all, being honest he would not act wickedly; and being vested with so much power (*potentia*) he could not be coerced. In this fashion originated the custom, which eventually acquired almost the strength of law, of exempting the ruler from the laws (*Principem legibus non tenerit*) and accepting that everything disposed by him would itself have the force of law.[58] In time, however, and as the human race worsened, the original ruler was succeeded by other princes, sometimes hereditary, sometimes elected by the people in their insanity and corrupted by anger, greed, or some other questionable motive. Princes, then, came to rule who in no wise could be compared, either in goodness or in prudence, to their predecessors. And those rulers demanded for themselves the same privileges granted by the community to their predecessors. But whereas the latter had used them sparingly, the former abused those privileges to the point that the old *Principem esse solutum legem* was now replaced by *Principem licere quidquid libeat*—to the prince anything, without restriction, is permitted. "Who will not be terrified by so much strength and license concentrated in the hands of one single person? It is tantamount to giving a sword to a homicidal maniac."[59]

With political society properly constituted and the necessities of life suitably met, the human mind moved from *necessitas* to *commoditas*. While man was besieged by want and fear he had no other thought but to free himself from them; but once that necessity was overcome he began to think of those things that produced pleasure and contentment. The results were catastrophic, for soon the body was snared by pleasure (*voluptas*) and his mind in thrall to *superbia*, both of which now claimed the greatest share of sovereignty over man. Through the former he was enslaved to pleasure and invented numberless things to serve it; he became prey to pride and created whatever he felt necessary to decorate himself and thus enhance his stature in the eyes of other men. But although serious, this aspect was as nothing compared to the harm wrought by his mental *superbia*, for it represents what Vives considers one of the great crimes committed by mankind: moving from *ratio practica* to *ratio*

---

[57] *De disciplinis* VII i *Opera* VI 224.

[58] Ibid. 225.

[59] Ibid. 224-25.

speculativa, from *actio* to *contemplatio*. This aspect of *commoditas*, embodied in man's all-consuming *curiositas*, caused his mind to turn from the "theater of man" to the "theater of the world," where he had been placed by God; in short, reversing the seminal process begun by Socrates.[60] The heavens, the elements, animals, plants, water, metals, rocks, even the contents of his own mind: everything became grist to the mill of his curiosity. Pushed on by *curiositas*, then, he felt great pleasure upon discovering something new, followed by an enhanced opinion of his intellectual prowess as the discoveries mounted. Soon, however, things got out of hand, and many elected to abandon all the duties of life (*vitae officia*) to devote themselves, as if preyed upon by an addiction, exclusively to a constant search for deeper knowledge.[61] Seeing that, inevitably, someone's findings contradicted someone else's, enmities developed and crystallized into sects (*sectae*).[62] Eventually, as the mad race for knowledge continued unabated, some men of reflective intellect sought a means of arresting it, attempting to ascertain precisely what the goal of that frenetic pursuit ought to be; a question Vives invariably stresses as deserving of careful examination. For, what is indeed the point of that strenuous activity if it only generates a renewed thirst for further efforts that lead nowhere but to total exhaustion? (and, of course, to the very Nemesis of society, *discordia*). And that search, the investigation of what the goal of knowledge ought to be, is in Vives' eyes indeed worthier than delving ceaselessly into the measure of the heavens or inquiring about the virtues of plants and stones. And yet, Vives admits, it is a quest very difficult to carry out, because the human mind cannot possibly find, by the weak and trembling light of its own intellect, the ultimate meaning of man's existence. So it was that thoughtful men, looking for that elusive answer, in that fashion came to have need of God, both to point the way and to guide us along it.[63] And that need for God was answered in the form of religion,[64] a ray from His light, a force from Him who is

---

[60] DTD I i *Opera* VI 246; Watson 15-16.

[61] "No man, however, should be so taken up in the search of truth, as thereby to neglect the more necessary duties of active life: for, after all is done, it is action only that gives a true value and commendation to virtue." Cicero, *De officiis* Book I Chapter vi p. 9.

[62] DTD I i *Opera* VI 246-47. Watson 16.

[63] Ibid. 247-48; Watson 17-18.

[64] It is to be noted that the upshot of this is to make religion into another art, although of course Vives goes on record against such notion; one resulting from a natural process similar to the one that, through *necessitas* and *commoditas*, yielded other arts. Vives' religion, in other words, is as natural a phenomenon as the mind of the Renaissance is capable of conceiving. But remember that Vives specifically says that knowledge of God

omnipotent. It alone returns us to the source from which we issue and toward which we move. There is no other perfection to man, for perfection, after all, consists in reaching that for which he was fashioned. Man was not created for food, clothing, or the seeking for hidden and troublesome knowledge. He was created for participation in eternity and God's divine nature. And religion alone can secure that participation for him. Everything else is superfluous. Religion alone is indispensable (*pietas nulla pacto potest*), for religion alone is capable of revealing man's true reality, his own divine nature. It alone is man's road to perfection.[65] Such is the reason why all other arts are in the absence of religion but children's games.[66] In short, man reached the conclusion that the realm of *sapientia* belongs to *pietas* alone.

Conclusion

From all that we have learned so far in the preceding pages, we can unquestionably conclude that Vives identifies three well-defined stages—pre-social, social, and political—in the evolution of mankind, and in the process suggests several points of considerable importance for us. Since in this study we are not explicitly interested in Vives' political views I shall, in what follows, confine my remarks to the first two.

In the first stage we meet man as a solitary wanderer leading a life guided by unrefined instinct and indistinguishable from that of the beasts. The second stands on the twin foundations of a discovery and an invention, both equally revolutionary. First, the discovery. Hitherto but a beast, man becomes gradually aware that he is ill-equipped to function

---

is not an art.

[65] "Sola utique pietas via est perficiendi hominis." Ibid. 248.

[66] It will not do, however, unduly to stress the argument for Vives' "modernity" on this issue. True, the point is strongly reminiscent of Toynbee's conclusion concerning the function of civilization as chrysalis for universal religion, but it probably has its conscious origin elsewhere. In Letter 88 2-3, Seneca, discussing the nature of true learning—one of Vives' own favorite topics—argues that the liberal arts "are worthy of a free man. But only one study is fully liberal in making a man free, and that is the study of wisdom (*sapientia*), with its strength of purpose and its noble and exalted ideals. *All the others are trivial and childish* [italics mine] (*cetera pusilla et puerilia sunt*)." And *sapientia*, according to Vives the skeptic is something that man can attain only through *pietas*. Religion, then, goes beyond all other forms of ultimate knowledge that man yearns for but cannot attain through reason. And the *civitas* is the achievement of reason. "The single task of philosophy is to discover the truth about things divine and human." Seneca, Letter 90 3. In Vives' Christian scheme of things the truth about the former comes from practical philosophy, the latter through *pietas* or religion.

alone and that his chances for survival will improve immeasurably if he associates with other beings similar to himself. Of course the discovery automatically insures that man will indeed survive, but not as a beast, for the very process of discovery has transformed man into something different: a human being. And herein lies one of the points mentioned above and worth underlining now, for all this is not merely a Thomist conceptualization elegantly designed to gloss with some credibility over the thorny issue of how man in fact came to be a social being. Rather, as far as Vives is concerned the stage during which man existed as a beast is historically real and concrete. Man once lived like an animal because he was once an animal. And for Vives, the hand–in–the–wound enthusiast, what man empirically learned during that bestial existence is precisely what enabled him to cross the threshold separating man from animal. God may have intended all along for man to be human, and he may indeed have planted that seed in him; but the actual process that caused the seed to blossom into fruit took place in time and must be credited to man alone. Clearly, Vives places a noticeable, if implicit, emphasis on one crucial assumption that those who would see the emergence of society from an organicist perspective had considerable difficulty in coming to terms with: man as human being is the end product of an evolutionary process. Man did not, as the organicists would have us believe, start out as a being endowed with all the attributes associated with life in common, and this simply because it would defy logic to think otherwise. It is not necessarily true, in other words, that the chasm separating man from beast is unbridgeable, for man was himself a beast once; there are not two natures separate, distinct, and irreconcilable. Rather, as Ovid and the Stoics would have it, man (social man) is but the refined consequence of a single nature—not unlike the metallic nature of the alchemists— unfolding, slowly and painfully, from the primeval ooze of bestiality to sociability.

And close on the heels of man's fateful discovery came an invention. Upon becoming aware of his own humanity, man devised society, the container alone capable of holding man the brute turned human. And, again a point well worth emphasizing, man's creation is the result of his own initiative. True, *necessitas* compelled him to do so; but the act of the will that endowed with actual reality what necessity suggested was man's and man's alone, a conclusion plainly unacceptable to the organicists. For them society, after the Pauline notion, is a body comprising different members. And as a living organism society does indeed function as a body. Each and every one of the individual members is a part of the whole, which by definition is more than the mere sum of its parts. Separate from the whole the individual constituents lack meaning. The relation between the parts and the whole is as close and intimate as that binding together the organs and the members of a living body. Society, therefore, cannot be the result of a conscious human effort, an exercise of the separate will of individuals to create a collectivity; rather, it has to be the result of organic and natural growth independent of human will. But there is more. For Vives, in addition to interpreting the transition from the first stage to the second as a historical instance of man's will at work, now proposes that man, organized in families and clans, lived and thrived contentedly and peacefully for a long time in the absence of political authority—something, according to Francisco de Vitoria, that only the gods can do. Although I have no evidence that Vives saw the state as an institution contrary to natural law and in effect an usurpation of man's God-given freedom, it is obvious that, in this at least, he has much in common with those who like Alonso de Castrillo believed that man is naturally meant to function in what can properly be called a state of anarchy. To be sure, introducing the subject at this juncture may be premature, but it will acquire such relevance when we come to Castrillo and the Spanish Neoscholastics that it is worth noting its presence, if only by implication, in Vives. Finally, all that has been said so far by way of conclusion suggests that we attempt to place Vives' two pre-political stages in the context of the phrase—state of nature—that would, in the language of early modern political discourse, become a useful shorthand commonplace to signify man as he existed before creating a government.

Broadly speaking, and strictly confining the discussion to the themes of interest to us here, it is possible to identify three different meanings associated with the phrase "state of nature." In the first it signifies an early, primeval stage in the historical development of humanity. The chronological element is a dominant factor in this interpretation, in that it insists that there existed a moment (a pre-social moment, to be sure) in the dawn of mankind when man lived under purely non-cultural constraints; namely, in an environment ("natural") structured and guided by self-love, a context other than the one defined by the sum total of what man himself creates through purposive action. In the second all references to time are omitted and it is used to designate a manner of living that might indiscriminately apply to an isolated individual or man organized in society. The outstanding earmark of the state of nature understood in this fashion is an existence guided preeminently (albeit no longer exclusively) by the instinctive, spontaneous, unpremeditated (the "natural"); a human state, in other words, in which the contrived, invented, artificial (the "artful") has not yet appreciably become a factor in man's life. Finally, in its third meaning "state of nature" has often stood, especially since the early modern period and after acquiring a pejorative implication at the hands of Hobbes, for the condition of human life antedating organized government when man, in short, organized in society had not yet set political authority over himself.

It is beyond question that all three variations to the theme of the state of nature are present in Vives. Given his historical approach to man's evolution and the time-discrete way in which both pre-political stages are fashioned, however, the first and third apply best to the humanist's own scheme. It should moreover be noted, since toward the end of the period covered by this monograph "state of nature" came to have a negative connotation as a state of naked brutality from which man could be rescued only by the state, that neither of Vives' two pre-political stages is intrinsically good or bad. Both are presented in the morally neutral manner reserved for true historical periods. Of course, given the notion of progress obviously present in Vives' discourse, man as savage beast is far less desirable to the humanist than man living in the company of his peers; nor is the decline of social harmony that made inevitable the rise of coercive power in the form of the state to be seen as anything but regrettable. Still, Vives' vituperative moral indignation is reserved for a stage in man's evolution well beyond the boundaries of the earlier two; the moment, in other words, when, after *ratio* has created the arts (the *sine qua non* of society), he willfully and perversely begins to dismantle what had taken him so much effort to build. And even then, with Vives' formidable indictment of man's perverse nature (and in the same work, *De disciplinis*) comes his formula for mankind's rebirth: educational reform. Under the circumstances, and given Vives' obvious reliance on the tales of classical primitivism, it would appear almost unseemly not to ask: is there any room in his vision of society for the notion of the Golden Age?

The Golden Age and the assumptions of what is often known as chronological primitivism[67] are inseparable, a fact that both brings the former into close proximity with the likes of "state of nature"[68] and gives rise to a terminology far from precise, constantly shifting in meaning, and guided—or perverted—at all times by the author's own goals and idiosyncrasies. St. Augustine's (and St. Thomas' after him) sponsorship, for instance, clearly tilted "state of innocence" in the direction of a meaning associated with a pre-lapsarian existence, thereby obviously limiting the options open to his successors in the use of the phrase. "State of nature," however, remained a more versatile expression and source of a much wider spectrum of meanings; witness, for example, the positive and negative connotations attached to it in the political thinking of

---

[67] For an extensive discussion of classical primitivism, see A. O. Lovejoy and G. Boas, *Primitivism and Related Ideas in Antiquity* (New York, 1965).

[68] Although we have fragmentary evidence that some ancient historians explored the conditions lived under by primeval men, most of the classical sources discuss the subject of natural man in the context of the Golden Age and the Age of Saturn (Kronos).

Antiquity and early modern times. At its most neutral (and most closely related to chronological primitivism) "state of nature" stands for man living in the "natural state," a pre-political stage in the evolution of mankind when social life was guided by the hand of the *pater familias* or the clan's elder; a time, in other words, before the advent of coercive laws and their obligatory sequel, political institutions.

Now, Vives is a chronological primitivist in that he implicitly subscribes to a point of view (the Christian version thereof) that insists that at one time in the past man attained to his most excellent condition of being. Man, therefore, was originally good, "natural," although subsequently he degenerated from that excellence. To explain this lapse an additional factor must be added to the existing equation: man carries with him an internal flaw that makes it inevitable that his history shall be an ever-growing departure from the original, or natural, state. Given these premises and Vives' own account of human evolution following the collapse of the state of innocence, it is difficult to avoid the conclusion that his Golden Age, if indeed he had it in mind at all and intended to link it to the state of nature, must be man's pre-lapsarian state.[69] No other seems to fit the particulars of the case convincingly. For one thing, the pre-political age of the clan cannot, strictly speaking, be said to be a golden state. True, it represents a considerable improvement on man the solitary brute, and in the absence of Christianity it would be as good an approximation to the Golden Age as we are likely to find among the Ancients. But in fact we are squarely in the midst of the Christian tradition, and so that stage represents a definite decline from the glory of an innocent yesterday. For another, even setting aside the pre-lapsarian age of innocence altogether and beginning with God's implementation of His new provisions the very structure of Vives' own narrative still leaves

---

[69] Solitary, wandering man first perceived his plight through instinct, not reason. Only after instinct had exhausted its potential, did reason come into play. The sum total of what self- love, *ratio*, and, much later and as a disruptive element, *commoditas*, bring about is society. I do not see, given these facts, how society could have existed in a state of innocence. Every man, to be sure, is a social being and to live in society is a dictate of reason, but not of the pristine, unpolluted reason of yesterday. It is rather a command of fallen reason. Compare Vives' version of man before the Fall with Tacitus' state of nature—the Golden Age according to a classical historian. "Mankind in the earliest age lived for a time without a single vicious impulse, without shame or guilt, and, consequently, without punishment and restraints. Rewards were not needed when everything right was pursued on its own merits; and as men desired nothing against morality, they were debarred from nothing by fear. When however they began to throw off equality, and ambition and violence usurped the place of self-control and modesty, despotism grew up and became perpetual among many nations." *Annals* III 26, in *The Complete Works of Tacitus*. The Church and Brodribb translation. Edited by M. Hadas (New York, 1942).

us in a quandary. For the humanist informs us in no uncertain terms that man reaches his utmost excellence of being in this life—his *summum bonum, bonitas*, good life—not in the family/clan stage but in that of *civitas*, the acme of politically organized society. And it can be said with absolute certainty that even the most tolerantly flexible definition of either the Golden Age or the state of nature cannot possibly accommodate the *civitas*. One final consideration: despite his Thomist confidence that human will and reason, if properly channeled, will redeem man in the eyes of God, there is an Augustinian streak in Vives that makes a Golden Age outside of Paradise both irrelevant and impossible. The flaw in man's character introduced by the Fall is ineradicable. History tells us, and this is what *De disciplinis* is all about, that the pristine commands of the law of nature have been blunted by sin and are no longer up to the task of keeping man's turbulent passions effectively in check. In the end only coercive laws backed by the force of political authority will be able to suppress the anti-social proclivities of man. In a world where the state is a permanent necessity, there is no room for an age of gold. It is the supreme irony of the situation that in this scheme of things for man to come closest to the good life implicit in his state of nature (here understood as his pre-lapsarian existence), the very instrument, the political side of organized society, which further distances mankind from the Golden Age, must be made correspondingly stronger.

Chapter Four: The Arts: fundamenta societatis

Origin, Nature, and Classification

i

SO FAR IN THIS MONOGRAPH we have explored the following topics key to the architecture of Vives' social thought: (1) God's first provision endowed man with the epistemological potential to contrive an *ars vivendi* embodying the *bonitas* gateway to *felicitas* (2) God, fully aware of the need for a context to permit *lumen*'s unfolding, planted in man the seeds of *societas* (3) Man, driven by instinct/*necessitas*, caused the seeds to sprout and became a social being. There remains one more crucial step to be taken. Man's reason, guided by his God-given *lumen*, must now invent the arts, the fertile soil alone suitable to turn the tentative flowering child of instinct/*necessitas* into a luxuriant garden for man. We established, in our study of God's first provision, that from Vives' perspective only a species of knowledge bounded by *opinio* and *verosimilitudo* remains open to man. It necessarily follows that as man creates the society mandated by God's second provision its foundations must be, somehow, carved out of that epistemological bedrock. Vives calls those foundations "arts," and once again commits himself to the task of educating the human actor; this time the subject is art: its origins, nature, and classification, and the method used to fashion it.[1] As always

---

[1] *De disciplinis* I i *Opera* V 8-9. One step above experience in the hierarchy of Aristotelian "intelligence" lies art, which "is produced when from many notions of experience a single universal judgment is formed with regard to like objects. To have a judgment that when Callias was suffering from this or that disease this or that benefited him, and similarly with Socrates and various other individuals, is a matter of experience; but to judge that it benefits all persons of a certain type, considered as a class, who suffer from this or that disease...is a matter of art." Metaphysics I i 981a 5-7. Art is therefore the knowledge of practical rules resting on general principles. "It would seem that for practical purposes experience is in no way inferior to art; indeed we see men of experience succeeding more than those who have theory without experience. The reason of this is that experience is knowledge of particulars, but art of universals; and actions and the effects produced are all concerned with the particulars. For it is not man that the physician cures, except incidentally, but Callias or Socrates or some other person similarly named, who is incidentally a man as well. So if a man has theory without experience; and knows the universals, but does not know the particular contained in it, he will often fail in his treatment; for it is the particular that must be treated." Ibid. 7-10. Art is therefore superior to experience. Knowledge and understanding are more properly said to belong to art than to experience. And so we assume the practitioner of art to be wiser than the man of experience, "which implies that in all cases wisdom depends rather upon knowledge; and this is because the former [artists] know the cause, whereas the latter

the humanist's undertaking is of the utmost urgency, for in his view art is what ultimately enables man to function in society—what makes it possible, in other words, for the actor to offer a creditable performance on stage—and saves him from the ignorance that Vives equates with damnation.

First, the origin and historical evolution of the arts. Man, we are told in *De disciplinis*, was given (or, if we remember the central thrust of this monograph, left with) but one gift: the sharpness (again, a term to be understood in a relative fashion) of his *ingenium*. From that gift emerged all human creations (*inventio*), the good as well as the bad.[2] And the first creations of that *ingenium* were, as is invariably the case, the result of compelling need. *Necessitas*, then, sharpened the mind to produce whatever was required for the survival of man. In other words, man's creativity was, and remains, the result of pressing circumstances in which he is placed by his own frail nature victim to necessity. In the beginnings of human society each man individually and on his own solved his problems as the contingencies[3] of his own living created them for him. Afterward, in moments of idleness and with the help of both his own past

---

[men of experience] do not. For the experienced know the fact [that the thing is], but not the wherefore [why the thing is], but the artists know the wherefore and the cause." Ibid. 10-12. To use an example given by Vives, the artist knows the elements that enter into the work of art, while the man of experience (Vives' "uninitiated" observer) sees only the finished product. In brief, we consider a man wiser not because he is able to act, but because he knows the theory and the causes. A word of caution: in the case of Vives this applies to the invented arts, not the natural ones; for in the latter case man cannot know the causes.

[2] *De disciplinis* I i *Opera* VI 8.

[3] An important concept that will acquire its full significance when later in this chapter we study prudence and history. Prudence sees into the future. But it sees into the future out of what the past gives it in the shape of experience/history. But the past was built on the basis of dealing successfully with contingencies peculiar to the time and place uniquely characteristic of that past. Therefore, if the prudent man is to foresee, and so shape, the future out of the past, he must keep in mind the contingencies of the past that history is a record of. So out of history the prudent man will not take everything—contingencies and the nature of man—but the latter alone; by the nature of man meaning the reality of the emotional/passional makeup that is his psychology. Nature, true, is unchanging. At least in theory. But in practice the actual behavior of man will not be solely constrained by nature; it will also be conditioned by his circumstances and his will. In short, as in everything else the teachings of history, the knowledge derived from history, will be for Vives a question of *probabilitas*, not of certainty. The greatest testimony to Vives as a historical thinker is *De disciplinis*, where it is clearly shown how all that man has created in the way of institutions and knowledge has emerged out of a fluctuating interaction between his own nature and his circumstances.

experience and his ability to think, he attempted to provide solutions for future contingencies. In time this gave rise to a body of experimental or empirical learning (*experimenta collecta*), which an individual gathered from his own experience or compared with that of others; this body of learning inspired norms (*praeceptae*), which in analogous circumstances might serve other men lacking the benefit of personal experience in dealing with problems arising out of those circumstances. Altogether, many of those norms affecting one aspect of human existence came to be known collectively as art.[4] In short, "experience created art" (*per varios usus artem experientia facit*).

Still in *De disciplinis* but one chapter later Vives offers us an additional version of art's origins. The seeds of all arts as well as their potential usefulness, we are told, were placed in nature by God pursuant to His plan for man.[5] But given the weakness of the human intellect man

---

[4] Ibid. 8-9. Such is the origin of art, a development born out of necessity and taking place in time. Since this process of creation is one that according to Vives never ends, it means that each art has its own history, the history of one aspect of human activity. When all the arts are seen together we have the totality of human activity, the entire spectrum of human challenges and responses; the history of the human race. But the activities of the human race, both individually and collectively, are absolutely conditioned by circumstances; that is, every step is the creation of an art, i.e., its history, is a contingency. The collectivity of arts, therefore, can never be anything but contingent. Is this an implicitly historicist position? Perhaps not, because if we define historicism in the modern sense it would seem that there is no more to history than this aspect of contingency. But in Vives there seems to be more, because in addition to this historical aspect he insists that history has elements universal in character, namely, that all the changes so far explained in terms of contingency—accidents—must additionally be understood in terms of a constant that itself never changes: man. So we seem to have two things here: an entity, man, which remains the same; that entity subject to circumstances that are themselves ever changing. The question, however, is: is the circumstances' potential for change finite or infinite? If infinite then, of course, regardless of our knowledge of man's psychology we cannot predict his future behavior in terms of past conduct. If, on the other hand, the changes are finite, then it is possible to predict, on the basis of historical evidence, what man's reaction to similar future-recurring—for if the possibilities are finite the circumstances must recur—circumstances will be. From what Vives says about the lessons of history (see the last topic in this chapter) he takes the finite position. Indeed, is Renaissance man willing to accept the existence of a formal infinite outside God?

[5] It would be difficult to exaggerate the role that nature plays in Vives' scheme of things, and time and again, throughout his writings, the author emphasizes his determination to seek in nature the roots and foundation for his ethic of man—meaning that religion is avoided as much as possible as a tool to exhort man to follow the ethical path built by Vives. In the Preface to *De disciplinis*, for example, Vives takes pains to announce that in his presentation of the origins and evolution of the arts he will propose reasons sought in

can reach to those seeds only with the utmost difficulty. In fact, the task of nurturing them would have been impossibly arid and insipid to man were it not for several factors designed to encourage him.[6] First and foremost, we have already noted, was necessity. And so not only did each and every man launch himself into the search for what he needed, but he sought to help other men involved in similar endeavors. Particularly prized was the help of some men of natural talent whose assistance became highly esteemed by the rest. Such men were given rewards—money, honors, private and public relevance—to entice them into devoting themselves fully to the arts needed in social life.[7] In this fashion Vives introduces us to the useful or practical arts, one of the three categories (see below) into which he will divide them. Other men, however, followed a different path that led to the creation of an entirely different, in the sense of the end pursued, group of arts. These lofty spirits, seekers after truth, found themselves compelled to study the causes of what they saw "by mining the truth out of nature's vein." Fascinated by the world surrounding them, then, such men forever sought to delve deeper into its causes. They were guided by an "inner light," the penetrating power of the mind that, complemented by diligence (experience and study), enabled them to move gradually from the simple and easy to the more complex and difficult toward the appointed end. These outstanding intellects eventually left the heights and, thinking that much of the light they had seen might be successfully communicated to the rest of mankind, proceeded to do so with all diligence. In short, it happened that some minds, motivated by material rewards and the needs of emerging society, studied (and invented) some arts, while others, out of the pure pleasure of learning, studied others, trying to fathom the mystery of a world that changes with every instant without prejudice to its eternal immutability.[8]

So far, Vives has emphasized *necessitas* as the moving force behind

---

"nature, not in Holy Scripture."

[6] Ibid. ii *Opera* VI 13.

[7] Ibid. This, for instance, is how the Egyptian priestly class developed geometry (here understood as the surveyor's art), for the periodic rises of the Nile obliterated farm boundaries.

[8] Ibid. 11-16. The arts thus created are not perfect, and the culprit is again our own flawed nature. "The strength of the human mind is not so great that it will create a perfect *opus* free from the need to be further refined." The point is that additional progress is not only mandated but possible by means of additional discoveries. The latter have not only added to the store of each art, but have further shown the errors committed by the very Ancients to whom we owe the arts themselves.

the genesis of art—the other, *curiositas*, we have already mentioned. In the long pages that follow Vives will chronicle in considerable detail the rise and fall of the arts that serve as the foundation of civilized society. What we have noted so far, in other words, is but a brief introduction to that historical unfolding of the arts that parallels the evolution of human society. But there is far more to the arts than their origin and history. There are also the metaphysical roots that nourish them, the human and natural wellsprings from which art flows. To find them we must go to *De prima*, where the old problem of cognition is now restated with reference to the arts.

Reason, searching after truth, advises the will, which in turn acts in function of the good. As reason becomes practical, that is, applied to something within or without itself, it must know both the end to be attained and the means of reaching it. "This reason we call industry and art, *solertia* (skill, dexterity) if art, a faculty to do or to inflict something upon oneself or others that is either innate or acquired through study." To speak, for instance, is natural, but to speak Latin or Greek is the result of one's own diligence.[9] Inside of both nature and art there lies a potency or force—"imitation"—that when manifested or actualized becomes *actio* (for nature) and *passio* (for art), and endeavors to reproduce God and nature, respectively; to be sure, the effort to mirror the model of perfection falls far short of the mark in both cases. "Art is the emulation of nature; it strives mightily to reflect it, but it never wholly succeeds because whereas nature penetrates to the core of things art cannot go beyond a mere skulking at the fringes."[10] As it endeavors to carry out its task art creates "artificial things," which are invariably a pale reflection of their natural counterparts. The making of a watch, for instance, belongs to the watchmaker's art, and so the watch is an artificial thing; but time itself remains natural. The medical art teaches how to determine and prepare a suitable dose of a given medication, although the effect of the drug on the human organism is caused by nature. The sound produced by the lyre is natural, the tune alone is artful and hence artificial.[11] It stands to reason, under the circumstances, that the process whereby art is created in imitation of nature should in some way parallel that nature uses to emulate God. As nature sets out from crude beginnings, which little by little lead to perfection, so does art polish and perfect slowly; nature works by influencing the innermost essence of things, art by

---

[9] DPP II *Opera* III 229.

[10] Ibid. 228.

[11] Ibid.

molding the outside, adding, subtracting, changing, as the case when a bronze statue is melted down to manufacture a cauldron. And this technique holds true not only for the manual arts but also in activities and disciplines that sink their roots in the soul: knowledge, the virtues, prudence for instance.

How is this process of creation, whereby art elaborates the artificial things, simulacra of those in turn brought into being by nature in imitation of God, carried out? To start with, both nature and man embark upon their respective creative processes (nature creating "natural" things, man "artificial" things; and, always, nature *ingignendo in intimis*, art *vero addendo exterioribus*) out of rough beginnings that are then gradually improved upon. Behind that deceptively simple facade, however, lies a series of complex operations common to both nature and man and involving two important concepts: *propositum* and *actio*. Just as in what is proposed (*propositum*) or planned by nature, that which emerges first is the perfect *opus*, and in *actio* what is sought after is the simple elements that will be put together into the composition of that same *opus*, so the human artificer must first conceive the work or end to be created/achieved and then carry out its execution. In both nature and man, then, conception of the perfect *opus* must precede execution—it is worth keeping this in mind, for what Vives means here is that in the creation of a practical art speculative precedes practical reasoning; this idea will become clear below, when we explain how in the practical arts the contemplative knowledge yielded by *scientia* becomes the springboard for their creation. And precisely because of these operational characteristics of nature and man, the human mind, as it strives to comprehend (*intelligere*) the work of nature (that is, understand what it is about to imitate) does not follow the path of nature's *actio* (the actualizing of its potential to imitate God)—from simple elements to the composite synthesis, that is, the *opus*—but rather one akin to nature's own *propositum*, since it first apprehends the synthesis and only then penetrates to the simple and recondite elements (from the outside to the inside).[12] In other

---

[12] Ibid. 228-29. In nature there lies the potential to imitate God, in art that of emulating nature. *Actio* is the actualization of the first potential; *passio*, the second. In both cases the imitation is possible because both nature and art carry within themselves, potentially, the possibility of imitating. When that possibility becomes a fact we speak of *actio* or *passio*. Vives defines both as follows: *actio est explicatio potentiae in aliud minus, passio explicatio potentiae ad aliud maius, minus voce infirmius et invalidius.* *Actio* (nature to God): the resolution of the *potentia* "into" something less, that is, something less than God, for nature cannot reach God. *Passio* (art to nature): the resolution of the potentia "toward" something more, that is, something more than art, even though art cannot reach nature. Vives appears to use the words *actio* and *passio*, here, as synonyms for deduction

words, the mind first grasps the outward mixture of the thing created by nature; obviously a first level of understanding generated by the interaction of the senses with the observed things. Only then is the human mind ready to penetrate to the simpler and internal structure of the thing. This explains why man stands in awe when confronted with what nature has wrought: he sees clearly wonders whose intimate essence he can barely perceive. And of course, given the affinity between nature and man discussed above, in his relation to nature man stands as the uninitiated observer ("ignorant peasant") who knows the artificial whole created by the artificer better than he does the simpler elements entering into the composition of the finished product.[13]

ii

Finally, the arts as the practical creation of man and their classification. We must now move on to *De tradendis* to see how Vives views art from the standpoint mandated by the pedagogical purposes of the treatise. And let us begin by understanding what the author says in Chapter Three of Book One, where he offers us an Aristotelian classification of the arts based on the relation between *materia* (subject-matter) and *finis* as the process that individually creates them in practice unfolds.[14] In arts such as agriculture the subject-matter is sought after because of the end, while in those pertaining to the contemplation of nature we desire the end because of the subject-matter. In some arts the end of knowledge is knowledge itself, and these are called *inspectivae*, such as geometry and the contemplation of nature. "The end of other arts is action, as in music, when, after the action, nothing is left. These are called the 'active arts.' The end of still other arts is some work or effect besides the action, as in building, medicine, that are termed 'practical.'

---

and induction, respectively. "In natural actions *actio* and *passio* differ in their *termini* but not in their reality—like, for example, the road from Louvain to Paris—for *actio* goes from A to B and *passio* from B to A." Ibid. 229. But in the arts the situation is different. Man the inventor must first go from B to A (induction)—synthesis—and then from A to B (deduction)—analysis. And herein lies the key to Vives' method as we shall see below. Speculative reasoning rises on the foundation of the information provided by the senses, going from the effects to the causes or general precepts; practical reason intervenes immediately and reverses the order, moving from synthesis to analysis on the path of induction, explaining the effects and using them, singularly and individually, to verify or falsify the universal norms. Everything so far said points to and illustrates that conclusion.

[13] Ibid.

[14] DTD I iii *Opera* VI 252; Watson 24.

Some are instruments for affecting other objects, e.g. grammar and dialectics."[15] Vives concludes with the following noteworthy observation: "Those that are not brought together under rules and precepts are not arts at all, but, to use a general name, are experiential knowledge [*cognitiones et peritiae*], e.g. knowledge of history and the contemplation of God. Wherefore an art is defined for us as a collection of universal rules brought together for the purpose of knowing, doing, or producing something."[16] But beyond the singular end of individual art endowed with a unique subject-matter lies, according to Vives, something far more significant: the collective end of art in general and the end sought by the practitioner. To practice an art means simply to carry out its precepts; but inasmuch as the artificer actually does the executing, it is plain that the precepts are more his instruments than they are the art's. The end of the artificer is therefore to set the precepts in motion (to accomplish a specific task or objective: to cure that man); the end of the art is to achieve the intended *opus* in as superlative a fashion as possible (to accomplish a universal task or objective: to cure man). Consequently, what for art is the means, namely, the precepts, for the artificer is the end. Art never regards things singly or cases as separate instances, but regards them collectively; the practitioner, on the other hand, acts on or toward things individually. Art, in brief, does not act; it merely teaches.[17]

In its inception, it follows (and this point we will develop more rigorously when we speak of Vives' method), that art is nothing more than a set of universal precepts inductively arrived at by natural/ spec-

---

[15] Ibid.

[16] Ibid. *Collectio universalium praeceptorum parata ad cognoscendum, agendum, vel operandum, in certa aliqua finis latitudine.* This definition goes back to Zeno (who in turn elaborated it on the basis of the Socratic doctrine of *techné*): "a cluster of perceptions exercised together to bring about an end useful to life." It would appear that the Renaissance takes the definition from the satyrist Lucian of Samosata, whom Vives often mentions (in *De tradendis*), sometimes recommending that he be read, while at other times judging him dangerous for young students with a penchant for scoffing and jeering. Given that Vives leans toward Skepticism and the latter is the enemy of Stoicism (to which Vives' ethics owes much) it is necessary to point out the following. According to the Stoic definition, "perception" must be understood in the sense of "cataleptic apprehension," that is, an irresistible impression leading to total certainty—precisely what Academic Skepticism rejected. In Antiquity the various translations of the Stoic quotation remained faithful to the original epistemological meaning. But it seems that during the Middle Ages *perceptio* became *praeceptio*, a meaning that the Renaissance, despite its awareness of what had happened, decided to follow. See N. W. Gilbert *Renaissance Concepts of Method* (New York, 1960) and Noreña, op. cit. on this.

[17] DTD I iii *Opera* VI 253.

ulative reason. Those precepts create the framework that within each individual art enables the artificer to handle or explain, through deductive inferences, the phenomena (taking the word in the technical sense of appearances) that make up the internal domain of the art in question. Gradually, the resulting process of testing the precepts against the demands of sensory reality both increases the subject-matter of the art and serves to verify/falsify those same precepts. The original hypothesis/set of precepts is in this fashion tested against each singular occurrence; if confirmed, the hypothesis remains intact; if denied, it is modified to conform with the evidence. This is precisely the reason-led procedure, known as experience, that simultaneously enables the art to enrich and widen its scope, broadens the artificer's own experience, and sharpens his wit as he endlessly tests the validity of the hypothesis/precepts against the testimony of reality. Vives implicitly accounts for this essential feature of art by returning to the old and ever-recurring theme of man's flawed nature: art, as practiced by man, is but a simulacrum of the ideals that can be approximated but never reached. As on an earlier occasion he emphasizes that the weakness does not lie with the nature of art but with the hopeless manner of our execution. And this is precisely what he means when he says that just as nature can only imitate God, so art shall at best endeavor to imitate nature. All of which logically leads Vives to remark that "beyond the end of art and that of the artificer lies the end of man himself." The latter end is of course hidden from us as if by a veil. Still, while man awaits the final act of the drama, to have the veil torn and the end both revealed and attainable, he will propose many and personal ends to which he will aim the arts—"Whence it happens that since the opinions of men are different, one fixes on one end in his pursuit of the arts; another one another; each for himself." Dignity, power, renown, greed, love of friends and family, the common weal, prosperity: such are the most common goals sought. There are even those whose pursuit of the arts leads them to "prudence and experience."[18]

iii

Now, beyond the Aristotelian ordering of the arts already mentioned, Vives proposes a second, and very much his own, classification, whose context is given by the human mind and society, one that he has already partially suggested, and we have noted, in the introductory pages of *De disciplinis*.

---

[18] Ibid. 254; Watson 24.

In the mind there are especially two functions, the power of observing (*vis intuendi*) . . . and the power of judging (*vis iudicandi*) and determining with regard to those things that the mind has seen. The former is concerned merely with observation, but the latter has regard to man's actions. The human mind ranges over the heavens, elements, stones, metals, planets, animals, man; the last named it regards not merely in a single relation, but it investigates man's mind and body and those things that happen to both of these, in their permanent states, and their vicissitudes at various stages. The mind then passes to consider human inventions, which open a new field of observation. Thence it goes on to study spiritual things, and eventually is led to the supreme and all-powerful God.[19]

On this double foundation Vives rests the three fundamental categories into which he divides the arts: (1) Arts that observe the external aspects of nature (empiricism); (2) Arts that aim at the intimate aspects of nature (*scientia*) and knowledge of the spirituality that finally leads to God (*sapientia*); (3) Arts that man, compelled by his own sociability, invents and develops; these last beget the *prudentia* that in turn makes the creation of *bonitas* possible. Let us look at each in turn.

First we have those arts that concern *aspectus naturae* and imply a reflexive observation (*contemplatio*) of the outward face of nature by means of the senses. It is not, however, in these early pages of *De tradendis* but in the chapter introducing Book IV, that Vives explains this important category in greater detail. Following some pertinent recommendations concerning the need to study what he calls the "critique of truth,"[20] Vives counsels that the young student be exposed to the "knowledge of nature." The statement with which he wishes to justify his advice is for us of considerable interest.

> The youth will find it [nature] easier to understand than all the things pertaining to *prudentia*, for natural things he can grasp by means of his own inherent sharpness of mind; whereas that which pertains to prudence can only be taught by the experience of life, much knowledge, and a faithful memory. What we know of nature has been gained by our senses or the fantasy, backed by reason as the controller of the senses. Petty and miserable is indeed, in view of the darkness that envelops us, the knowledge gained in this fashion. For the same reason that knowledge is more *verisimilitudo* than

---

[19] Ibid. v 262; Watson 37.

[20] *Censura veri*, about which we shall speak extensively later.

certain truth.[21]

Meaning, of course, that we are dealing with knowledge reckoned as probable rather than absolutely true. Under the circumstances, the first "precept in the observation and discussion of nature is that since we cannot gain any certain science, we must not indulge excessively in the examination of those things to which we can never truly attain; all our studies should instead be applied to the necessities of life. . . .Thus the contemplation of nature is unnecessary and even harmful unless it serves the useful arts of life."[22] Which arts belong in this category? Evidently all those that directly or indirectly are related to the observation of nature. But it is possible to be a little more specific, because bearing in mind the treatises that Vives recommends to the student interested in the contemplation of nature, we may conclude that among such arts are astronomy, agriculture, geography, botany, the study of animals in general (it is to be noted that Vives is an enthusiastic advocate of pisciculture), and mineralogy.

The next category of arts emerges as the observational process just mentioned moves away from the outside of nature to its innermost workings and no longer with the aid of the eye but through the mind—"although observation begins with the eye." Such is the origin of metaphysics. The observer moves on to those transcendental things that, escaping the net of the senses, can be grasped by thought alone; this is the only way of investigating the *res spirituales*,[23] whose discipline is known as *spiritualitas*.[24] "Out of all this we extract an exacting and extensive

[21] Ibid. IV i *Opera* VI 347.

[22] Ibid. 348.

[23] Ibid. I v *Opera* VI 264-65. Those who decide to go beyond the external aspects of nature will be taught how to reach its intimate aspects by means of metaphysics, which Vives defines as a scrutiny or investigation of how things and actions having their origin in the essence and intimacy of any thing are linked. From this we move on to the external causes, and thence we rise to God, for God's invisible things are offered to the eyes of the mind through the things made by Him, including His eternal power and divinity. But to reach this last, these "invisible things of God," means to acquire *sapientia*, something that we have already pointed out man cannot reach by reason. And so Vives warns that nature, from which, as stated above, we rise to God, must not be examined "by the poor and tremulous light which is the knowledge of the gentiles," that is, by the light of natural reason, but instead by the "brilliant torch" brought by Christ to chase away the world's darkness. Or, to say it differently, what we pointed out earlier: *sapientia* can only be had through *pietas*. Ibid. IV ii *Opera* VI 351.

[24] From this we conclude that, properly speaking, neither metaphysics nor *spiritualitas* are arts. And neither can be considered arts the disciplines which help us to understand

narrative that embraces not only the effects but the causes as well, although more in the manner of explaining the latter than inquiring about them. We call this *historia naturae*."[25] So far Vives has sketched in *De tradendis* the cognitive categories itemized in *De anima*: as it ranges over the subjects of the sublunar world, including man himself, and their spiritual archetypes of the intelligible world, the mind creates a manner of knowledge called *scientia*; while what lies beyond is *sapientia*. As for what happens when "the mind passes to consider human inventions," it is never made explicit in *De anima*. It is otherwise in *De tradendis*, for it will eventually become clear that what Vives has in mind is the notion that such human inventions are precisely what may be properly termed art. This is how he proceeds to account for the third and last category.

The constraints imposed on man by his natural sociability, he begins, are responsible for the creation of various tools needed by him to preserve the rational structure of society. "Laws were instituted, and the limitations of rights promulgated. . . .Certain instruments also were sought for, with which we should be more easily and pleasantly led to the paths of reason . . . an art was thought out that is called geometry . . . arithmetic. . . . In the close investigation of the truth, which has become so obscured to us, the judgment is advanced by a canon of probability; in forming an opinion that is based on conjecture, the instrument of dialectic is useful . . . music . . . poetry."[26] All these instruments or arts were created by the human mind as it put to use, "on its own initiative and industry," God's gift, natural reason. But given the human condition natural reason alone cannot go very far on its own; "we must apply a great deal of diligence to discover and extract, by the light of that vacillating candle gift of God, what is useful to us out of nature." Such is the material and such are the ends of those *cognitiones* or arts which, "far from being incompatible with piety or religion, are instead of great

---

nature—unless, and such is the key condition, they contribute, directly or indirectly, to what is practically profitable to man. For that reason, and even though to avoid confusion we shall continue to use "invented arts" or "practical arts" to mean disciplines that are the true and only arts and "natural arts" to signify that modality of knowledge that speaks of nature to us, it must be remembered that "art" is what man discovers, elaborates, or invents to live profitably in society.

[25] Ibid. I v *Opera* VI 265; Watson 41-42.

[26] Ibid. 263-64; Watson 39-40. For Aristotle dialectic is a theory that in practice becomes rhetoric (itself aiming at persuasion by means of probabilities). If diverted from its legitimate object, dialectic becomes sophistry. The normal use of dialectic has three functions, one of which leads to the discovery of first principles. This is how Vives views dialectic here.

service to the body."[27] Medicine, for instance, is the art that cares for the health of man. There are also precepts on how to achieve the inner balance proper to man; when gathered into an art, such precepts receive the collective name of ethics. Others teach how to manage and conduct oneself in one's household (economics), while still others are the guidelines for a citizen's behavior (politics). Rhetoric, grammar, and philology are arts pertaining to the language. "Practical knowledge of life, the examples of our elders and the past, and acquaintance with the present we call *prudentia*." Then there are the arts that are themselves but the instruments of other arts: geometry, arithmetic, probability, music, poetry; and theology, the art that concerns itself with sacred matters.[28] Vives has now established a clear and working distinction between those disciplines that study nature, the realm of natural/speculative reason pursuing truth and overseeing the senses, and the arts that, seeking the good usefully, concentrate on man's needs, the province of practical reason; reason, that is, assisted by experience.

The boundary between the natural and the invented arts, however, is not an inflexible one, as Vives himself reveals with his own "unless it serves the useful arts of life." Indeed, there exists an important relation of cause and effect between the arts that study nature and the invented or practical arts. The basis of that relation is that *all* arts imitate and therefore reflect nature; even when man is inventing the practical arts he is still imitating nature. Strictly speaking, therefore, the practical arts emerge as the result of an exercise in the imitation of nature that is in no fundamental sense different from the exercise that created the first two categories of art. Natural reason is involved in all cases, and in all cases also what is sought is to imitate nature. Where, then, is the difference between the creation of the natural arts and the invention of the practical arts? The difference lies in that in one case *scientia* is the end sought, while in the other it is but a means. This is what I believe Vives has in mind. When man applies his natural reason to the study of nature for its own sake, he arrives at a manner of knowledge harvested by natural reason in its *speculativa inferior* mode. On the other hand, when man's primary goal is not enjoyment of the yield of speculative reason but the creation of practical arts, he does not stop at *scientia*; on the contrary, he

---

[27] Ibid. 264; Watson 40. Herein lies the key difference between Vives and the French skeptics. For the latter not only is natural reason sufficient, but it is essential that it be left alone, with no intervention on the part of "artificial reason." As far as Vives is concerned, on the other hand, the latter complements the former through its unique creation, the arts.

[28] Ibid. 265-66; Watson 43.

uses its speculative knowledge as the stepping stone to move on to his true end, practical knowledge. In this fashion, from being an end unto itself *scientia* becomes a means, an instrument, a method to invent the practical arts. Cases in point are arithmetic and geometry, the two parts of mathematics that in turn branch off, each into two: one, "remaining within the boundaries of contemplation is called speculative, while the other, issuing into the external world is called active. From the former is born the latter, as one would expect, for in all things human the idea precedes the action."[29] This accounts for geometry being included, within Vives' educational scheme, among both the contemplative arts and those invented by man, a creation of the mind until applied to practical matters. In other words, we have here an instance of the plan theoretically developed in *De anima*, whereby speculative knowledge can become, through *experientia, actio* or *ratio practica* in the guise of practical art. But the relation between the natural and invented arts remains nonetheless an uneasy one. And, Vives warns, woe to the student who fails to remember the strict conditions placed upon speculation! "Anxious inquiry into such mathematical problems leads away from the problems of life, and estranges man from a perception of what conduces to the common weal. ... Studies should not draw a man to vain and profitless speculation."[30] Scholars should indeed study mathematics, but only "to lead up to their applications in the affairs of life." In the specific case of geometry the benefits are clear inasmuch as from it "are developed optics or perspective, and architecture, and the art of movement, all of which have great usefulness in ordinary life."[31] While the distinguishing trait of art is intrinsic usefulness, such is not the case with speculative knowledge, which alone can be tolerated insofar as it yields a practical result. "Learning is unsullied and fruitful only if directed to its proper end, virtue (that is to do good)."[32]

It would seem, given what has just been said, that man should have no difficulty in approaching the task of acquiring knowledge with sure-footed discrimination. Unfortunately, in Vives' scheme of things nothing seems to be easy for man. The realm of nature, like that of the knowledge I have tied to *opinio*, is the domain of cognition yielding at best probable truths, knowledge of which, while teaching us about the

---

[29] Ibid. IV v *Opera* VI 369; Watson 202.

[30] Ibid. 369-70; Watson 202.

[31] Ibid. 371; Watson 204.

[32] IAS, in *Vives' Introduction to Wisdom*, ed. M. L. Tobrinner (New York, 1968) 102 *Opera* I aphorism 134.

effects and describing the cause, nevertheless does not explain the latter. Although the subject will be explored with greater rigor in pages to come, it is still possible to conclude here that insofar as Vives uses the term "science" outside the context of *scientia*—that I have taken to mean method—he applies it to those disciplines, the study of nature, in which, paradoxically in view of what today we have come to understand by science, knowledge is only probable. And, even more important to the subject at hand, no more could those disciplines hope to bear "true science," i.e. Aristotelian science *simpliciter*. We broached this subject earlier, in the context of our examination of God's first provision. Let us repeat it, now for the concrete case of the arts. Man would like to know God, but *sapientia*, which *pietas* alone can yield, lies outside of his natural powers. Ultimate wisdom is therefore beyond man's reach. Nature offers the next and best hope, for nature imitates God and therein are locked the images of the latter. By understanding nature, man tries to derive knowledge of them. This goal he pursues armed with instruments known as the natural arts, instruments that by means of speculative reasoning attempt to probe into the intimate being of nature. What they in fact produce is at best an explanation of causes, not an understanding of them. Man, in other words, cannot perceive God's images; he can explain that there are so many heavenly bodies, but not the why of their number. Seeking now a limited truth (the truth of nature, and one far less exalted than *sapientia*, for it deals not with Reality but with the images of Reality), man finds out that even this less ambitious goal is not fully within his reach; he has truth, but not the whole truth, let alone the ultimate Truth. All this, through constant reiteration, has become an article of faith for Vives. But it is also perfectly clear that man's existence is not limited to grasping the truth of nature (or of his own divine reality); he also has needs. And those needs can be satisfied only by imitating (as opposed to knowing) nature. In essence, and such is precisely the problem to which I wish to call attention in this paragraph, man is then engrossed in a twofold and simultaneous undertaking: understanding and imitating nature.[33] Paralleling the course of action whereby the latter imitates God, man now "invents" arts that, imitating nature, aim at the

---

[33] Nowhere is this dual ambition better embodied than in the tradition of Renaissance magic. In alchemy, understanding of the processes whereby nature purified metallic nature in its womb would hopefully enable the adept to reproduce them in the laboratory to yield the philosopher's stone. And beyond understanding and imitating lay the even loftier goal akin to the search for Vives' *sapientia*: the purification of man's soul, the ultimate and truest goal of the alchemist.

good of his kind.[34] And this is precisely the source of those apparent
ambiguities that often cloud our understanding of Vives' thought. For
the humanist, man's fundamental task is to seek out the good. But man's
reason "not only leads to the good, it also discriminates between what is
true and what is false"—although what is true is in fact what man's flawed
judgment tells him is true. This peculiarity unique to man is in Vives'
view also the source of his tragedy, for he thus cannot reach out for the
good without simultaneously searching for an absolute truth he cannot
see "clearly," which in the last analysis is but the opinion created by his
own judgment. It is a tragedy because he cannot reach the whole truth,
while he must have the good, and so some men will be misled into
singlemindedly hunting after truth to the detriment of the good.

Finally, we must ask: what are the invented arts? Still in *De
tradendis* and still discussing the orderly progression to be followed in
mapping out a youth's course of studies, Vives significantly prefaces their
introduction (that immediately follows the discussion of mathematics to
which I have repeatedly alluded above) with the following words: "By
this time, a man of age, ability, learning has become ripe in knowledge
and experience of things. He should now begin to consider more clearly
human life and to take an interest in the arts and inventions of men."[35]
The statement is important because Vives clearly implies that maturity
and experience are essential prerequisites for the study of the arts invented
by man; it will acquire an added dimension later on when Vives insists
that prudence and youth are mutually exclusive. The realm of the
invented arts is virtually boundless (and some of them we have already
met above). Dietetics, agriculture, veterinary medicine, architecture,
cloth manufacturing, navigation, medicine are but a handful among those
suggested. And learning about them—by questioning the sailor, farmer,
baker, smith, shoemaker, and observing them as they ply their trades—is
"a most honourable occupation and one clearly worthy of a good citizen.
By such observation in every walk of life, practical wisdom (*prudentia*) is
increased to an almost incredible degree."[36]

---

[34] This last aim cannot be accomplished without man first knowing himself. Such, as we
shall soon learn, is the reasoning that lies at the foundation of Vives' emphasis on
prudentia, the one idea that gives unity to his entire scheme.

[35] DTD IV vi *Opera* VI 373-74; Watson 208

[36] Ibid. 375; Watson 210. Although this monograph is clearly not the place to determine
what, if any, place Vives deserves in the history of the Scientific Revolution, it is
nevertheless equally obvious that, if we consider the numerous statements quoted
heretofore, his assertions concerning reason and knowledge imply a point of view on
cognition and the manner of its acquisition deserves examination. Indeed, the themes so

iv

To sum up. The contemplative arts, embracing the study of nature and insofar as they seek no end other than themselves, are not *bona fide* creations of man. He, in turn, his mind clouded by sin, cannot hope to penetrate to the indubitable truths that nature doubtless hides within itself. By contrast, the practical arts, relating to mind and body both, man has methodically—in the absence of method they become merely "experiential knowledge," such as history—constructed and can, therefore, be, again methodically, used to understand the truth of all the singular instances that are part of their respective wholes. Because the subject of the inquiry is man, the end result is knowledge of self. And self-knowledge, Vives has stated in *De anima*'s dedication, is the first step toward wisdom. What, then, does he understand by wisdom? Wisdom, obviously, cannot be *sapientia* (unattainable by rational man) or

---

far noted here suggest that from a philosophical perspective Vives is far from moving within the age's rational current. But very often he has been characterized as an empiricist *à outrance*, a conclusion that in my view is the result of a superficial and incomplete reading of his work. Vives does not belong to that group of thinkers pilloried by J. H. Randall, Jr., as "the many humanist seekers" who, "revolting from the scholasticism of the Scotists with their technical 'terminist' logic, seem to have displayed all the customary ignorance and futility of intellectual revolutionaries, and to have proposed new methods distinguished chiefly by the novelty of their ignorance" ("The Development of Scientific Method in the School of Padua," *Journal of the History of Ideas* I [1940] 177-206). There is no doubt, on the other hand, that for Vives, interested in manufacturing the useful and reaching to the good, understanding and knowing aim, immediately, to the perfecting of the practical arts and, mediately, to the creation of the *vir prudens*. In other words, Vives is wholly resolved to emphasize the transcendence of practical knowledge and how it can be acquired though observation and experience. But he has no interest in getting to the first causes, in reaching what Cartesian rationalism would one day call indubitable truths attainable only through one concrete modality of *scientia*, physics. His only goal is to strengthen the means to reach what is his authentic end, the good. Like Socrates before and Vico after, and unlike Descartes, Vives is interested in the nature of man, not in that of the world surrounding him. Randall further misrepresents Vives' position when he states that "a Vives and a Bacon, recognizing no useful knowledge in the investigation of the mathematicians and astronomers of their day, might counsel experience and more experience." Op. cit. Far more than "experience and ever more experience" is involved in Vives' method. But an even more significant error is to bracket Vives and Bacon together in the same breath. Vives' purpose is never to study nature, to pursue knowledge for its own sake, or to arrive at new paths leading toward a certain apprehension of knowledge. He is not, in other words, a "scientist." Rather, he belongs with Erasmus and More to a tradition of social reform. As such, his goals are eminently practical, and so must the paths leading to them be. In lieu of nature, he is interested in knowing man; an eminently practical pursuit, for only as man knows himself so will he be an harmonious part within the social order.

indubitable knowledge of nature or *scientia* (in essence a method to reach an end). It must be practical wisdom or *prudentia*—not an art but the ultimate beneficiary of all arts. All roads, regardless of how seemingly diverse or unrelated, appear eventually to lead to one single destination: prudence. Practical wisdom is the ultimate justification for the many paths followed by man as he seeks to increase his store of knowledge. We may now state more precisely what Vives understands the *virtus* of man to be: man is a being whose function is to acquire *prudentia*, an instrument whereby his *virtus* becomes actualized into *bonitas*. The senses as the source, reason as the tool, the arts as the means to accumulate and organize (and here is where experience plays its role), according to Aristotle's recommendation,[37] the needed knowledge, prudence as the universal expression of that useful knowledge: everything projected and executed as part of the divine plan to allow the potential of human *virtus* to become reality in *bonitas*.

Method

"The practical arts man has methodically constructed." Let us say it differently. Vives believes that *ratio practica* can give us the knowledge needed to lead a normative life. Where does that knowledge come from in practice? Man "invents" it; its sum total is the arts. But how do we know that the probability of the invented arts is strong enough to warrant their use in mapping out man's moral life? Certainly the haphazard, intuitive responses of early man to his needs are not enough to answer the question. They must eventually, therefore, give way to some orderly scheme for the acquisition and organization of knowledge. "Not every kind of knowledge is called an art, but only that which becomes a rule for doing something."[38] Earlier in the same treatise Vives had defined knowledge as "a kind of close inspection that either consists in the contemplation of each particular object, e.g., when the eye observes closely the distinction in a variety of colours, and again when the mind ponders over the memory of events, or considers closely and seeks after some end; if it collects general aspects or norms to a definite end it is called art."[39] Before we can properly have art, therefore, we must have knowledge organized in function of a rule or norm. And to organize

---

[37] See *Posterior Analytics* II xix 100a, 100a 5-10, 100b; *Prior Analytics* II xxiii 68b 15-25; *Topica* I xii 105a 15.

[38] DTD I ii *Opera* VI 251; Watson 22.

[39] Ibid. 249; Watson 19-20.

knowledge to that end we need a "method." The answer to the question posed above is therefore method. Clearly, then, Vives' method must be a whole made up of the instruments or criteria used to gain the kind of knowledge he thinks man can both reach and profitably use. And since I believe that in the case of Vives that whole owes a great deal to Cicero, it would seem pertinent to introduce Vives' method with some brief considerations concerning Ciceronian dialectic—considerations that assume and accept that besides the syllogism there exist other forms of inference that can profitably be used in discussion and debate, and that also obey philosophical as well as rhetorical reasons.[40]

i

The orator, explains Cicero in *De partitione oratoriae*, has at his disposal personal resources such as things and words that must before anything else be found (*invenienda*) and ordered (*collocanda*). Once the process of inventing and ordering has been completed the orator moves on to attain the end aimed at by his travail. An end that according to Cicero is to convince and to influence by means of instruments called *argumenta*, "something probable with the intention of persuading (*probabile inventum ad faciendam fidem*), which are extracted from the *loci* (the Greek *topoi*) or compartments where such instruments are stored."[41] To persuade (*ad faciendam fidem*)—meaning to capture the good will and attention of the audience—the orator makes his case in terms of confirmation (proving his own point of view) and refutation (demolishing his opponent's). In every disputation, moreover, what is being resolved is either the reality of the question at hand or its identity or its qualities; to arrive at the first, the valid method is inference (*coniectura*); for the second we use definition, and for the third, reason. Inference is therefore the study of that by means of which we succeed in persuading.[42] And the orator's method clearly aims at verisimilitude, precisely the objective of Academic Skepticism.[43] In essence, then, Ciceronian rhetoric is not

---

[40] L. Jardine, "Lorenzo Valla. Academic Skepticism and the New Humanist Dialectic," in M. Burnyeat (ed.), *The Skeptical Tradition* (Berkeley, 1983). According to Jardine it was Lorenzo Valla who first noted the intimate relation that binds Ciceronian rhetoric and philosophy together. Whether Vives may have come to similar conclusions from his knowledge of Valla or his own Ciceronian studies is irrelevant to our interests here.

[41] *De partitione oratoriae* I-II 1-6, trans. H. Rackham. The Loeb Classical Library (Cambridge, Mass., 1968).

[42] Inference is wholly based on probability (*in verisimilibus*) and the essential characteristics of things. *De partitione oratoriae* X 34-35.

[43] This is how Cicero interprets and translates the terminology of Greek Skepticism. "For

something isolated and conceived solely for purely literary ends, but is in truth an instrument designed to infuse life into a philosophical posture.[44] And *ratio argumentandi* is the method, procedure, or strategy that according to Cicero the Academics used to determine which was the most probable from among two or more opinions—although of course it cannot be known whether the most probable alternative dictated by this method is really the true alternative[45]—thereby justifying *actio*. And it is clear, once we juxtapose Cicero's rhetorical and philosophical works, that the method he develops for the orator, the *ratio disserendi*, derives from the *ratio argumentandi*. Both in turn are, in Cicero, intimately associated with Aristotle's theory of topics and dialectic, materials all used by Vives, like Valla before him, to erect the structure of a skeptical dialectic.

Cicero's *ratio disserendi* is divided into two parts: the *ars inveniendi* or art of the *topoi* ("those *loci* where the arguments are ordered and ready to be utilized") and the *ars disserendi*.[46] The *ars inveniendi* looks for arguments and orders them, "and [this science of Topics] saves one from always having to drone out the same stock arguments on the same subjects without ever departing from one's notebooks. For one who knows under what general heading a particular case comes, and how to lead up to it, will be able to bring out any argument however far out of sight it lies, and always takes a line of his own in debate."[47] The *ars disserendi* or *ars iudicandi* is the dialectical judgment or rules of inference, and consists in ordering what has been achieved through *inventio* to convince or persuade. For its part, Aristotle's applied logic, namely, logic

---

they [the Academics] hold (and this in fact, I noticed, excites your school extremely) that something is 'probable,' or as it were resembling the truth, and that this provides them with a canon of judgment both in the conduct of life and in philosophical investigation and discussion." *Academica* (II) X 32.

[44] *De oratore* III xxi 80.

[45] "The sole object of our [the Academics'] discussions is by arguing on both sides to draw out and give shape to some result that may be either true or the nearest possible approximation to the truth. Nor is there any difference between ourselves and those who think that they have positive knowledge except that they have no doubt that their tenets are true, whereas we hold many doctrines as probable, which we can easily act upon but can scarcely advance as certain; yet we are more free and untrammelled in that we possess our power of judgment uncurtailed, and are bound by no compulsion to support all the dogmas laid down for us almost as edicts by certain masters." *Academica* (II) iii 7-8.

[46] *De finibus* IV iv 10. "Every systematic treatment of argumentation has two branches, one concerned with invention (*inveniendi*) of arguments and the other with judgment (*iudicandi*) of their validity." *Topica* II 6-8.

[47] *De finibus* IV iv 10.

as structured in *Topica* (whose content is dialectic as the science of reasoning about what is probable),[48] aims at how to use the mind in debate in the direction of allowing the participants to reach the desired conclusion starting out of acceptable premises. This aspect of logic concerns itself with inferential forms that do not lend themselves to being formalized and whose validity, therefore, is doubtful at some levels. We make use of applied logic when we develop forms of reasoning, that we then unfold to establish that a given position is more convincing than another.

Now, it is clear that from its very beginnings Renaissance

---

[48] For our purposes here we will divide logic into formal and applied. About the first, a theoretical and syllogistic logic explained by Aristotle in *Prior Analytics*, where he deals with the knowledge of that which is certain (the truth) and pays preeminent attention to logical formulas, we will not say much, for it is the second that interests us. In *Prior Analytics* Aristotle explains the doctrine of the syllogism in its formal phase and without reference to the matter in which syllogisms can be used. In *Posterior Analytics*, Aristotle discourses on the characteristics that reasoning must necessarily possess if it is to lay a claim to being truly scientific. In *Topica* are studied the reasoning modalities that, although syllogistically correct, do not fulfill the conditions needed to be considered as scientifically precise. Aristotle describes the end aimed at in *Topica* as follows. "The purpose of the present treatise is to discover a method by which we shall be able to reason from generally accepted opinions about any problem set before us and shall ourselves, when sustaining an argument, avoid saying anything self-contradictory." 100a 18. That is, the work seeks to enable two participants, he who asks and he who answers, to play their respective roles competently in a dialectic discussion. It is therefore possible to conclude that the subject of *Topica* is a dialectical syllogism based on premises that are only probable, as opposed to the demonstrative or scientific syllogism (*Prior Analytics*) rooted in premises both true and immediate. For our purposes here we will divide logic into formal and applied. About the first, a theoretical and syllogistic logic explained by Aristotle in *Prior Analytics*, where he deals with the knowledge of that which is certain (the truth) and pays preeminent attention to logical formulas, we will not say much, for it is the second that interests us. In *Prior Analytics* Aristotle explains the doctrine of the syllogism in its formal phase and without reference to the matter in which syllogisms can be used. In *Posterior Analytics*, Aristotle discourses on the characteristics that reasoning must necessarily possess if it is to lay a claim to being truly scientific. In *Topica* are studied the reasoning modalities that, although syllogistically correct, do not fulfill the conditions needed to be considered as scientifically precise. Aristotle describes the end aimed at in *Topica* as follows. "The purpose of the present treatise is to discover a method by which we shall be able to reason from generally accepted opinions about any problem set before us and shall ourselves, when sustaining an argument, avoid saying anything self-contradictory." 100a 18. That is, the work seeks to enable two participants, he who asks and he who answers, to play their respective roles competently in a dialectic discussion. It is therefore possible to conclude that the subject of *Topica* is a dialectical syllogism based on premises that are only probable, as opposed to the demonstrative or scientific syllogism (*Prior Analytics*) rooted in premises both true and immediate.

humanism exhibited an affinity for applied logic. In other words, the humanists interpreted logic in the sense of dialectic, as a form of reasoning adapted to a literary focus. Consequently, we find in humanist dialectic a tendency to move away from syllogisms and toward the analysis of statements in speeches and dialogues. It should not come as a surprise, then, that the medieval penchant for approaching logic from its purely formal side should have been profoundly repugnant to humanist reformers of dialectic like Valla and Agricola.[49] Because to those who made theirs the humanist and revolutionary posture toward knowledge and how to acquire it, the educational dogmatism implicit in the attitude of a Scholastic logic exclusively preoccupied with establishing valid syllogistic inferences was necessarily shocking. But even more important is the fact—and this, once we set aside the details (and invective) of the devastating criticism unleashed against medieval logic in several of his works, we find also in Vives' thought—that the medieval texts, exclusively emphasizing the formal aspects of logic, persuaded the student that once the statement had been reduced to a series of syllogisms adequately constructed, the truth of the inference in turn implied that the conclusion had to be necessarily true (given that, in such a syllogism, out of true premises there emerges a true conclusion). All this plainly carries with it the assumption that it is possible to reach the truth. But for those who like Valla and Agricola (and Vives) were far less sanguine concerning such an assumption, both the study of reasoning (through formal logic) as proposed by the medieval tradition and the means employed to arrive at an objective truth had to appear inadequate. And yet, once the possibility of reaching the whole truth is discarded, there remains open but the epistemological posture of the Academics: it is not possible either to arrive at indubitable knowledge or to formulate rules accepted as true by all, a stand that carries with it the conclusion that there exists no truth that cannot be debated with identical virtuosity by both sides. In retrospect it is obvious that there was nothing new about the humanists' quandary, for the Ancients themselves had been caught in the horns of a comparable dilemma. Authors like Quintilian, Cicero,[50] and Boethius had extricated themselves by making theirs the epistemological position of the Academy, and by building on its foundation the technique—*in utramque partem*— that enabled them to explore uncertainty. In turn, Valla creates a non-dogmatic dialectic understood as an alternative to the dogmatism of

---

[49] Authors of *Dialecticae disputationes* and *De inventione dialectica*, respectively. Agricola's work was first published in 1539, one year before Vives' own death.

[50] See *De fato* I 1-2.

the schools' formal logic, and rooted in Ciceronian Academicism.

ii

Vives' method[51] (and although I will use the word here it must be noted that I have been able to find *methodus*[52] explicitly mentioned only once)[53] aims, as is frequently the case during the age, not at the sciences but at the arts, the latter being a group of disciplines somewhere between the extremes of simple mechanical skill and of demonstrable knowledge, disciplines that emphasize that which is practically profitable for life (something traditionally part and parcel of the Socratic inheritance). Disciplines, in other words, that are as far removed from the mere dexterity, the province of the common artisan, as they are from the sphere of what is purely contemplative and theoretical (this last rooted in the Aristotelian scientific method based in turn in demonstration as a procedure proposed to go beyond what Socrates had already explored). Vives, therefore, admirably embodies what Neal W. Gilbert has called, in

---

[51] It is clear that Vives, despite being a "dialectician," that is, a humanist rebel against Scholastic logic, and despite Melanchthon's opinion that (*Erotemata dialectices*) "dialecticians have adopted the word *methodus* to signify the most correct way of explaining," does not discuss the subject of method. But it is equally true that he is a bitter critic of Scholastic logic and medieval pedagogy (like Agricola, who does not speak of method, either), and an educational reformer. Therefore, if we take the meaning of "method" in the Platonic sense of the surest path to reach knowledge, or think of it as a *via* to reach an end proposed beforehand, or interpret it as proposed by Socrates when he compares rhetoric with Hippocrates' medicine, or understand it in terms of how deeply related to each other method and art are in Greek thought, or accept it in the Renaissance sense, that is, as a technique to formulate simple and clearly stated rules for any art whereby the task of learning the art in question is facilitated and accelerated for the student, then there is no doubt that Vives is a "methodic."

[52] It is well known that Aristotle did not write a treatise on method. The work that closest approximates a formulation of method is the *Posterior Analytics*, where he explains the conditions under which it is possible to affirm that something is known with scientific certainty. It would appear, however, that the *Posterior Analytics* aims at a limited objective: preparation for the study of geometry, arithmetic, and related disciplines such as optics and astronomy.

[53] It is possible that Vives refrained from using the word *methodus* because he shared the humanist contempt for Latin words of non-classical origin ("method" is a Greek word). Cicero himself never used *methodus*, although he might have had used *ars* and *ratio* in its place. St. Thomas always prefers ars. Boethius appears to have been the first to use *methodus*. Vives employs *ars, ratio* (in the sense of "procedure") in places where the meaning would seem to point toward *methodus*. For example, in *De disciplinis* he cites a few lines from *Topica* (I ii 101b 2-3) where Aristotle uses "method," which Vives translates as *viam et rationem* (III i *Opera* VI 111; Riber 426).

the introduction to his *Renaissance Concepts of Method*, the artistic methodology of the Renaissance. According to Gilbert, there is a methodology applied to the arts ("artistic") and a methodology applicable to the sciences ("scientific")—I use quotation marks in both instances because "art" means something totally different from the classical *techné* or the medieval *ars*, and because today's "science" is the progeny of the seventeenth century scarcely related to that of the sixteenth. According to the author's definition, the first category was aimed at the teaching of the arts; the second is Aristotle's own contribution in the shape of explicit criteria of demonstrative procedure.[54]

Obviously, the skeptical elements in Vives' thought would hardly have enabled him to embrace the scientific method defined in those terms, for it would have meant simultaneously accepting an Aristotelian brand of dogmatism. Evidently only the artistic methodology remains as a viable alternative; in other words, developing an educational structure enabling man better to learn and understand the arts. But given that learning and understanding imply, both for the teacher and for the student, grasping the subject-matter of the art in question, it is clear that the ability to investigate its content is essential. To that end a systematic procedure must be found that will enable, simultaneously, the finding and evaluation (*inventio* and *censura*) of the arguments leading to the probable truth of the question under discussion. It therefore follows that the artistic method includes (1) finding arguments; (2) evaluating those arguments by means of several kinds of reasoning, one of which, induction,

---

[54] Science ("We consider that we have unqualified knowledge of anything [as contrasted with the accidental knowledge of the sophists] when we believe that we know [i] that the cause from which the fact results is the cause of that fact, and [ii] that the fact cannot be otherwise." *Posterior Analytics* I ii 71b 10- 15) or scientific knowledge *simpliciter*, according to Aristotle, starts out from first principles. In other words, science is demonstrative ("Reasoning is *demonstratio* when it proceeds from premises which are true or primary or of such a kind that we have derived our original knowledge of them through premises which are primary and true. Reasoning is dialectic which reasons from generally accepted opinions. Things are true and primary which command belief through anything else, for regarding the first principles of science it is unnecessary to ask any further questions as to 'why,' but each principle should of itself command belief. Generally accepted opinions, on the other hand, and those which commend themselves to all or to the majority or to the wise—that is, to all of the wise or to the majority or to the most famous and distinguished of them." *Topica* I i 100a25-100b25) knowledge arrived at through syllogisms ("A syllogism is a form of words in which, when certain assumptions are made, something other than what has been assumed necessarily follows from the fact that the assumptions are such." *Prior Analytics* I i 24b) from first principles or premises that themselves are not and cannot be known by demonstration. To arrive at those principles we obviously need something other than demonstration.

gives us the universal rules that are the foundation of any art; (3) using the process developed in this fashion and applicable to all arts, to offer the student the opportunity to learn, swiftly and efficiently, their contents; and (4) communicating with the student and persuading him (dialectic tells us how to create the arts, rhetoric how to expound them). And all this, of course, with the emphasis carefully placed on efficient teaching and application to life of the useful arts. Like other Renaissance advocates of the artistic method, Vives, with his feet firmly planted in the Socratic preoccupation concerning whether virtue can be taught as art and whether knowledge can be conveyed by someone capable of speaking persuasively (Socrates calls "dialecticians" the practitioners of dialectic and rhetoric), maintains a point of view contrary to the position adopted by contemporary proponents of scientific method in several fundamental aspects: (1) Socrates, not Aristotle, as guide; (2) greater emphasis on *Topica* than on *Posterior Analytics*; (3) impugning of the dogmatic aspects of Aristotelian thought; (4) preference for rhetoric (without forgetting Vives' fondness for experience) when philosophy reaches dogmatic extremes (with the proviso that rhetoric must be deeply rooted in philosophy); (5) the possibility of shaping a prudent man as alternative to the impossibility of creating a wise one.

In *De tradendis*, Vives, as he outlines a broad study-plan to be followed in the education of the young, offers us an example of how training in grammar, dialectic, and rhetoric must always precede instruction in the arts. First, "from the study of language the young pupil" should be led into "a method for examining the instruments of the true and the false[55] by means of simple and composite statements[56] and known as the critique of truth (*censura veri*) . . . .This art, or better still, *organon* or tool, is the part of dialectic known as critical, meaning *iudicium argumentationis*."[57] Next, as mentioned earlier, comes "the knowledge of nature" (*rerum naturae cognitio*). Little previous

---

[55] *Ratio examinandi instrumentum veri et falsi.*

[56] *Enunciata simplicia et composita.*

[57] DTD IV i *Opera* VI 345; Watson 162. Contrary to what one day would be the practice among the Stoics, Aristotle's classification of knowledge leaves logic out of the running. Logic, then, is for Aristotle not strictly a science but rather the instrument (*organon*) of science. Presumably, therefore, logic emerges variously as a general introduction to teaching, a general liberal education imparted to the average citizen, the training undergone by those preparing to become scientists. Logic, in brief, is the study of the structure of rational thought conceived as a means or tool for the attainment of truth. And knowledge and the means to attain it are precisely the twin Aristotelian themes that are relevant to our present inquiry.

preparation is needed here, for the youth's natural perspicacity and the
sharpness of his senses are enough—in contrast to what happens in what
pertains to *prudentia*, where much knowledge, practical experience of life,
and excellent memory are required.[58] Once the fundamental study of the
outside of nature is concluded, those who wish to delve more deeply into
the subject must endeavor to penetrate to nature's inner being. In other
words, the next step in the educational process involves the study of
metaphysics.[59] Here, the student must possess the kind of talent "that will
enable him to rise above the senses into the causes and origins of things
and reach the synthesis of the universal out of the singular. . . .Care must
be taken to begin with what is most simple and elemental, namely, that
which is best known, what the senses can verify most accurately, and that
can later be subjected to examination by the mind."[60] After "a portrait of
nature" has been outlined the teacher shall emphasize instruction in the
"*instrumentum probabilitatis*, that is, the method of finding arguments (*de
ratione inveniendi argumenta*). . . .*Argumentorum inventio* is one of the
two parts of dialectic, the other being, as stated earlier, judgment or
testing of the truth (*veri censura*) of the arguments discovered."[61] In other
words, for Vives dialectic (the subject of his logical works) has two phases:
(1) discovering the arguments leading to the truth; (2) judging those
arguments. Let us begin with the former.

iii

The first phase of Vives' dialectical program is outlined in *De
instrumento probabilitatis* (1531).[62] The author begins with some broadly

---

[58] Ibid.

[59] For Aristotle, metaphysics is the noblest among the sciences whose end is knowledge
for knowledge's sake, whose goal is Being for being's sake.

[60] Ibid. ii *Opera* VI 354.

[61] Ibid. Simultaneously, the youth will be taught the art of speaking (*de ratione dicendi*)
or means of presenting the question under discussion. Vives emphasizes that only by
following the prescribed order (from *rerum naturae cognitio* to *ratio dicendi*) is it possible
to create the needed context for the proper acquaintance with all these disciplines. It
would be pointless to teach how to create arguments and how to put them forward to
anyone who does not know the subject-matter to which they aim.

[62] Despite the title, it is in *De disputatio* and not in *De instrumento probabilitatis* that Vives
formally defines probability. "Probable is that which seems so to everyone, not because
the reason is certain and evident but simply because it is more verisimilar than the
contrary reason." *De disputatione Opera* III 70-71. Properly speaking there are two kinds
of *disputatio*: (1) the quiet discussion or soliloquy that every man carries on with himself;
(2) the debate that confronts our own points of view with those of others. Of the second

general considerations intended to serve as introduction to the problem that caused dialectic to be in the first place. "The human mind, which is the faculty used to know the truth, has a certain affinity with those preconceived truths (*anticipationes*) wherefrom all others are born." From these seminal truths the mind gradually garners all the rest, "as the stalk grows out of the seed."[63] Each newly uncovered truth merely whets the mind's appetite for more, thus encouraging it to further search. The task is entrusted to *iudicium*, whose action determines whether we assent to the truth or dissent from what is false. Assent may in turn be simple (*simpliciter*): "this is, this is not," or doubtful and cautious: "I suspect, I believe." More often than not, however, neither straightforward path is open to *iudicium*, either because the evidence is sufficiently ambiguous to justify a suspension of judgment, or because neither extreme is supported by proofs strong enough to warrant accepting one at the expense of the other.[64] The role played by *iudicium* is obviously fundamental, as Vives reiterates in *De disputatione* (1531). Buried deeply within the body, the mind cannot fully intuit the truth. To make matters even worse, shadows of our own making darken the things themselves, with the predictable result that everything appears to us as if concealed behind an impenetrable veil. Fortunately, to free the truth of its man-created impurities the *ingenium humanum examinandae veritatis facultatem a Deo accepit*. Its function, *disputatio*, Vives defines as "a comparison of the *argumenta* proposed by both sides to prove or refute something" closely tied to the

---

Vives is not fond, for he is well aware how it tends to degenerate into acrimonious and pointless debate. It should be noted that *disputatio* is a medieval method of approximation to the truth profoundly influenced by Aristotle's *Topica*. Much of its popularity suffered an eclipse during the Renaissance, the result, no doubt, of humanist criticism; this, however, should not lead us to conclude that what *disputatio* owes the *Topica* was also rejected. The main objection was not to the *disputatio* as method, but to the manner of its use by the schools.

[63] DIP *Opera* III 82. See also the very beginning of *De disputatione*. Although all this is accompanied by the phrase "there had its origin Plato's opinion," Menéndez Pelayo does not consider this position of Vives to be Platonic. "These *informationes naturales* are not Platonic innate ideas ... such an admission is impossible for anyone who like Vives held to an essentially sensualist theory about the origen of ideas. Vives' *informationes naturales* ... are not ideas, but merely forms of thought, 'anticipation' or 'catalepses,' which existing potentially only lack reality; they are, therefore, not true knowledge but simply seeds of knowledge" ("De los orígenes del criticismo y del escepticismo y especialmente de los precursores españoles de Kant," in *Ensayos de crítica filosófica*, Edición Nacional de las Obras Completas de Menéndez Pelayo, XLIII [Santander, 1948] p. 167).

[64] DIP *Opera* III 82.

five *animi functionis*: *mens, cogitatio, opinio, phantasia,* and *sensus.*[65] *Disputatio*, in other words, stands on the functions of the soul mentioned above. The senses are of course the ultimate source of information, feeding both *opinio* and *phantasia*. Our thoughts are in turn fueled by what the mind suggests or what fantasy and opinion place at their disposal. The mind provides, within the measure of its own possibilities, what is truest and what has been carefully scrutinized. "The general axioms, natural knowledge, and natural impressions common to all men" thus generated are all linked with syllogisms ("wherein science lies, if in fact it lies anywhere"). The ultimate result is ratiocination. For its part, *opinio* contributes that which is "believable, but at times true and often false, hence the existence of syllogisms characterized by verisimilitude from which doubt is not totally absent." Finally, the fantasy supplies all the "images, dreams, deceitful conclusions, and impostures."[66] It follows from all this that the development of a suitable instrument of analysis is both mandated and conditioned by three sets of circumstances: (1) the unfree nature of the human mind and its tendency to project its own insufficiencies into the very things it observes; (2) the failure of the sources feeding our thoughts to convey clear and unbiased images; (3) the inability of *iudicium* to discriminate with utter precision between what is true and what is false. Given these conditions and what was said above, we must first ask: how does the mind in fact proceed in its search for the truth?

The first "order of credibility" belongs to the senses. "The mind follows the lead of the senses, although at times it does not hesitate to modify the knowledge derived from them. Using the information harvested by the senses the mind probes deeper, into the nature of things, uncovering what is hidden and abstruse." The process must be slow and rigidly gradual, for it would be absurd to move from one extreme to another without first passing through the middle. The mind, then, with what is certain as its point of departure, moves onward into the realm of what is uncertain; it must enter into the unknown through the known, penetrate the realm of things that engender doubt—but only after starting out from what is credible and verisimilar and always one step at a time.[67] What we have explored to the point of certainty or seems to us to be probable, and then use to examine other things, endows the latter with the same conditions of either uncertainty or verisimilitude inherent in the former. "That which we believe to be [either certainly or probably]

---

[65] DD *Opera* III 68-69.

[66] Ibid. 69.

[67] DIP *Opera* III 84.

becomes the demonstration [certain or probable] that supports our faith in something not yet believed."[68] Clearly, the process, as implied here, whereby a proposition or group of propositions provides grounds or support for the truth of another proposition is an argument (*argumentum*: Cicero's *probabile inventum ad faciendiam fidem*). The provisions made by Vives concerning the certainty or probability of the premises necessarily imply that the conclusions will be either deductive or inductive. "All arguments are drawn either from certain, verified, and necessary things or from probable realities that themselves depend on conjectures. Properly speaking, however, those names correspond more to the way in which we view things than to the things themselves, for while some men see them as certain and indubitable, others do not."[69] It must be remembered, however, that everything said so far is based on the senses. And, how much credit can the senses, and hence the premises therefrom, be given? According to Vives different circumstances may cause the senses to derive erroneous information; they cannot, therefore, be considered as entirely reliable. But however frequent the senses fail, "it does not justify the Academy's flat abrogation of all faith in them as if they were unable to perceive things correctly. The occasional error of which they may be guilty now can be remedied at other times, and what one man perceives erroneously is set aright by another."[70] In addition to the senses, the passions play a substantial (*secundus fideis locus*) role in shaping an argument, and so "the degree of certainty or credibility inspired into a man by his own passions" must be taken into account.[71] In Vives' eyes the "passional process" tends "to blunt the sharpness of the mind and the penetrating quality of judgment," and in effect destroys the latter's objectivity to the point where it becomes impossible to evaluate the matter at hand, because passion both anticipates and destroys critical analysis.[72]

But Vives is here interested in neither the senses nor the passions as "sources of credibility"—after all, "the senses are creatures of nature and so not subject to teaching, while the passions are carried onward by their own impetus and remain deaf to reason."[73] He wants, instead, to know how to avoid the errors to which we may be led by the senses and the

---

[68] Ibid.

[69] DD *Opera* III 70.

[70] DIP *Opera* III 84-85.

[71] Ibid.

[72] Ibid.

[73] Ibid. 85.

passions. The means to achieve that goal consist in arranging, orderly and systematically, the arguments leading to probability. He begins by explaining the value of arguments and authority[74] as a means of discovering the truth, for "*argumenta* and reason carry with them their own persuasive strength, as does the authority that is the source of what is being said."[75] Still, *argumenta* and *auctoritas* are bound to affect different men differently. Some rely for their judgment exclusively on arguments, be they apodictic or merely verisimilar; others insist "that the arguments be fully demonstrative (*necessaria*). Obviously these men have complete confidence in the powers of their own intellect. On the other hand, for those less self-assured the authority of others is held in high esteem." The weight of authority is of course not always the same, but whenever a man draws from that source, what he accepts as true ought to be considered as "belonging to the realm of probability." The importance of arguments as paths to the truth, Vives readily grants, is well known to men of learning. "All who starting out from clear and certain things launch themselves into an investigation of what is dark and uncertain use

---

[74] The preface to *De disciplinis* is nothing short of a critical manifesto conceived for the purpose of guiding the author's steps as he ponders on the value of Ancients and Moderns as authorities. Knowledge, Vives says, shall be better served and its advancement assured if we adopt a critical attitude toward the writings of famous authors. After all, nature is not such an exhausted vein that it cannot, if adequately mined, provide as abundant a stock of news today as yesterday. In truth, and given the knowledge and experience accumulated through the centuries, it would not be too bold to state that today we extract more than it ever yielded in times past. It would seem, then, that after such prolonged observation of past and present knowledge, we should be in a position to put forth views and forge opinions about nature superior to those of Aristotle and Plato. If Aristotle can criticize the opinions of his predecessors, should the same privilege be denied to us? "I do not presume to elevate myself to the level of the sages of Antiquity, but I do demand that their reasons be compared to mine and that the best be heard." Still, we must not forget that Vives (bitter critic that he also is of the erudition of the schoolmen of his own day), as so many other Europeans until the very end of the seventeenth century, also finds in Aristotle the anchor needed to secure his own ideas. And nowhere is this better highlighted than in the question under consideration here. It is moreover important to note that (1) Vives belongs to a generation of humanists that no longer believes that what the Ancients achieved could not be surpassed by the Moderns, and (2) he nevertheless does not condemn the former as Montaigne two generations later. These facts will once again validate what we have repeatedly stated throughout the pages of this monograph to be Vives' postion: the acquisition of knowledge is a task neither useless nor pernicious; we must persevere, but judiciously, weighing what authorities say and using our own critical faculties to reach, slowly but inexorably, the heights of knowledge our intellect, defective but not blind, allows us to reach.

[75] DIP *Opera* III 85.

identical instruments. . . . The jurist, physician, geometer, rhetorician in search of the essence, accidents, causes, effects. . . . All this is readily available to experienced minds through the clarity and penetrating power of the intellect."[76] But inasmuch as "other, less gifted men need the aid of authority and consultation," Vives concludes that it would be useful "to observe, note, catalogue into precepts, and turn into an art (*quam de inveniendo nominarum*) the very rational inquiring and gathering of probables generally used by us all."[77] Within this art, a method woven around a core of arguments, the latter and all their attendant elements are orderly contained in niches known as *loci*, "a name that pleased Aristotle who, if we are to believe Cicero,"[78] invented this faculty. *Locus* signifies the "instrument by means of which we catch a glimpse of the probable reason," namely, the grounds of proof, the point or points on which the proof is founded.[79]

Vives has then arrived at the dialectical means, a judgment of probability, to test the true and the false. When the *argumenta* or proofs are based on realities or things our senses confirm as either probable or bound to the proof itself by a nexus that is not clear, our *iudicium* constructs an *argumentatio* (defined by Cicero as *explicatio argumenti*) that is known as probable or credible and called dialectic by Aristotle— "probable being that which seems to be so to every observer, not because the reason is certain and evident, but simply because it is more verisimilar than its opposite."[80] As Vives reviews in *De disciplinis* the many and different ways in which learning has become contaminated through the ages at the hands of both Ancients and Moderns, he particularly deplores the fate suffered by dialectic. For the latter is precisely the one subject that ought to have remained unsullied, since through it alone can we hope to enter into all remaining arts and disciplines. What in fact happened was that the corruption that infected dialectic spread to numerous other arts.[81]

> The ancients created two arts relative to the language: dialectic, *quam "artem disserendi" vocat* Cicero, Aristotle "*logicam*"; and rhetoric, *quam "artem dicendi."* Dialectic puts together the proof *(argumentum)* with a handful of brief points; rhetoric broadens it and

---

[76] Ibid. *Opera* III 85.

[77] Ibid. 86.

[78] See Burnyeat, op. cit. p. 264.

[79] DIP *Opera* III 86.

[80] DD *Opera* III 70-71.

[81] *De disciplinis* III i *Opera* VI 110.

accommodates it to the judicial, deliberative, and demonstrative causes. For that reason Zeno was fond of saying that dialectic is the fist and rhetoric the open hand. In the creation of the mansion housing the language, grammar cuts the timber and lays down the foundations, dialectic builds the house, and rhetoric founds the city . . . dialectic advances up to argumentation [*argumentatio*].

Vives next proceeds to translate the passage (*Topica* I ii) where Aristotle explains the threefold usefulness of his treatise. We are particularly interested in the third application, which Vives quotes as follows (insisting that he is translating from the original Greek). "It is impossible to say anything about the first principles of any art, since they are the earliest of all principles. The investigation of any one thing must therefore find its point of departure in the probable about the thing; a process to which dialectic is most fittingly adapted because, being naturally inquisitive and inclined to investigate, it owns both the path and the method leading to the origins of all arts."[82] Vives, however, balks at Aristotle's interpretation, objecting that he has turned dialectic not only into a means of reaching what is probable but into a treasure trove of instruments suitable to all sorts of investigations as well; while Vives himself believes that no single art can be so efficacious, and that if in fact any such existed it would not be dialectic but metaphysics. His own view is that of "those who thought dialectic to be no art at all, but the tool of the other arts."[83] Let us now move on to *De censura veri* and the second phase of dialectic.[84]

iv

As the artificer seeks within the subject-matter of his own art for the statement or proposition (*enuntiatio*) aptest for explaining either the truth or the rectitude of the procedure followed in his investigation of the truth through probability, he is in fact using an additional instrument—an

---

[82] Ibid. 111.

[83] Ibid. 112.

[84] By reason of the deep shadows surrounding it and the veil that as a barrier separates it from the things themselves, the human mind is incapable of clearly intuiting the truth. To cleanse it of all the impurities that so limit its scope, man has at his disposal the function of the *facultas examinandae veritatis* known as *disputatio*. The examination of the truth expurges the falsehoods, ambiguities, and uncertainties, and like a ray of light illuminates our mind. The latter, on the basis of the truth thus reached, is now able to clear up or refute what is doubtful. For its part, this last operation is carried out by means of arguments that demonstrate the probability; and these arguments are precisely what *disputatio* compares and examines—"*argumentum ad aliquid probandum aut improbandum, comparatio.*"

"*instrumentum examinandae veritatis* applicable to each and every one of the disciplines or arts and analogous to that other instrument employed in the search for probability."[85] However, the operation of *censura veri* embodies two "extremes" (studied by Vives in two related pieces): simple statements (*enuntiata*) or declarations that do not as yet fit within the framework of *argumentatio*, and *argumentatio complexio*. With the first extreme or case he deals in *De censura veri in enuntiatione* (1531), with the second in *De censura veri in argumentatione* (1531).

In the first treatise, Vives takes pains to explain the nature of words, the structure of sentences, and how "complete and perfect sentences" may come to constitute propositions—that he calls *enuntiata* or axioms and "wherein lies what we are trying to ascertain: truth or falsehood." He classifies them as (1) singular when one single subject is involved, (2) particular if they refer to several, and (3) universal when all are concerned. Strictly speaking, therefore, *enuntiata* involve propositions that have not as yet been linked into arguments. When association has in fact taken place and we wish to inquire into the validity of the arguments thus created, we come to the contents of the second treatise; in other words, we are now involved in a critique of propositions structured into *argumenta* through the process of *argumentatio* (what we ordinarily and in a non-technical sense call "argument").[86] Vives points out that there exists no sure procedure whereby to assess whether a given *enuntiatio* is true or false—by itself dialectic cannot determine whether propositions are true or false. The only viable guide is a man's own criterion within the subject-matter of his own competence. What dialectic can do is to provide man with an instrument with whose assistance to achieve that determination. For instance, in what pertains to the *vita communis*, the judgment of the *vir prudens*—"practiced in affairs, experienced, abundantly endowed with common sense and great intelligence"—is best.[87] Nevertheless Vives pledges to offer an *instrumentum* that will enable all, within their respective professions and after a thorough examination of the facts, to inquire into what is true and what false in the *enuntiata*. He begins by defining the two terms. "A true proposition is one that enunciates what the thing truly and really is: 'Christ shall judge all men'; the proposition is false when it states what in reality is not."[88] Various circumstances may be involved in determining the truth or

---

[85] DCVE *Opera* III 142.

[86] Ibid. 148-53.

[87] Ibid. 155.

[88] Ibid.

untruth of anything. Some are part and parcel of the things themselves; others reside in us. Within the thing itself lies what is immutable (and in the immutable resides the necessary), possible, contingent, used, rare, frequent about it; what is possible is found throughout, but it has greater tendency to become associated with that which is specifically mutable, and it is what may happen—so long as it is not contrary to nature. Necessary is what must happen or cannot happen otherwise, given the essence of the things in question.[89] When starting a proposition care must be taken to purge every ambiguity inherent in the words themselves. About this there are no rules; each man has to judge by himself, although the *vir prudens*, endowed with practical experience, is particularly skilled in this endeavor.

With all this in mind Vives proposes three *formulae* affecting the classification of propositions mentioned above. We are particularly interested in the first. "Everything subsumed in the universal renders the latter true if congruent with both what is enunciated and the manner of the enunciation. And incongruity falsifies it." Moving "from the universal to the singular implies *descensus*; the opposite signifies *ascensus*." The latter process—that in both *De disputatione* and *De argumento probabilitatis* Vives also calls *enumeratio* (the repetition of an experience)—adds to the universal; the former weakens it. It is imperative to insure that both in *ascensus* and *descensus* all singular propositions be indeed of the universal, that the time be taken into account, and that connected singulars be taken connectedly. As we move from the universal to the singular and vice-versa, care must be taken, as we build up the truth, that in either process all the elements of the universal be contained within a general clause such as *sic et ceteris*, or "nothing has been observed to the contrary." Vives offers the following illustration. To command a ship, run a school, and break in a horse, the surest hand ought to be chosen; therefore, to rule a commonwealth the best man should be elected. This series of statements Vives calls a *genus inductionis* (wherein lies implicit the universal), which in fact comprises an induction *ascensus* and a *descensus* or deduction in this fashion: if for a ship, school, and horses, the most skill is desirable, so it will be for all other cases inasmuch as "nothing has been observed to the contrary." From the universal thus established Vives now in effect "inductively descends" to conclude (after warning the reader that in *descensus* one single obstacle suffices to wreck the entire sequence) that what applies to ship, school, and horses holds equally true for the republic as well. To please those who might object to this deductive reasoning

---

[89] Ibid.

from universal to singular, Vives grants *sit sane inductio non univer-salitatis, sed similitudinis, et exemplorum.*[90]

In the second piece (*Censura veri in argumentatione*) of *De censura veri*, Vives deals with the theory of argumentation, which he defines thus: *argumentatio est connexio enuntiationum*, in such a way that what is prior follows from, and after a fashion is born out of, what is posterior, and maintains a quasi-necessary connection with it.[91] The first proposition is called "antecedent, reason, argument, premise; what comes after is the consequent . . . which Cicero called conclusion and is commonly referred to as consequence." *Argumentatio* then is an adducing of proof or simply the reasoning alleged to support a conclusion. And by prior is meant of course not what comes first, but what contains the other, the posterior, that which is inferred. All forms of *argumentatio* fall into two broad categories: particular and universal. The former embodies *argumentationes*. In some cases the particular are also temporal: they exist and are valid only within a limited time frame. For example, " 'this man earned the enmity of Octavian; therefore, he will die.' Such was the case before the establishment of the monarchy, but not afterward." Still other particular *argumentationes* must not or should not exist in the absence of some additional ones. "Such is the origin of conjecture among clever spirits who gather what shall happen from what already took place."[92]

Having finally linked propositions into arguments, Vives is now ready (in this treatise and in *De disputatione*) to itemize the various kinds of possible "connections." Enthymeme he defines as an imperfect syllogism, and example as "that which is used to prove something similar."[93] *Inductio* Vives sees as including *ascensus* and *exempla*, "a procedure by means of which all the arts were discovered. From particular experiments carried out by the senses the mind formed the rule of art."[94] Elsewhere, calling induction *enumeratio*, he points out how thanks to it "were discovered all arts; that is, the many experiments were synthesized into a formula. Should any one particular instance fail to fit within the latter, however, the whole thing collapses. But since it is impossible to cover all

---

[90] Ibid. 156.

[91] DCVA *Opera* III 163.

[92] Ibid. 164-65.

[93] Ibid. 167. "Example and enthymeme are the theoretical forms answering to induction and syllogism respectively." *Posterior Analytics* 71a 9-11. Example differs from (perfect) induction (1) in not proceeding from all the instances, and (2) in finishing by applying the general conclusion to a new particular (*Prior Analytics* 69a 16-19).

[94] DCVA *Opera* III 167.

singularities, some we take for the whole, adding at the end '*sic in ceteris*,' or 'nothing has been observed to the contrary'. . . . In this fashion it will be possible to include cases which, once thought to be certain, are shown not to be so by the passage of time . . . the conclusion is verisimilar when despite intense investigation no one finds anything to the contrary."[95] This is clearly an empirical inductive generalization based on simple enumeration. Gradation occurs "when many things are taken in such a fashion that the second can be inferred from the first, the third from the second, and so on." In *sorites* (given the premise, the conclusion cannot be drawn by a single syllogistic inference) "I add or subtract, endlessly accumulating and so proving that the process neither comes to an end nor is it ever destroyed . . . as in the example of the heap of wheat where if any one grain does not make up the pile, neither do two nor three, nor any number."[96] In *De disputatione*, Vives refines the example as follows. "The pile of wheat is neither created nor destroyed by any of its constituent grains."[97] The dilemma (an important form of argument at a time when logic and rhetoric are so closely related) embodies a situation in which given two alternatives, the opponent, no matter which he chooses, becomes trapped.[98] Socratic induction is an argument by analogy defined as "an *argumentatio* that conforms to nature. 'If such is the case in other and analogous instances, so it must be in this one.' In a sense this form of induction is akin to *exemplum*, but its strength is greater by reason of the many examples adduced."[99] When *argumentatio* is "true, genuine, and perfect, it becomes syllogism, called *ratiotinatio* by Cicero." Vives defines it as "a collection of three enunciations or statements of which the third one, meaning that which is to be inferred, emerges naturally out of the connection between the other two."[100] The entire demonstrative value of the syllogism lies in that out of the universal it is possible to infer either the universal or the particular, "a negation from a negation, and affirmation from an affirmation."[101] The rest of the treatise Vives devotes to a discussion of eighteen syllogistic forms.

---

[95] DD *Opera* III 73-74.

[96] DCVA *Opera* III 168. The sorites, in the shape of the heap of wheat, seems to have originated with the Megarian School. It was an argument used by the Academic Skeptics.

[97] DD *Opera* III 67.

[98] DCVA *Opera* III 168.

[99] DD *Opera* III 74.

[100] DCVA *Opera* III 169.

[101] Ibid. 170.

V

In conclusion, Vives' method fundamentally implies four major and distinct phases or stages. First, the process actually begins in an introductory fashion with what in practice is a tentative, preparatory step of transitional value. A series of general concepts, "not invariably valid" and constituting the realm of *opinio*, is derived on the basis of sense-perceived evidence drawn from individual[102] things; drawn, in other words, from the component parts of what is essentially the synthesis presented to us by nature, in the same manner as the craftsman offers the finished masterpiece to the eyes of the uninitiated. Such is the theory; in practice, however, things are more complicated because several additional and important considerations must be kept in mind. To begin with, Vives certainly grants (indeed, insists) that sense-perception is both fundamental and indispensable; but it does not necessarily follow, as what has just been said above might appear to suggest, from his admission that sense-perception and universal precepts must be bound to each other by a strictly immediate relation of cause and effect. Or, to put it differently, universal rules are not induced directly out of individual impressions collected by the senses, no matter how large the number of objects observed might be; everything we know about Vives indicates that in his view the nexus between facts and universal rules is remote and indirect, and time and again we are told that universal statements cannot be derived inductively from less than universal evidence. In short, sense-perception and the evidence thereof are indeed the crucial raw material, but before the latter issues into universal norms it must pass through two filters: the imagination-fantasy and speculative reason. The former both fulfills its appointed function within the circumstances of this the introductory phase of Vives' method presently under discussion, and is the second among the considerations mentioned above. The intervention of the imagination-fantasy implies that from the start the observed facts must be subjected to a gradual and systematic process of abstraction leading from the observed composite to the abstracted simple, from the unique qualities of objects singularly observed to the collective characteristics, or class, of things. All the internal senses share in this procedure. There is, however, more, because inasmuch as we are in effect endeavoring to penetrate beyond the accidents into the substance of things, we are also inevitably drawn into ground where the certainty associated with individual things directly observed by the senses wanes, to be replaced by a more

---

[102] "Out of each and every one of the things perceived by the senses, our minds established universal *praecepta*." DPP I *Opera* III 192.

problematic verisimilitude that is both inherent in the realm of *opinio* and is the inevitable companion of man's judgments. Obviously, then, and this brings us to the final important consideration to keep in mind, the delusive probabilities peculiar to this stage and responsible for its transitional character must be weeded out before we may proceed to the next phase; such a crucial task is performed by dialectic, in itself an instrument by no means infallible since neither its premises nor its conclusions are necessarily true. Certainty, it must therefore be borne in mind, should not be expected; only a higher order of probability.

Second, induction. This is surely the heart of Vives' method, with the second filter mentioned earlier, speculative reason, playing the leading role. The mind now takes over where the external/internal senses leave off and through induction attempts to bring into being a specific body of knowledge, *scientia*, embodied in precepts of universal value. The path now followed—in other words, the path leading from *opinio* to *scientia*—has been cleared by dialectic, thus making possible the application of induction guided by reason in its *speculativa inferior* mode. The process here involved is outwardly closely associated with Aristotle's own search for scientific knowledge: on the basis of general statements wrought by *opinio* and buttressed dialectically, Vives intuitively reasons the main premises or first principles from which science makes its start. But outward parallels do not tell the whole story. It is well known that Aristotelian scientific investigation consists in extracting from particulars what is common to them all, their form, and only as the individual is dissected into a set of universals—laws, types, qualities shared in common with others, and the like—can it be said to be known. And this is also what is involved in the Vivesian process leading to *scientia*. Evidently, as remarked earlier, since universals are involved and universals cannot be created by the imagination-fantasy, reason—inductive reason—must be a part of the process as well. Vives' path so far moves along Aristotle's own. But there is one important difference. When Aristotle combines intuitive knowledge of first principles with demonstrative knowledge (necessary knowledge derived deductively from first principles), the result is cognition of things that are necessary, universal, and eternal. This knowledge Aristotle calls wisdom. In Aristotle, therefore, apprehension of first principles necessarily creates the realm of knowledge known as philosophical wisdom. For Vives this significant outcome is out of the question, because *sapientia* cannot be attained by any means other than *pietas*; his goal is consequently far more limited than Aristotle's own. In other words, Vives' universal precepts, truths, or laws are limited in that they only reveal (and imperfectly at that) the images of God embedded in nature (after all, man cannot cognitively transcend the latter); they do not penetrate to God's own Self. This of course we were told in *De prima philosophia*, when Vives pointed out in no uncertain terms that his metaphysics was indeed a first philosophy (the study of the natural world) but not a theology.[103]

Third, deduction. Out of the principles thus found by Vives as he elaborates *opinio* into *scientia*,[104] *ars* is created, and the investigator, armed with knowledge of causes, proceeds deductively to explain the effects; once the precepts have been learned, to practice the corresponding art means to carry out its precepts.[105] In other words, following the formulation of those universal precepts or norms (the collective intelligible behind the simulacra belonging to any genus or species in the world of nature) that are its objectives, reason—hitherto speculative reason methodically applied—must choose between two alternatives. On the one hand, it may remain speculative and withdraw into contemplation to enjoy the fruits of its labors so far generated by induction, namely, the truth inherent in the discovery of universal norms; in that course of action might (if those norms were indubitably true) lie the path to wisdom deemed possible by Aristotle but denied by Vives. Or it may, on the other hand and starting from universal precepts, opt for shifting into a deductive mode, which makes possible the transition from speculative to practical reason.[106] The ultimate result of this process is the creation of

---

[103] For Vives, then, that induction by means of which intuitive reason grasps the first principles mentioned earlier is an "imperfect deduction" that reaches merely a probable conclusion, not (as in Aristotle's case) a universal truth seen then and afterward as self-evident.

[104] Principles, it must be emphasized, in no way identical to those yielded by Aristotle's scientific knowledge inasmuch as they are probable truth at best.

[105] Writing on the division of the arts, Vives points out that "out of this," meaning the norms found inductively, "we extract an exacting and extensive narrative which embraces not only the effects but the causes as well, although more in the manner of explaining the latter than of inquiring about them." The passage is of interest to us now for two reasons. First, because the bulk of what Vives says and proposes about the arts is aimed at the "natural," not the "invented" arts. This, however, in no sense detracts from the importance of discussing Vives' method in a context heavily weighed toward the study of the practical arts; after all, a natural art, namely, one aimed at the investigation of nature, is admissible only insofar as it is the progenitor of a practical art. Secondly, the very last sentence of the cited passage, emphasizing "explaining" rather than "inquiring" about causes, again sets the tone for what is Vives' thoroughly consistent approach to the kind of knowing open to man.

[106] And, of course, the transition (1) from *contemplatio* to *actio* and (2) from "natural" to "invented" or practical art.

art, practical art—"from what is general, it is possible to establish rules and precepts out of which we can form an art."[107] If, therefore, a man who has trodden the path to *scientia* (the very path that leads Aristotle to philosophical wisdom) is to refrain from wasting his time and effort in useless contemplation, which according to Vives necessarily leads nowhere, and instead is to work toward the creation of that productive goal that in the end is the one thing that alone lies within the power of man to do, he must veer away from speculative to practical reason. Aristotle had pointed out that within the rational part of the soul there exist two faculties, which he designated as scientific and calculative.[108] The Philosopher's statements, given the nature of the things that are the rightful operational domains (and result in two distinct sets of virtues) of the two faculties, clearly preclude the passing from one faculty to another. To my knowledge, the closest Vives comes to Aristotle's classification is when he divides reason into natural (speculative) and deliberative (practical); and seemingly nowhere does he appear to suggest the kind of Aristotelian inflexibility that would prevent the mind from going from a speculative to a practical mode of reasoning, from *scientia* to *ars*, truth to good. In fact, one might suggest that this presumed flexibility is precisely what affords man the opportunity to reconcile (insofar as this reconciliation is possible given the handicaps attendant to his rational capacity) the two seemingly incompatible impulses doing battle within his soul: to seek after truth and to find the good. And unquestionably, for Vives, who more than once judges contemplation to be, at best, useless, and at worst near-criminal self-indulgence, the ideal life consists in *actio*. It is of further significance that when Aristotle discusses deliberative reasoning as the source of both arts and practical wisdom, he establishes a distinction between things made and things done; for him "making" is art, and "doing" is prudence or practical wisdom. For his part, Vives from the start uses "doing" in the context of art; not an unmindful distinction, perhaps, inasmuch as he will eventually make the arts into prudence's wherewithal.

Speculative reason, then, inductively fashions the universal out of which are derived the less general norms (by reason now practical), that in turn make the individual arts possible. It is obvious that if we were to

---

[107] DAV II ix *Opera* III 379. Elsewhere this definition is reaffirmed in even stronger terms. "That which has fixed, constant, and invariable precepts is subsumed in art. . . . Art is therefore 'the collection of general formulas which orient towards a result.'" Ibid. x *Opera* III 382.

[108] *Nicomachean Ethics* VI i 5-7.

define deduction as a process leading to conclusions of a generality less than that of the premises, we would be compelled to admit that a deductive step has been taken when going from *scientia* to *ars*. Science is general knowledge "firm and indubitable," and "out of the general we may derive rules and precepts that in turn may serve as a basis for some form of art." But "not every kind of knowledge is called an art, but only that which becomes a rule for doing something. . . . For art is the means of attaining a sure and predetermined end. Every art has an end, which it keeps in view, toward which it aims everything."[109] "What is general" is science (understood within the limiting parameters repeatedly underlined by Vives' conditional approach to the term), the universal to be transformed, through a deductive process, into "that which becomes a rule for doing," the norms or rules of the individual arts. But as we shall see, deduction is for Vives an ongoing process which, after creating the "less" universal norms that generate a given art, moves on to account for the reality of individual cases within the purview of the art in question, a process known in fact as verification/falsification.

Fourth, verification/falsification. To start with, enough evidence is needed. True enough, the contributions of many men created a repository of available information, which serves to restrain us from hastily judging as universal that which in reality might be supported only by limited and insufficient evidence. We are therefore now obviously in a position to explain, from general principles that both define and limit the radius of action of a given art, each and every occurrence, object, or phenomenon part and parcel of that art. But it is also equally clear that for such a program to be fully met, the original repository must be constantly enriched with new evidence;[110] and the resulting accumulated data in the domain of those things whose nature is to be explained by the universal norms will themselves serve to test (verifying/falsifying) the norms.[111] Next, we must go back and scrutinize the record of earlier experiments, namely, the information contained in the repository handed down to us by our predecessors; because each individual occurrence or object within the art may have singularities given to it by time.[112] Before the occurrence in question can be explained and accounted for by the norms ruling the

---

[109] DTD I ii *Opera* VI 251-252; Watson 22.

[110] Vives argues that rhetoric never establishes universal norms before having paid all possible attention to the "cunning of nature" (*naturae artificio*) and taken into account all experiences as norm. DPP I *Opera* III 193.

[111] Ibid. 192.

[112] Ibid.

art, therefore, the time-given singularities must be purged or the norms themselves further falsified, meaning that the hypothesis must be changed to explain the observed reality of individual things.[113] Finally, since besides time, place may also be partially responsible for the singularities in question, we must additionally endeavor to understand how the occurrence or phenomenon in question might manifest itself in different places—"what *opus* did nature produce and in which place; and how each local miracle of creation can be revealed to us."[114] To that end Vives (and here we reprise a theme already broached earlier), speaking now in *De tradendis* and addressing himself to any man who might wish to study nature at any level beyond the elementary, reminds him that he "must study outward nature by close observation . . . he will observe the nature of things in the heavens, in cloudy weather, in the plains, on the mountains, in the woods. Hence he will seek out, and get to know, many things from those who inhabit those spots. Let him have recourse, for instance, to gardeners, husbandmen, shepherds and hunters . . . whether he observes anything himself, or hears anyone relating his experience, not only let him keep his eyes and his ears intact, but his whole mind also, for great and exact concentration is necessary in observing every part of nature, its seasons, and in the essence and strength of each object of nature."[115] And by way of quantity, time, and place we inevitably reach experience ("after this fashion, we begged the few crumbs to sustain our minds in their poverty"), either firsthand or that derived from others or both. And, we shall soon see, without experience there can be no prudence.

---

[113] Vives invariably stresses the element of sense irreducibly present in knowledge. "All our knowledge goes through the gate of the senses; we have no other source of knowing, imprisoned as we are in our body. True, as the mind knows, it moves beyond the senses, and from that vantage point it induces other things but does not see them." Vives, of course, values universals—"oftentimes we so follow the senses that we sentence according to what they tell us, even though the mind is suggesting something entirely different. . . . We must judge of things not out of their characteristics but through our estimation and judgment." But apparently he loves them less than the individual thing, which for him is unquestionably the cornerstone of cognition. He therefore will not hesitate to modify his universal norms as mandated by the reality of the individual. In fact, according to Vives, when we state that such is or is not, we are merely establishing a conjecture based on the perception of our *animus*. It is an assessment forged by the mind and not by the things themselves because, to us, they are not their own measure. Similarly, when we say good or bad, profitable or useless, we are not making an objective but a subjective judgment. Ibid. 193-94.

[114] Ibid. 192.

[115] *De tradendis disciplinis* IV i *Opera* 350; Watson 170-71.

Prudence and History

i

Let us begin with Vives' understanding of wisdom, whence *prudentia*[116] must ultimately derive. In *Introductio ad sapientiam* he implicitly agrees to interpret *sapientia* in terms both human and divine.[117] In what concerns wisdom, therefore, there are two grades or chief stages: a *vera sapientia*[118] defined at this point as the "ability to judge a thing correctly and to know it for what it in truth is,"[119] and a *sapientia* or knowledge of God.[120] We are here of course interested only in the first one. Two fundamental assumptions both underpin and condition the workings of Vives' entire system: (1) man must seek God, (2) the path to Him necessarily passes through society (meaning an ascending hierarchy of orders: self, household, community, mankind). Not surprisingly, therefore, to approach Vives' notion of *vera sapientia* correctly implies understanding it with reference to man as man, man as social being, and man as God's creature. That in turn obviously means that man's path to God, from beginning to end and in all three stages, is inseparable from wisdom: wisdom or self-knowledge in the first, the stage unique to man as man; wisdom or *humana sapientia* in the second, as the man who knows himself becomes integrated in society; wisdom or *perfecta sapientia* in the third and last stage, when man, an individual entity in full knowledge of self and a social being living in harmony with his own kind,[121] is aided by *pietas* to reach the ultimate goal. Clearly, then, in the

---

[116] For Aristotle's definition of prudence see *Nicomachean Ethics* VI v 1-7.

[117] According to Cicero (with whom wisdom had been transformed into an *ars vivendi* which Seneca would later define as the relentless search for virtue and a zealous desire to attain the good which have tranquillity as their reward), "that wisdom which I have given the foremost place is knowledge (*scientia*) of things human and divine, which is concerned also with the bonds of union between gods and men and the relations of man to man." *De officiis* I xliii 153.

[118] In contrast to *mundana sapientia*, which reduces wisdom (and prudence) to mere astuteness.

[119] Which is what Vives, in other works where the aphoristic format of the *Introductio ad sapientiam* does not inhibit lengthier and more detailed analysis, explains to be *iudicium*.

[120] This is what Vives also calls *divina* or *perfecta sapientia*, something that is not achieved intellectually but through religion. To know the latter is perfect wisdom; to live in accordance with it is perfect virtue; but no one who fails to live in perfection can hope to know it perfectly. IAS aphorism 283.

[121] In other words, the man who has fully achieved what in the following pages will emerge as prudence: the *vir prudens*.

race toward *vera* or *humana sapientia*, that occupies man's entire life and for which he must prepare himself since early childhood, "the first step is that aphorism so dear and celebrated by the Ancients: 'Know thyself.'"[122] And if to that condition we now add the definition of *vera sapientia* quoted earlier, we must conclude that there are—or so it would seem at this stage in the discussion based on the *Introductio ad sapientiam*—two indispensable pillars on which Vives' *vera sapientia* must rest: self-knowledge and *iudicium*.[123] Let us begin with the first one.

In the dedication of *De anima* to the Duke of Béjar, Vives insists that he who has not yet explored his own self will hardly be in a position to act righteously—"before anything else we must know the artificer [man] because that is the only way to determine what can be expected of him and to ascertain what he can and cannot do." And so it happened, he further adds, that the ancient oracle commanded, as the first step to be taken in the direction of *sapientia*, that every man should know himself. But this knowledge, warns Vives, who apparently feared that the injunction might be taken to mean solely physical awareness, necessarily implies much more than simply a detailed acquaintance with one's body. It means also to know "the nature and structure of the soul, its *ingenium*, faculties and passions, and all its complex operations."[124] Clearly, then, a significant aspect of the process leading to self-knowledge must be devoted to learning about one's passions. But it is equally plain that the passions, in addition to being known, must be restrained, for they may constitute the greatest obstacle found on the road to self-knowledge. And the reason lies with the very meaning of sin, a violation of that natural order that

---

[122] Ibid. aphorism 11. There are other, additional, and somewhat more secondary "steps" to be taken: distrusting that which the vulgar holds to be wisdom, familiarizing oneself from infancy with the habit of forming true opinions about things, an early education in the art of differentiating between good and evil. Ibid. aphorisms 1-11.

[123] Although Vives' understanding of prudence is perfectly clear, the terminology used is at times confusing. Thus he often uses *iudicium* (as in the definition mentioned above) and self-knowledge as synonyms for prudence.

[124] DAV *Opera* III *praefatio*. Speaking of the soul in *Introductio ad sapientiam*, Vives divides it into two parts: a superior part, known as the soul proper, which understands, remembers, knows, and uses *ratio, iudicium, and ingenium*. IAS aphorism 118. The other—by virtue of its attachment to the body—is lacking in reason, brutal, bestial, cruel; those movements known as passions or perturbations: arrogance, envy, anger, fear, etc. have their seats in it. Ibid. aphorism 119. Although Vives repeatedly, here and elsewhere, blames the body for much that is distasteful in man, it would be a mistake to conclude that he views it as totally devoid of merit. "In the body we find beauty, health, strength, uprightness, agility, and also their opposites . . ." Ibid. aphorism 14. By the same token, in the soul also coexist learning and ignorance, virtue and vice. Ibid. aphorism 15.

demands that all things obey wisdom. Because when the passions or affections rebel—and the Fall, explains Vives, has caused man to be extremely prone to this kind of openly mutinous behavior—against the superior part of the soul, and compel it to serve them and the body, they are in effect forcing man to stand outside the order of nature.[125] What to do? The obvious solution seems to be to restrain the passions.[126] But how can we achieve that goal? According to Vives, the interaction of three faculties—*ingenium*, *estimativa*, *voluntas*—yields the sought-after result: the control, but not the annihilation, of the passions. *Ratio* finds the truth; *iudicium* contributes the process of *censura*, that examines the validity of that truth; *voluntas* seeks the good. They are the faculties, in other words, that make self-knowledge possible.[127] Let us now examine in what concrete way the first two (the last one, the will, we have already discussed elsewhere in this monograph) of these faculties contributes to man's knowledge of himself.

First, reason. *Ratio naturalis* plays in this instance a somewhat unexpected (in that it brings Vives closer to Montaigne) role as the instrument that, no longer pretending to probe the divine nature, successfully awakens in us the love of God. In *De veritate fidei Christianae* (1543), his posthumous work, in which he insists that religion is the result of an instinct nature has embedded in man,[128] and that only the shape and

---

[125] IAS aphorism 126.

[126] They neither can nor should be destroyed. Vives chides the Stoics for having attempted to uproot the passions from the soul; because in so doing they simultaneously tried to separate man from himself. The only effective method of eradicating the passions is that which places man above the human condition, that is, a procedure that causes a "mental eclipse or the soul's perpetual convulsion." DVF V vi. The Aristotelian theory of the golden mean, fundamental to the Philosopher's concept of virtue (*Nicomachean Ethics*) is also applicable to the passions. And Vives in this instance follows the Aristotelian path.

[127] It is to be noted, if we are to avoid confusion, that *iudicium*, which in *Introductio ad sapientiam* Vives aphoristically tagged as *vera sapientia*'s supporting pillar, becomes in the reasoning followed in *De anima et vita* an integral part of self-knowledge.

[128] DVF 1433. This is worth remembering for future reference, because it gives the reader the impression that Vives seeks to make religion into natural religion and, implicitly, Christianity into a natural religion. Now, for Vives the *vir sapiens* becomes so through natural reason; he turns into the *vir civilis* through a process that involves his transforming himself into a *vir prudens* assisted by *ratio naturalis* become *ratio practica*. But inasmuch as Vives' fundamental premise is that the *vir civilis* becomes so because only in this fashion can he eventually partake of the *divina sapientia*—the ultimate goal for which he was created—it is clear that as *vir* becomes *vir sapiens* becomes *vir prudens*, he must also become *vir religiosus*. The instrument that regulates his becoming *vir religiosus* is also natural reason—because, remember, religion is a natural phenomenon. Essentially, then, *ratio naturalis* adopts several guises: *ratio naturalis* properly speaking to create the

form it adopts are the actual creation of man, Vives argues that there is a cure for the man whose inner being is kept in constant turmoil by the unruly passions; a means, in other words, to bridle the passions, which, in addition, is easily accessible to Christians. For, reasons Vives, what if one of the passions were stronger than the rest? Would they not be then subject to its control? Obviously, if this hypothetical passion were in addition a good one, its ascendancy over the others would be correspondingly beneficial—"All spiritual teachers agree that there exists one passion that is supreme over all the others: love. And what love is stronger and firmer than the love of God?" Whoever loves God is free from bewilderment and perturbation, and is admirable in his serenity and composure. "There is no virtue except in that love, because virtue will not be revered in good faith unless man can experience the emotion of divine love."[129] And this circumstance, Vives explains, is why the philosopher's precepts on virtue[130] invariably fall short of the mark: they are not rooted in truly firm soil.[131] The elixir to quiet the inner turmoil caused by the unruliness of the passions, in other words, cannot be created by means of precepts only the few can grasp; it must on the contrary emerge from teachings so fully developed, so simple, so congruent with the human mind and nature that they will easily reach all: men, women, and children. Because natural reason (weakened by original sin, to be sure, but still fully up to the task)[132] is of course what awakens in us our love of

---

vir sapiens; the *ratio naturalis qua ratio practica* to yield the *vir prudens/vir civilis; ratio naturalis qua ratio religiosa,* which we call *pietas* and which produces the Christian man in the most accomplished and fullest sense of the word. In this sense Vives fully deserves the name of Christian humanist. The growth of man from plant to *homo* described in the *Fabula* must be paralleled at a spiritual level by his growth as a Christian man.

[129] Returning to the discussion of the *Fabula,* the last stage in the evolution of man—his ethical growth, as it were—culminates in man becoming one with God: through love.

[130] Prudence is virtue and virtue is love. Hence the dovetailing of Vives' system: prudence is love of God; now, through prudence, man has taken the final step in the direction of becoming one with God. Ethics is prudence is virtue is love of God.

[131] Is this a confession that Socrates was ultimately incomplete because he was not a Christian? (Remember the nature of his work and how close Vives is to death.) Then it would seem that Socrates could not have been a prudent man. From Vives' other works it is possible to draw another, more likely conclusion. See Chapter Five, where I suggest, in the context of *caritas,* that Socrates might be included among those who according to Vives help other men "walk along the path leading to virtue."

[132] Natural reason is still fully able to recognize religion; but as in everything else, it needs the help of practical reason, which, just as it creates the arts, creates the religions, viz., Christianity.

God, which in turn the corrective synonymous with virtue, which, as it gives man control over the passions, makes possible the consummation of the process leading to self-knowledge. In works not so directly concerned with Christianity and its value, Vives outlines a somewhat different, if related, answer to the problem of the passions as the most significant obstacle capable of thwarting the search for self-knowledge. However viable and commonplace the binomial natural reason/love of God may ring in Christian ears, it becomes meaningless when we move into the pagan context of classical learning, that no humanist can possibly ignore. Clearly, Vives has this difficulty in mind when, in *De tradendis* and while discussing the merits of history, he establishes a distinction between "the examples and virtues" of pagan philosophers and Christian saints; the former became exemplary by the practice of virtue through the "light and guidance of nature alone," while the latter achieved their proverbially "heroic probity by the grace of God."[133] When Vives therefore elects Socrates as his paradigm, natural reason emerges as the only instrument used by the Greek sage to focus all his powers of observation inwardly. And by first studying his inner self by the light of natural reason alone, Socrates acquired his knowledge, and so presumably the means to restrain the affections as well, to restructure and to reorganize his soul, a denouement that in turn led to the discovery of his own perfectibility and potential for beatitude.[134]

Second, *iudicium*. To prevent the passions from subjecting the soul to the control of the body, the former was endowed with "the intellectual strength required to examine all things, and so to discern what is good and should be acted upon and, contrariwise, what is evil and must be avoided."[135] This *ingenium* can be sharpened and polished through divine and human arts, which provide it with such knowledge. Thanks to the latter the *ingenium* becomes more precisely acquainted with the qualities

---

[133] Having said this, however, it should also be noted, once we have remembered Vives' definition of religiosity as a natural force within us all, that it would not be unreasonable to point out that pagan philosopher and Christian saint alike are operated upon by the same basic impulses, albeit under different guises.

[134] But Socrates believed in the possibility of acquiring ultimate knowledge. Vives does not. So for Vives, Socrates, after attaining to self-knowledge through natural reason, must have switched to practical reason to create, out of the awareness of self-knowledge, the social ethic that according to Vives is his gift to mankind. Socrates, then, did not reach beatitude—he lacked the knowledge of God that only Christianity can give. He reached awareness of God through natural reason, and ethics through practical reason. He became, in short, man, *vir prudens*, but not *vir religiosus*.

[135] IAS aphorism 122.

and values part and parcel of each and every thing.[136] And *iudicium* is a
capacity given to man by his intelligence or *ingenium* and begotten in the
facultas estimativa of the soul—"the estimative faculty is that which, on
the basis of sense-perception, produces the art of judging."[137] Within that
faculty the function of *iudiciun* is to accept or reject conclusions arrived
at rationally. *Iudicium* itself, therefore, *est censura*; that is, *approbatio et
improbatio rationis*.[138] Once reason has done its part, man's judgment
mounts the stage, and if, as it contemplates the relative merits of the
rational process, it estimates the latter's discourse to be flawed, it may
decide to reject the conclusions.[139] But, given his conviction that the
human mind is far from perfect, Vives willingly grants that it may often
lead to mistaken judgments. It follows, he insists, that if one's judgment
is to be clear and healthy one must take care to examine calmly and
precisely all aspects of the business at hand. And this is precisely the facet
of intellectual equanimity that Vives prizes above all others; for it is the
quality—and "not experience, the knowledge of many things, erudition,
science, or art"—that separates the "high-minded from the low-minded."
When judgment is applied in this fashion the resulting stand, positive if
iudicium agrees with the findings of reason and negative if it rejects them,
Vives calls *opinio*.

ii

Natural reason, judgment, will: the man who knows himself and has
cleansed his own being by admitting the universal and fundamental
freedom of his *iudicium*, now commits himself, voluntarily and
irrevocably, to guide his life by the dictates of reason. What happens next?
To answer that question, we must return to Socrates. As Vives tells it,
Socrates went (presumably compelled by the will and shunning
contemplatio) beyond self-knowledge, and starting from his own
introspection invented moral philosophy, enabling others to follow the
same path guided by his example—"[He] externalized what he had
wrought internally into a means capable of bringing well-being into one's

---

[136] Ibid. aphorism 123.

[137] DAV I x *Opera* III 328.

[138] Ibid. II v *Opera* III 362.

[139] Ibid. I x *Opera* III 328. In the midst of the bewildering diversity that Vives believes is
attendant on the human mind's acquisition of knowledge, the judgment stands, acting as
arbiter, weighing everything, sanctioning what it finds acceptable and rejecting what if
finds to be false.

private and public life; that is, into an instrument, ethics, whose aim is to introduce order into one's mores." This attribution, which in effect changes Socrates from a man at peace with himself into a universal teacher of virtue, and places his most intimate personal discoveries at the service of mankind, is a perfect example of Vives' own lifelong commitment to and abiding interest in education, the Socratic dimension to Vives' thought mentioned in our discussion of the *Fabula*. It is also a metaphor for something fundamental that has just taken place: the transition from self-knowledge to prudence. Having achieved self-knowledge, man is now free to follow the example of Socrates and undertake *actio*, "that we may follow the path of virtue." In other words, he is ready to take the next step, this time in the direction of placing a personality fully harmonious and under control at the service of mankind; and once the process has been successfully consummated, there rises the *vir prudens*, the virtuous man whose learning serves the common weal. Let us now examine more closely the nature of this *vir prudens*, because he is the culmination of that second step which, in turn, is both the prelude to *prudentia* and the final effort that makes Vives' *vera sapientia* a reality.

Everything said so far seems to underline Vives' conviction that natural reason, be it in the guise of Christian love of God or under a pagan format as moral philosophy, is enough to lead man to self-knowledge (total control of the passions). We may therefore begin our study of prudence with the following question: where does he go from here? Given Vives' views on the nature of man and the quality of his reason, only two options are open to him once he has achieved knowledge of self. Either he succumbs, with natural reason operating now *qua ratio speculativa*, to the temptation of boundless—and meaningless—intellectual enjoyment of contemplation of what he has so far discovered, or he chooses, through *ratio practica*, to follow the *via activa*. For the former, *contemplatio*, we have already seen that Vives has nothing but contempt. It is the latter, therefore, the way of the *vir prudens*, that concerns both Vives and ourselves. And to understand properly the nature of the second option we must first do two things: (1) outline the general contours of the man who has succeeded in carrying out the first phase of the process leading to wisdom; (2) understand what is expected from the man thus defined.

The Vivesian sage, the man who knows himself, distrusts authority, rejects what passes for learning in conventional circles,[140] treats with

---

[140] What Vives, with the usual humanist contempt for Scholasticism terms the "knowledge of the schools."

disdain what the vulgar embraces as wisdom, and maintains a relativistic posture in all matters pertaining to human knowledge. Above all, and this we wish to underscore carefully, he never wavers in his willingness to confess an error or to accept a valid, albeit new, point of view, regardless of what effects the resulting reconsideration may have on opinions previously held; in other words, the Vivesian sage understands and accepts that changing circumstances may well demand a change of attitude or opinion. And what must the man so defined, the man who like Socrates has succeeded in ordering his soul, do? Unless he wishes to opt for the unproductive path of *contemplatio*,[141] he is obligated to enlist everything so far harvested in the service of a second effort that will make possible his insertion into the society of his peers. Given these circumstances, it plainly follows that the instrument, *ratio naturalis*, which has so far carried him forward, must now be replaced with a "different" one, *ratio practica*, more suitable to the changed circumstances into which the sage is about to plunge. There is no other possible conclusion to be drawn, because in the process of explaining who the Vivesian sage is and what he must do Vives has implicitly introduced a new factor into the equation that is inseparable from practical reason—knowledge. Thus it is true, on the one hand, that the Vivesian savant understands and accepts that at a given moment circumstances may effectively compel him to discard as useless, conclusions hitherto accepted as valid. But, on the other hand, now that besides being wise he is a man of action as well, he remains absolutely committed to follow the path beaten by evidence firmly rooted in what after all is the only soil at man's disposal, that is, *opinio* born of probability. Why? Because as a man compelled to act in the real world and guided in this his fundamental function by what is probable, the Vivesian sage, now clearly a man both of action and of affairs (*vir prudens*)—that is, a social being—has no alternative but to act on the basis of that probable knowledge. In short, we have just admitted that the wise man now conducting himself in the manner of a *vir civilis* needs knowledge;[142] knowledge, that is, made available by the arts methodically

---

[141] Clearly, Vives refuses to take seriously the possibility that a man as right-minded as a sage will waste precious time pursuing *igniis fatuus*.

[142] The reason is not hard to find. The Vivesian sage, let us repeat it, the man who knows himself, is now a *vir practicum*. But the capacity of such a man for *actio* is directly proportional to the probable knowledge at his disposal. It is eminently desirable, under the circumstances, that we do our best to enhance the probability of that knowledge, for in that fashion man's *actio*, namely, his ability to discharge his social obligations, shall be correspondingly broadened. And, finally, there is no doubt that the order of probability

developed and taught by education. The role of the former is self-evident: the whole body of the arts invented by man was created for that very purpose, to provide man with the knowledge needed to survive as an efficient social being.[143] As for the latter, it is obvious that not all forms of knowledge are equally useful in enhancing the quality of *opinio*'s probability, so education remains the best means available to insure that man shall indeed receive the knowledge most suitable to the purpose in question. Or, to put it in a different way, the wise man who becomes *vir prudens* reaches that goal because he has at his disposal an adequate educational system.[144]

"We have now traversed the road that leads to a knowledge of the nature of things—and to the knowledge of bodily nurture, and to the antidote for the diseases that menace men, and the remedies for those illnesses that have actually befallen them." Vives has, in other words, surveyed the world of the contemplative and practical arts; concluded that contemplation alone is hardly enough, but must in turn be aimed at some end of practical value; and offered man the means of arming himself with useful knowledge. What is expected of the man who has achieved self-knowledge? Nothing less than complete commitment to the world. "Now we approach that other question; how, in fact, man is to prepare for the task of committing himself to the world." In this fashion Vives introduces *prudentia*, the subject-matter of *De tradendis*' Book V Chapter I,[145] because it is clear that the nature of man's "commitment to the world" is defined by and irrevocably tied to society, whose well-being in

---

rises proportionately with the volume of knowledge acquired.

[143] At the head of this procession made up of the arts marches, of course, moral philosophy, the very same discipline whose invention Vives attributes to Socrates. After all, moral philosophy teaches us how to deal with our own selves, with others, and finally (because it enhances our piety), with God himself. It is, in other words, virtue; for, if we cannot be equitable with ourselves and merciful toward our peers, how can we hope to aspire to render unto God the piety owed Him?

[144] A fact that in turn ought to give us a fair idea how important it is for Vives to reform Europe's educational structure. He insists at all times that little can be expected in the way of imparting the right kind of knowledge from what passes for education in his own day.

[145] But not for the first time. On several occasions in earlier chapters he has presented prudence variously as "springing from reason"; being "like a rudder for guiding a ship. . . . By it the very order of life ought to be regulated"; "practical knowledge of virtue"; something "increased by experience, which is supported by memory"; and "that which makes a many-sided man."

turn hinges on reason.[146] And it is precisely from that same reason that prudence issues. By *prudentia* "the whole order of life ought to be regulated, and at no stage of his life could [man] be without it, nor indeed can he be if he lives humanly; for all the humanities come under the head of wisdom; from it spring those sciences that the Greeks called Ethics, Economics, and Politics. These are subjects that the human intellect and the whole nature of man with impulses aroused by the Creator, necessarily found out and built up into organized knowledge. If they were excluded entirely, man would not live at all, and if removed in part he would live not a human life, but the life of a wild beast or a savage."[147]

iii

What, then, is prudence? Clearly, it is not wisdom. Under the heading "Prudentia quid sit," Vives makes explicit a fundamental distinction that sets *prudentia* and *sapientia* on two different foundations. "In the affairs of life, *prudentia* stands at our side, ready to be an ally; in matters of religion, we have *pietas* to teach us who God is, and how it behooves us to act toward Him. This latter kind of knowledge stands alone and has a special claim to the name of *sapientia*."[148] If not wisdom properly speaking, is *prudentia* perhaps *ars*? Vives himself had defined the end of art to be the useful (at least immediately, although he frequently suggests that mediately its objective is also the good), and that of prudence to be the good (evidently there exists a relation, at least mediately, between art and prudence); in other words, art is making (*facere*) while prudence is doing (*agere*). In Aristotelian terms, it follows, prudence cannot be art.[149] Nor is it *scientia* because, again like Aristotle, who believed that prudence deals with human conduct (that is variable), Vives reiterates now the earlier association made in *De anima* between *prudentia* and *opinio*: prudence "is the skill of accommodating all things of which we make use in life, to their proper places, time, persons, and

---

[146] "In human society, in which it is right for men to use moderation and reason, it was fit that each person should act, not rashly, nor violently, nor in the manner and fashion of wild beasts, but modestly, as far as reason, well and fittingly trained, might prompt him." DTD I i *Opera* VI 245; Watson 14.

[147] Ibid. 246; Watson 15.

[148] Ibid. V i *Opera* VI 386; Riber 645; Watson 227.

[149] "Making and doing are quite different activities. . . . Consequently the rational faculty exercised in doing is distinct from that which is exercised in making." *Nicomachean Ethics* VI iv 2-3.

functions."[150] While neither *sapientia* nor *ars* nor *scientia*, *prudentia*, we are told, is "the moderator and rudder in the tempest of the [passions], so that they shall not by their violence run the ship of the whole man on the shallows, or on the rocks, or let it be overwhelmed in the magnitude of the waves,"[151] and that it is born out of *iudicium* and *usus rerum* (experience). "Judgment must be sound and solid. . . . Experience is either personal knowledge gained by our own actions, or the knowledge gained by what we have seen, read, heard of, in others. Where either of this sources is lacking, a man cannot be practically wise."[152] Theory without practice and experience avails nothing, and experience in the presence of "confused judgment" fails to yield prudence.[153] Two chapters later, as Vives reflects on the consequences of original sin, *prudentia* fully comes unto its own as *humana sapientia*. Man is an eternal battleground[154] where the soul endlessly struggles with the body to retain its rightful supremacy. "Within the soul itself, reason seeks to subject the passions to its authority, a quest that, involving as it does the whole man, demands total knowledge [of him], internally and externally."[155] Inwardly (man's

---

[150] DTD V i *Opera* VI 386; Watson 228. The doubt originating from changes in "places, times" is not, apparently, the same caused in the study of the natural arts. Evidently, then, *opinio* is prudence and *opinio* for the instance of the natural arts are not identical.

[151] Ibid; Watson 228.

[152] Ibid. 386-87; Watson 228. "It is true that *iudicium*, like everything else which in prudence is natural . . ." Ibid. 388; Riber 6471.

[153] In other words, here as elsewhere Vives argues that nature alone is not enough, and just as natural reason must be complemented by practical reason, so must *iudicium* be accompanied by *experientia* if *prudentia* is to emerge at all.

[154] "On that account [prudence] is not to be looked for in youth, nor in young men whilst they lack experience, nor in older men, who are slow, dull, or depraved in judgment." Ibid. 387; Watson 228. *Ratio naturalis, iudicium, voluntas, ratio practica*: we meet them all as man became aware of his own self and embarked upon a course of action demanded by his own nature; but now Vives is more specific with respect to *ratio practica*. Whereas before it involved knowledge in general, he now insists on dividing it into theoretical and experiential or practical. Moreover, theoretical knowledge—actually originating with ratio speculativa and thus associated with despised *contemplatio*—is now de-emphasized in favor of experientia said to flow from two sources: (1) one's own practical knowledge, (2) that of others.

[155] "Through sin all things were inverted so that man's lower nature desires the higher position for itself; the passions contend for attention in place of the reason; reason, conquered and overwhelmed is put to silence, and is made the slave to the temerity of the passions. Thus there is an eternal . . . battle in man, in which he has a perpetual toil and struggle not to let the maid get the upper hand of the mistress." Ibid. V iii *Opera* VI 402; Watson 250-51.

"private life"), we must know by what things "they are restrained, calmed, removed. This enables a man 'to know himself.'"[156] But, Vives insists, we are not interested here in self-knowledge (*se ipsum nosse*); rather, the task at hand aims at the external knowledge of man (his "public life"): to show how the passions of the mind should be subordinated to the authority and judgment of reason.[157] The instrument that will enable us to accomplish that task, it turns out, is moral philosophy. But as was the case when Vives discussed the question of how best to become intimate with man's "private life," that is, self-knowledge, the humanist also chooses to approach the subject of moral philosophy as the means to understand man's "public life" from two different angles; angles that reveal their kinship with Erasmus' own infallible remedy for ignorance, itself the root of society's ills: a simple piety and classical learning.

First, religion. Man is in dire need of clear, penetrating reason. But our intellect, groping in the dark shadows with which reason has been shrouded by the passions, slaves to sin, cannot fully penetrate the veil. Under the circumstances, the divine reason is his sole remaining hope. And where better than in Christianity can man avail himself of its bounty? In Christianity, therefore, we find the best version of the precepts of moral philosophy. "We must obtain the precepts from God's own teaching. . . . We have as the interpreter of God and as mediator, Jesus Christ. . . . The interpreters of the Son are His disciples, and afterwards the other holy men. . . . From the teaching and words of these men should be gathered, as it were, remedies for the diseases of the mind, so that the passions may be subjugated to the hand and power of reason. When this precedence is established, and as far as is permitted it is firmly grounded, man then bears himself rightly towards himself and towards God, and towards those higher, lower, and equal to himself in station, whether we speak of private individuals, of families, or of the commonwealth; whether we speak of public life at home or abroad."[158] Second, secular knowledge. Although clearly the preeminent source, Christianity is by no means the only *fons* from which the precepts of moral philosophy flow. And so it came to pass that men who wrote on the subject of human wisdom (*humana sapientia*) divided the discipline (*moral philosophy*) most apt at dealing with human mores into ethics, "which concerns itself with the mind and the formation of individual morals"; economics, the province of those concerns appropriate to life

---

[156] Ibid; Watson 251.

[157] Ibid; Watson 251.

[158] Ibid; Watson 252.

within the family; politics, "which studies the principles of groups and gatherings of peoples"; and the "treatment of those intermediate duties of life that would not be found in the training of nature so much as would be posited in the custom or education of each region and people."[159] Moral philosophy is therefore a fourfold trail strewn with thorns that the *vir prudens* alone can travel in safety. It is the very realm of *prudentia*: man as he discharges his obligations to self, family, and country; a path leading to right living or virtue. In such consists precisely human wisdom (Aristotle's "practical wisdom"), the virtues whereby man fulfills his own humanity. Prudence is human virtue or goodness.[160] But there is far more to prudence than a mere canon to guide man as he weaves a pattern for right living out of the choices and challenges inherent in his daily existence, because as Vives understands it *prudentia* projects its impact well beyond the present into the future. It follows, then, that there are two aspects to prudence. One, moral philosophy, is predicated on a premise we have encountered repeatedly in the course of these pages: in the absence of a well-organized, smoothly-functioning society free from strife, man will inevitably suffer the full spiritual consequences (the human actor of the *Fabula*) of the Fall. And of course Vives is convinced that the conditions prevailing in his own day make it impossible for European society to meet those requirements. His life's work, therefore, is Socratic, wholly aimed at convincing his contemporaries that prudence in the guise of moral philosophy is the ideal instrument to remedy the current failings of that society. This fact, I believe, is significant enough to warrant the conclusion that Vives' thought, insofar as the explicit evidence of his writings to all appearances indicates, is overwhelmingly social.[161] But, beyond the present obstacles lying in the path of society as

---

[159] Ibid; 403. Watson 262. There is a very important point to understand here. Whether man is dealing with himself, family, or commonwealth, the values or precepts of moral philosophy that must guide his steps are all uniquely derived from an identical source: Christianity. There is no ethical division here. Whether man acts as private individual or political persona—prince or pauper—he is guided by Christianity.

[160] "The queen and principal mistress of this world is virtue. All other things, if they are to meet their own ends, must be at its service." IAS aphorism 17.

[161] Vives' most explicit attempt to reform society is recorded in *De subventione pauperum*. Within the framework of his favorite political entity, the *civitas*, Vives outlines a blueprint for coping with some of the age's most telling social and economic evils. In fact, *De subventione pauperum* might easily occupy in Vives' thought a place comparable to that taken by *Utopia* in More's. It is, however, a measure of Vives' temper as a reformer that he proposes no Utopia for Bruges, but hardheaded, practical measures feasible within the existing institutional structure. Perhaps his outlook in this instance can be best summarized by saying that whereas More's Utopian society can be only

it strives forward toward internal harmony and balance, Vives perceives, as inhering in the human condition, a very real potential for future contingencies spelling possible danger for that society. How does Vives suggest that man may cope with this problem? Prudence, of course, is the answer; but prudence in its second aspect, whose aim is to acquaint the *vir prudens* with those contingencies. And by the path trodden by *prudentia* as it endeavors to plumb the uncertainties that the morrow will inevitably bring, we arrive at history.

iv

Let us begin with the following proposition. "The best part of [*prudentia*] consists in the conjectures that we form of future things from the combination of past events. [Prudence] is then a certain kind of divination."[162] Plainly, then, the primary, and highest, function of prudence is now to provide fallen man with the wherewithal to foresee the future, thus affording him and the collective *aedes*—society—of which he is a part the means to prepare against the contingencies of tomorrow. Evidently, the question now is: how and by what means can prudence fulfill that fundamental obligation? The answer is undoubtedly history. We have already noted how the conjectures that result from prudence's prognosticating power derive from knowledge of past events. And in Book I, Chapter X of *De anima* we are further told that "that which changes with circumstances or because of the diversity of subjects— meaning changes according to place, time, people, or some such[163]—falls under the jurisdiction of prudence." I believe that if we examine Vives' explicitly stated views on history within the context of these two statements, we will conclude that the impact of history on his social and political thinking is formidable indeed.

Taking his cue from Cicero in *De oratore*, Vives defines history as "witness of the ages, light of truth, life of memory, mistress of life, messenger of Antiquity."[164] History, Vives emphasizes time and again

---

achieved at the expense of the destruction of the passions [is it fair to say that it is the passions that have built the old order rejected by More?], Vives' reforms are predicated on achieving a measure of control over them.

[162] DTD VI i *Opera* VI 387; Watson 229.

[163] The same parameters according to which the arts change.

[164] *De disciplinis* II v *Opera* VI 102. "And History, which bears witness to the passing of the ages, sheds light on reality, gives life to recollection and guidance to human existence, and brings tidings of ancient days, whose voice, but the orator's can entrust her to immortalize?" *De oratore* II 9 36.

both in *De disciplinis* and *De tradendis*, is a well-nigh inexhaustible reservoir of important qualities. It tells us about the past, it delights with its narrative of bygone events, it teaches by example. History is the image of life; an image, Vives insists, which must be utterly precise, without making reality either larger or smaller. And so he pours scorn on historians who, like the Greeks, "make an elephant out of a mosquito."[165] But, most important to us, history renders immense service in everything concerning the commonwealth and the administration of public business,[166] a fact that accounts for the inability of philosophers to rule: they have always been deficient in historical knowledge. In short, history is *prudentiae nutrice*.[167] And for precisely that reason Vives rejects the conclusion of those who insist that knowledge of the past is useless because time has wrought profound changes in everything, particularly in what pertains to the waging of war and the ruling of cities and peoples.[168] To be sure, Vives concedes, many things indeed suffer alterations with time insofar as they are subject to our will and tastes, but not human nature. One thing thus remains immutable: the causes of the affections of the mind (*causae affectuum animi*), as well as their actions and their effects, because they are rooted in nature.[169] This is what we must know, and precisely what history must teach. "For what greater [prudence] is there than to know how and what the human passions are: how they are aroused and quelled? Further, what influence they have on the commonwealth, what is their power, how they can be restrained, healed, put aside, or on the contrary, aroused and fomented, either in others or in ourselves? What knowledge can be preferable for the ruler of a state, or more expedient for any of his subjects to know? And . . . what more conducive to the happiest kind of [prudence]! For how much better it is that a man should be warned by the evils that have befallen others, than await the experience of them in his own person? So history serves as the example of what we should follow, and what we should avoid. Even a knowledge of that which has been changed is useful; whether you recall something of the past to guide you in what would be useful in your own case, or whether you apply something, which formerly was managed in such and such a way, and so adopt the same or

---

[165] *De disciplinis* II vi *Opera*.

[166] DTD V i *Opera* VI 389; Watson 231.

[167] Ibid; Watson 232.

[168] Ibid; Watson 232.

[169] Ibid; Watson 232.

similar method, to your own actions, as the case may fit. Indeed, there is nothing of the ancients so worn out by age and so decayed, that it may not in some measure be accommodated to our modes of life. For although now we may employ a different form, the usefulness just remains. This could easily be shown by discussing customs one by one."[170] What do all these statements tell us about Vives' conception of history and its role in and contribution to shaping his social and political thinking? Clearly, they contain several things of interest to us here.

To begin with, according to Vives what sinks its roots in nature never changes, meaning in this instance that the *causae* of the affections of the human mind undergo no alteration, and neither, therefore, do the actions (and their effects) brought about by those affections—actions, incidentally, which have an impact on the commonwealth and its social and political life. In short, the essential nature of human beings is timeless. From history, moreover, we derive knowledge of events and their general causes; events and causes that, rooted in human nature, must share in its fundamental characteristic: permanence. Obviously, history understood in these terms can easily provide the sagacious statesman with a clear window into the future, precisely the unique condition that makes history the ideal nurse of prudence in its prognosticating mode. Are we, then, given all that has just transpired, to conclude that political knowledge rooted in the study of history is a science? To my knowledge, Vives never answers the question explicitly. Nevertheless, it is clear from everything that has been said so far that the essential ingredients to make history into the mainstay of a science of politics are all in place. Convincing proof of this fact, so significant for the study of Vives' political thought, is easily forthcoming once we notice the striking parallels between Vives' premises and the thought of Baltasar Alamos de Barrientos, the late-sixteenth-century founder of Spanish political Tacitism and staunch advocate of politics as a science. According to Alamos, the precepts, rules, and advice relating to political questions or, for that matter, to the "whole governance of human life," result and proceed from the knowledge of human passions. In effect, Alamos reduces politics to a set of rules or criteria rooted in human psychology.[171] But human nature is constant: the names and the times may change, but not the nature of man, which means that today the passions have the same

---

[170] Ibid. 389-90; Watson 232.

[171] *Dedicatoria* to the author's Spanish translation of Tacitus, in my *Baltasar Alamos de Barrientos. Aforismos al Tácito español* (2 vols., Madrid, 1987), 19.

consequences and produce the same effects as they did yesterday.[172] Obviously, Alamos does not mean that each generation is the identical twin of its predecessor. There are indeed changes wrought either through accident or through necessity; man, in other words, cannot be totally divorced from his circumstances. But the point is that these changes are largely superficial, cosmetic, and, above all, temporary.[173] But how does the statesman acquire the crucial skill that will enable him to consider in all his calculations both what is temporary and what is permanent in human nature, and, above all, how does he know that what takes place today indeed happened yesterday in similar form? Alamos' answer is simple and straightforward: history will tell him.[174] And "knowledge of human passions" acquired from history "will make possible the prognostication of future events." There is no question, then, that Alamos, building on foundations indistinguishable from Vives', concludes that politics is a science. But how precise and certain is that science? Or, to put it differently, is this "prognostication of future events" based on information derived from the past absolutely reliable? Alamos does not hesitate: prognostication through knowledge of human psychology "shall not be infallible, because in matters relating to human discourse nothing is on account of free will." Still, in *ciencia de contingentes*, as Alamos calls politics, "most of the time we shall be correct, and rarely will we err, if we prove that in other men of the same condition the same thing happened."

---

[172] "For, as stated by Tacitus. . . .'Other are the men but not the mores.'" Ibid. 21.

[173] It follows that the statesman—or, for that matter, any prudent man involved in public affairs—must not place his trust in appearances (*accidentes*), for at any given moment what seems to be the true inclination of men may in reality be nothing but an intentional or accidental device cloaking their true nature; because once the emergency or convenience is past, the true and constant nature of man will again surface and those who trusted in appearances will come to rue their error. Ibid. 20. In short, "the principal thing in this science which they call of state is to know the passions, be they natural or the result of circumstances." Baltasar Alamos de Barrientos, *Norte de príncipes* Ms. Biblioteca Nacional, Madrid fol. 10r.

[174] "This knowledge of the passions to reach what one aims at (or to shun whenever necessary), to know the plans of others both in theory and in practice, to proceed with caution in all aspects of life, to attain to the rules and advice needed for the conquest of kingdoms, their preservation and their increase: without doubt all this is learned from history. Doubtless it is from history that one must derive the means needed to counsel and to decide in weighty matters of state." *Dedicatoria* p. 20. And in the same work Alamos further claims that "everything which I have pointed out can and must be learned from history, bearing always in mind the end and outcome of the occurrences which it reports, and fashioning out of this precepts, rules, and general advice with which to guide both our actions and counsel." Ibid. 23-24.

And of course the secret of this qualified certainty lies in history. "To learn of this we must read history, to learn about what happened to others, and to draw from that knowledge counsel, warning, and wisdom for the future."[175] Unfortunately, we have no similarly direct testimony from Vives concerning the limited "scientific" character of politics. But the question raised above plainly suggests a correlation between the failure of politics to be an infallible science, and history. And about the latter, our central subject here, Vives does have a great deal to say.

History is important to the "whole governance of life." But no sooner has Alamos made that statement than he plunges wholeheartedly into an explanation of why and how history is the keystone of politics—and indeed justifiably so, for Alamos' goals are strictly political. But such is not the case with Vives, a thinker whose interests invariably range through the entire spectrum of human activity and for whom, in this sense, politics as such can never be more than incidental, a part of a far larger whole (the whole, it must again be emphasized, that is invariably the singleminded focus of Vives' interest and attention), a partial means to the all-important end. That is precisely why, in Vives' scheme of things, history is significant, not because of its unquestionable impact on politics, but on account of the crucial role it plays in the whole governance of life. Man's present, his preparation for the promised life to come, is what it is because of a specific past event, the Fall. That present can only run its proper course if ordered on the foundation of a broad acquaintance with the future—a future whose ultimate culmination is everlasting salvation—which in turn can be fathomed only in terms of the past. And history is of course the tether that binds man's present to his own past and future. In the *Fabula*, as noted earlier, Jupiter had created a stage, society, where man could give free rein to his will. But everpresently dictating the script to be complied with by man stood Jupiter's own omniscient will. Metaphorically, then, we have a stage—human society, ordained of Jupiter and constructed by man as the domain of his free will—within a Stage, nature itself, governed by universal law (natural law) legislated by the Father of the gods. Insofar as

---

[175] Ibid. 22. And to that end no historian surpasses Tacitus, for, and Alamos is now quoting Justus Lipsius, "None tells things with more truth and brevity; nothing he leaves untouched in what pertains to customs; no effect or result proceeding from the passions does he fail to discover . . . because Tacitus' is not just history, but a garden and a nursery of political precepts." Ibid. 25. Vives shares with Alamos this admiration for Tacitus. "He is sublime, bold, and possesses much power." DTD III vi *Opera* VI 331; Watson 140. "Cornelius Tacitus is weighty in judgments and thus directs the reader to practical wisdom." Ibid. V ii *Opera* VI 396; Watson 243.

God chooses to make His will known to man, His Providence unfolds from nature to man in society through history. It seems, consequently, that history is the mechanism whereby natural law stands revealed to man. There is, however, one difficulty with the promise which, in my view, Vives would appear to be making metaphorically in the *Fabula*. One of the more telling and constant landmarks of Vives' thought is his skeptical attitude toward the possibility of acquiring absolute knowledge. He has already told us in another context, and in no uncertain terms, that man can fathom neither first causes nor the First Cause. The contradiction apparently implicit here resolves itself if we remember that Vives is a staunch advocate of free will; indeed, the profoundly normative (Socratic) nature of his thought as he endeavors to convince his audience that a well-ordered social life can in effect reverse the consequences of the Fall, would be meaningless in the absence of that commitment. And just as Alamos maintains that what makes politics into a *ciencia de contingentes* is free will, so Vives, implicitly, holds that Jupiter's script provides—through the human will—that history shall be something more (and less) than a revelation of natural law. To my mind, no single instance illustrates this better than Vives' approach to the arts.

Their seeds were planted in nature by God in compliance with the plan, the divine script of the *Fabula*, devised by Him for His fallen creature. The arts, insofar as they emerge—"unfold"—from those seeds must do so in a manner congruent with the dictates of natural law. It follows that their ultimate manifestation (a possibility, incidentally, that Vives implicitly rules out, as he maintains that they are in a constant process of evolution) would be the revelation of universal norm. Vives, however, has already explained that the arts do not emerge collectively but are instead "invented" individually by man, and in function of circumstances of space and time characteristically peculiar to each and every art. In short, the collective emergence of the arts implies and embodies an unfolding that (1) is determined by natural law, and (2) would result in the eventual revelation of the latter to man; but their individual creation hints at a process of development determined by a set of circumstances (a replica of Alamos' *accidentes* or contingencies) unique to each art. But, we must remember, nothing defines and sets society forth better than the arts. And society, in turn, is a human stage, the domain of man's will, inserted into a divine Stage, itself the realm of God's Will, just as any given art is part and parcel of the larger whole collectively constituted by Art. On the Stage, Art originates and, through History, unfolds to disclose the Will. On the stage, history, woven into the very fabric of each and every art, becomes the testimony to the development undergone by the individual art as a function of circumstances largely brought into being by the action of the will. The unfolding of Art, therefore, is the unfolding of History that unveils universal law; the evolution of the individual arts is the development of history conditioned by changing circumstances. And in conformity with Vives' skeptical approach to man's capacity for knowing, man cannot fathom History anymore than he can plumb the depths of Knowledge as nature makes it known through Art. How, then, does History tell him about his own nature? The question is clearly unavoidable, inasmuch as Vives has argued that therein lies precisely the usefulness of the discipline. The answer is that History does not, but history does.[176] Because the history of the individual arts is the history of man as he "invents" them, and into that process of invention go the contributions of man's will and the circumstances it creates. True, man's nature ought to be, by definition, constant. The actions taken yesterday to develop any given art—or, by extension, any other activity proper to man as a social being—should therefore have the same causes and identical effects as equal actions carried out today and tomorrow. But there is, of course, a problem. To be sure, the *fons et origo* of man's actions is his nature; their execution, however, involves also the unforeseen intervention of his unique gift, the will. And what would otherwise be a straight path to human nature becomes in practice a twisting and turning road dotted with uncertain signposts. Born of prudence and rooted in history, politics, like any other human activity, is therefore a game of probability issuing at best into *verisimilitudo*.

---

[176] History provides truth, history *opinio*.

Chapter Five: Charity: Vinculum Societatis

The Meaning of *caritas*

i

IF THE ARTS ARE THE GRANITIC FOUNDATION on which society stands, *caritas* is the bond that keeps it together by making all men aware of their mutual interdependence. I do not know, therefore, of any other single concept more suitable than *caritas* to bring to a close a monograph aimed at understanding Vives' social thought. For *caritas*, like the Aristotelian lunar world's aether, is the one idea that forms, permeates, and brings together everything in Vives' universe. It is the worldly embodiment of the divine love, that most potent passion, mistress of all passions, capable of taming the inherent unruliness of man's individuality, and the vital complement to the philosopher's virtue, whereby the man who has achieved *bonitas* rises to an understanding of his own divine persona. *Caritas*, obviously, is a strong bond; as it must indeed be, for even those things conceived and executed by society (the laws, an economic system, education)[1] are sooner or later twisted or corrupted. Man's self-centered arrogance, the very *superbia* that led him to covet God's divinity, will threaten to pull down whatever he devises in his desire to move forward toward God. *Caritas*, therefore, is inseparable from society, the arts, the state, man's individuality.

Society inevitably reflects the dual nature of its immediate creator. Its most enduring characteristic is an eternal dialectic between the internal forces struggling to preserve its integrity and those threatening to plunge it into chaos. To forestall such a dire outcome, we have already noted, society created the state. But God in His infinite wisdom soon realized that nothing that has its origins in man is impervious to subversion. Something else was therefore needed, something without any human roots and so potent that not even man could easily taint it. And so God commanded that "even in this life . . . men should succor each other through the reciprocity of love."[2] To explain God's decision, Vives once

---

[1] DSP I ii *Opera* IV 424-26.

[2] Ibid. I iv 431. In addition to the socio-political reasons that are the subject of this chapter, there is an additional one that explains God's command. "So that with that initial love men begin to prepare themselves for dwelling into the heavenly city, wherein nothing exists save perpetual love and indissoluble concord." Ibid. In other words, men must succor each other in this life because such mutual help leads to that concord which is a reflection of the most characteristic quality of eternal life.

more reprises a theme already familiar to us. After the Fall, man came to
need society (itself being, by definition, succor) to get that which God, in
His infinite mercy, resolved not to take away from him. It is well known,
moreover, that (1) society was engendered because man's sin perverted the
pristine individuality that had existed before the Fall, and that (2)
individuality, now hopelessly corrupted by sin into the *locus* of the
passions no longer under control, became a sword permanently aimed at
the heart of society, the agent of chaos utterly determined to destroy the
order that political society had so painfully achieved. Under the
circumstances, as it were, God decided "not to create any man so high in
Fortune's favor that he is free from imploring, even against his will, the
succor of another man inferior to him."[3] And, of course, absent *caritas*
the arts, society's foundation, cannot be. Their invention and unfolding
were exercises in human cooperation that only the presence of *caritas* can
explain. Conversely, their corruption witnessed the resurgence (a
temporary one, Vives hopes) of man's individuality at *caritas*' expense.
The lesson is not hard to learn: only after men come to their senses and
sacrifice their own ambitions on the altar of *caritas* will the arts be healed.
With its foundations thus restored society will be whole again.

Now, what began as an explanation offered by Vives of the
circumstances that led God to implant in man's nature the imperative of
mutual assistance, almost at once broadens to account for *caritas*' political
dimension. "Without the help of the *inferiores* the favor of fortune
neither grows nor survives. Sufficient proof is given by the example of
the great kings whose strength, rooted in their subjects, would crumble
into dust the moment the latter withheld their support."[4] The meaning is
clear: the prince's political power rests on the people. Which is but
another way of saying what more than sixty years after Vives' death will
become a premise fundamental to Francisco Suárez's political thought:
political sovereignty lies with the people. "In the consent of the subjects
are rooted the greatest empires; empires which would undoubtedly cease
to exist should all, in unison, cease to obey."[5] Although Vives
wholeheartedly agrees that a commonwealth (*respublica*) is just and its
government healthy when all the concerns and counsels of those who rule
are aimed at the public weal,[6] it is clear that this "cease to obey" implies

---

[3] Ibid.

[4] Ibid.

[5] Ibid.

[6] Ibid.

far more than the expected rebellion against an unpopular ruler. In fact it means that a commonwealth in which each one places his own personal concerns above those of the body social will surely be short-lived; and this holds true regardless of whether the outward form of government is monarchy, oligarchy, or democracy.[7] Of the three, Vives seems to think that democracy is the least susceptible to suffer from the ravages attendant on rampaging individuality, for he quickly warns that "if each man does everything lying in his astuteness, ability, or power to advance his own profit and cause, *even* [italics mine] in a democratic regime the people become their own tyrant and thus retain political liberty precariously and briefly, and eventually become slaves under the dominion and arbitrariness of another."[8]

Finally, man's individuality. By its very existence *caritas* both testifies to and wards off the dangers part and parcel of man as individual; it is, in other words, the only effective antidote against man's rampaging individuality. We know that the rise of society meant both the triumph and the defeat of the latter. Triumph because society was the last step in the gradual process of liberation from bestiality that assertive individuality alone could bring about. Defeat because as the goal of sociability came within reach, the enhanced degree of cooperation (rooted in *caritas*) among men correspondingly diminished their individual freedom of action. And of course the creation of the state institutionalized that defeat, for the state embodies the single most startling example of the shift away from individualism (in political terms, anarchy) to collectivism (a political order). With this in mind it is now important to remind ourselves, for it is a matter of no small consequence, that on the basis of a single premise, original sin, Vives has carved for *caritas* a niche as the one divine impulse imprinted in man, capable of safeguarding man's sociability. The future of both state and society, then, rests on the idea of mutual assistance. "In this fashion man was turned into an absolutely miserable being, internally and externally, in just punishment for his lusting after God's divinity. . . no animal in creation is weaker or of less intrinsic value. By himself man is nothing. His whole life, his health, depend upon the health of others."[9] Vives, in common with the likes of Castrillo, Erasmus, and More, whose *Utopia* is the ultimate expression of an outlook endeavoring to emulate, in human terms, the much-admired organization of the beehive,

---

[7] Ibid.

[8] Ibid.

[9] Ibid. I ii 425-26.

subordinates as a matter of course and sound socio-political theory the
individual to the whole. Indeed, we have repeatedly seen that he views
individualism with profound distaste. It is the force, the fatal human
impulse, both cause and effect of the Fall, a power for ill embodying the
arrogance, ambition, and selfishness that are the least attractive traits of
man. Far from admiring human individuality, then, Vives condemns it,
reflecting a deeply-held conviction that by himself man is fated to fail.
Man, therefore, neither is nor can be self-sufficient—be it personally,
socially, or politically; at any of the levels, in other words, of practical
wisdom. True, some men need help in one form and others in another,
but they all need assistance; for all *caritas* is an unavoidable imperative.
This is why Vives, in *De subventione*, a treatise outlining a plan to deal
with the problem of the urban poor, emphatically insists that "anyone in
need of outside assistance is poor and requires compassion . . . and charity
does not consist, as the vulgar seem to believe, exclusively in giving
money. On the contrary, charitable is any deed or work which
contributes to alleviate human insufficiency."[10] It is not, therefore, the
"poor" alone who are destitute; mankind itself is poor—again, personally,
socially, and politically—and in need of *caritas*, the only antidote capable
of neutralizing the venom inhering in human individuality. The goal of
Vives' essay, then, is far more than merely outlining a pattern of behavior
aimed at dealing with the needy as the word is normally used, for the
poor are all men, society itself vulnerable to the assaults of its bane, man's
individuality. To succor the poor, consequently, means to admit once and
for all that men need each other, and that the survival of society, itself the
sole and last hope of man, rests (1) on our full awareness of that fact and
(2) on our will and ability to act accordingly. Given these circumstances,
Vives must explain how and why man must be charitable to other men.
Let us begin with the "how."

ii

Vives' argument has a fundamentally naturalist character, and is
rooted in the very essence of society. And given the hierarchy of good
that serves as the primary scaffold sustaining his thought, it is not
surprising that man's *caritas* to other men should be aimed, in descending
order, at succoring the soul, the intellect, and the body. The greatest and
highest service that man can render another man is to help him walk

---

[10] Ibid. I iii 426-27.

along the path leading to virtue.[11] Some men, Vives believes, have been chosen by God to share in His light to the extent of knowing and being able to practice what is holy and salutary. When these fortunate men share with others their unique awareness of what the divine pleasure is, they are pointing the path of virtue to the less fortunate.[12] Is this uncommon gift to be understood in the sense of *sapientia* revelationally infused in the chosen few? The temptation to answer the question in the affirmative seems overwhelming, for Vives goes on to say that what virtue brings to the soul is precisely "the great benefit that Christ bestows upon those who are baptized in His name and who deposit their confidence in Him. The ministers and dispensers of this benefit were His disciples and after them the Apostles."[13] Obviously, both disciples and Apostles received *sapientia* directly from Christ's hand, but what they (and perhaps others equally gifted, for Vives does not explicitly close the door to that possibility) in turn offer others is clearly not *sapientia* but the potential to acquire it once the fundamental prerequisite, itself the goal of apostolic teaching, has been met: a moral life leading to *bonitas*. Undoubtedly, this first expression of *caritas* is teaching at its most sublime. And bearing in mind the boundless admiration that Vives felt for Socrates, one might understandably ask: would he have begrudged the Greek sage a niche among such distinguished educators? Arguably Socrates, alone among pagans, transcended the philosopher's virtue, that is, the highest goal to which a non-Christian could aspire. He, after all, was the man who achieved self-knowledge and then, freeing himself from the extreme individuality (and the consequences, according to Vives, attendant to it) that such discovery implies, shared his newly-found wisdom with his fellow men, thereby opening hitherto unsuspected new vistas for mankind (and in a sense affording man the worldly equivalent of Christ's own promise). What else but an explicit infusion of the love divine could have inspired in Socrates—pagan or no pagan—such a monumental act of *caritas*?

Next in importance comes *caritas* as teaching in the sense in which we commonly understand the word, which Vives defines as an activity "aiming at the knowledge of virtue which one man awakens in another."[14]

---

[11] Ibid. The end is "to bring composure and tranquillity to the soul, a goal partly achieved with the precepts of virtue."

[12] Ibid.

[13] Ibid.

[14] Ibid.

And here, as everywhere else throughout his writings, the humanist shows how overwhelming a passion education is for him. "How beautiful a task it is to indoctrinate, to polish, to adorn the intellect, the highest among the powers of the soul."[15] Those who bask in the glory they stupidly imagine reflects on them from the distribution of money among the poor would be far more justified in their pride if instead they undertook personally the task of enlightening them. Aristotle himself, Vives adds, placed the services rendered by teachers at the level with those men receive from God and children from their parents, and he further points out that it would be immensely beneficial for the community if a handful of wise men took charge of the education of the citizens at the most tender age, seeing that in their childhood human beings are more receptive to being guided along the right path.[16] It is indecent, he thunders, that rulers should be remiss in providing the best education available for their children; after all, it is upon the shoulders of the latter that the responsibility for continued survival of the community will eventually rest.[17]

To be sure, caring for the soul and the intellect of others is therefore a task of supreme importance. But it does not bring to an end the extent of man's obligation to man. The task of aiding the "poor" is not yet complete unless care is also taken of the body. For that reason, Vives insists, those who in the past endeavored with great success to insure the safety and material well-being of their fellow men were honored with the name of "liberator" and "savior,"[18] a fact that explains also why medicine was held in such high esteem by the Ancients. Finally, and pointedly placed at the bottom of activities mandated by Vives' broad understanding of the nature of charity, comes money.[19] The author himself confesses that he has intentionally left money for last to emphasize that what is often seen as the most important factor in dispensing charity is in reality

---

[15] Ibid.

[16] Ibid. 428.

[17] Ibid. As far as Vives is concerned, the commonwealth that cares to provide children with good teachers guarantees its own future. "In the initial upbringing of the child lies hidden a great and virtuous strength which lasts for life. . . . Undoubtedly, it would be wiser to concentrate resources on this, rather than on the ornamentation of the city; unless, of course, we conclude that it is worth leaving behind a bad future generation so long as it is wealthy." Ibid.

[18] Ibid.

[19] According to Vives, providing the needy with goods "establishes a certain resemblance between man's condition and nature and God's." Ibid. 429.

the least weighty. And his reasoning appears on the surface to be rather unusual. Thus he explains that giving alms can become addictive, a narcotic causing such euphoria in the giver that men so afflicted have been known to use foul means to raise the money needed to continue their charitable work among the needy. Herein, he cautions, lies precisely the gross error of those who despoil some men in order to give to another; because, what possible good can come out of doing charitable work through unjust means?[20] And the reason why some men embark upon this bizarre line of conduct is their failure to understand "the sweetness of giving for its own sake, without seeking any other further purpose."[21] These remarks, touching as they do on the sensitive issue of a Christian's right to give alms, are of considerable importance. Their full significance, however, emerges only out of Vives' plan for the eradication of beggary from his adopted city of Bruges. For that reason we will defer further examination of the remarks in question until such time as Vives' views on charity have been fully explained. For the moment, therefore, let us say the following, by way of summary, concerning Vives' position on the matter of how to aid the poor. Man has an inalienable obligation to share his material goods with his fellows. But he must, even more importantly, share with them other forms of property; the soul's patrimony, for instance, which for Vives means to offer advice, to teach precepts for right living, and to point out the road toward prudence to those who, less fortunate, lack in those important areas. Moreover, the truly charitable man will place his own body at the disposal of others; that is, he will be present among the poor, offering words of advice and lending his own strength whenever and wherever it is needed. And he will not hesitate to help also with external things, namely, things that are neither of the soul nor of the body, but can be obtained with the help of money: authority, dignity, influence.[22] And lastly, an important political message. Society, we know, is a structure invented by men out of seeds planted by God to make charity possible; understanding charity, of course, in the broad sense of indispensable mutual help defined by Vives above. And society must be protected at all costs. Hence the coming of the state led by a man, the ruler, who of all the men who help other men must stand at the forefront. Indeed, for precisely that reason what he heads, the state, was created in the first place. He leads his subjects in the direction of virtue

---

[20] Ibid. 430. See below, Vives' attack on the Anabaptists.

[21] Ibid.

[22] Ibid.

through his own personal example; he is teacher—and the teacher is indeed the greatest exponent of charity: to teach others is the greatest act of charity that a man can perform for his fellows—to his people, whose collective body his sword shields and protects; he sees to it that the economy of the commonwealth is healthy because he cannot suffer to see want among his charges.

Concerned now with the second aspect, the "why," of charity, Vives moves away from a naturalist position presumably independent of society's religious aspects, and toward another centered around the idea that Christ's fundamental teaching is the love that Christians owe each other.[23] Alas, he complains, despite the Master's clear injunction "We speak as if we believed in everything while living as if we believed in nothing."[24] Christ and His disciples emphasized the value of charity, and St. Paul went so far as to call avarice idolatry.[25] The Apostles themselves are said to have worried about the whole man, that is, his body and his soul. Both must be cared for, and so Christ's disciples cared for the body by way of miracles that healed its ills, while with the money they collected they aided the needy. Such is the calling of the true Christian, who will help the soul and the body of those in need.[26] And all these considerations move Vives to conclude that he is no Christian who fails to succor, to the extent of his ability, his indigent brother.[27] Having settled to his own satisfaction that Christians are indeed responsible for the physical and spiritual well-being of each other, Vives, now in the last chapter of Book I, moves on to explain a series of considerations that determine the criteria to be used when dispensing charity to the poor. And with these observations, the humanist brings to a close that part of *De subventione* in which he studies the problem of charity in the context of both its background, origin, and justification (divine and human), and its individual aspects—meaning in this instance the obligation that man, as a singular entity, has to be charitable to his brother. The individual's obligation to the whole is therefore the central theme of the first part. But it turns out that there is also a significant institutional network involved in *caritas*. Thus, as *caritas* touches upon the succoring of the soul, the institution on which this obligation would presumably devolve is the

---

[23] Ibid. I x 456.

[24] Ibid. 457.

[25] Ibid. 458.

[26] Ibid. 459.

[27] Ibid. 458.

Church, the heir to the Apostles. To this aspect of *caritas*, Vives, to my knowledge, does not devote any single treatise. Perhaps he felt the subject to be beyond his ken. Or perhaps in an age obsessed with the spiritual failure of the contemporary Church, the question had become too controversial for a man noted for his dislike of quarrels. A very different situation, of course, applies when we touch upon *caritas* as intellectual succor. In this instance Vives' belief that education is the business of society as an institution turned him into one of the most outspoken among the age's educational reformers. Finally, the state, conceived and executed to defend society, is equally bound by the duties implied in *caritas* as the succorer of the body. And this is precisely what Vives proceeds to discuss in the second part of *De subventione*: the role of the state in caring for the bodily wants of those members of society in need of material assistance.

Welfare Reform in Bruges
i

"Up to this point I have mentioned what each individual ought to do; hereafter I shall speak of what the commonwealth and its ruler, who is to it as the soul is to the body, must do."[28] And this very metaphor, a commonplace, to be sure, during the age and beyond, reveals to us an important political idea: just as the soul cares for the body as a whole, so also must the ruler care for every part of the community. "Consequently, a magistrate must never allow any part of the commonwealth to be neglected. Whoever cares only for the wealthy behaves like the physician who neglects to heal the hands and the feet because they are far removed from the heart and thereby endangers the whole man. Similarly, in the republic the poor cannot be ignored without peril to the powerful."[29] And for Vives it is this criminal indifference of the rulers that lies at the root of all the evils that afflict contemporary European society. In the first place, the humble and downtrodden are forced by need to steal; they feel indignation toward the mighty and their absurd luxuries, seeing that they are unable to feed their children; they are angered by the insolence with which the rich abuse the wealth they stole from the needy. And such have traditionally been the seeds of countless wars.[30] Second, the misery of the poor is responsible for the very illnesses that afflict them, and inasmuch

---

[28] Ibid. II i 465.

[29] Ibid.

[30] Ibid.

as those unfortunates have no alternative but to beg, the threat of contagion is always present; this is a fact that no magistrate responsible for the prevention or containment of the plague can ignore.[31] A third consequence following from a ruler's neglect of poverty and misery is the spread of thievery and crime into the countryside by the poor who for whatever reason have limited or no access to alms. All this concerns men; as for women, the common solution to the woes of poverty is prostitution for the young and pimping for the old, while the youths of either sex remain illiterate and find in vagabondage the only occupation suitable to their condition.[32]

Why is all this happening in a Christian commonwealth?[33] As if taking his cue from the first part of *Utopia*, Vives answers that the ruling classes have a mistaken notion of what governing is all about. For the humanist, good government means to do whatever is necessary to turn men into good citizens, whereas European rulers hold that their sole function is to restrain and to punish the wicked. While they insist that they must rid their realms of crime, in truth they should bend all their efforts to their true task: preventing it.[34] In short, the governments of Europe are doing a dismally poor job of ruling their commonwealths. What, then, is the solution? What should governments do to justify their power and authority? Vives thinks that the ideal solution is to return to time-honored measures. If, he asks, we change or renew the things that time and circumstances have made obsolete—walls, buildings, institutions, customs, laws—would it not be equally reasonable to return to that primitive canon of money distribution from which we departed? Vives himself, bearing in mind contemporary circumstances, suggests change along the lines of (a) reducing the various and onerous obligations and taxes that fall most heavily on the shoulders of the poor, and (b) apportioning public lands and funds (whenever the latter should become available) among the destitute. Both means are certain of restoring the old harmony achieved when money distribution is based on need. They are, in other words, measures ideal for bringing about a just society. Of

---

[31] Ibid. 466.

[32] Ibid. 466-67.

[33] For comments on beggary as a profession, see Erasmus' *Colloquies* ("The Beggars' Dialogue," 1524). According to Bataillon, Vives is an interpreter of the spirit of the cities of northern Europe that are beginning to move in the direction of organizing the public welfare and ending beggary. M. Bataillon, "J. L. Vivès. Réformateur de la bienfesance." *Bibliothèque d'Humanisme et Renaissance* XIV (1952) 141-58.

[34] DSP II i *Opera* IV 467.

course, Vives is fully aware that in practice the existing opportunities to carry out such a program are few and far between: "in these our times, it is therefore necessary to have recourse to more practical and lasting means."[35] The obvious question to ask next is of course: what are those means? As it turns out the means proposed by Vives are the remedial steps to be taken by the government—concretely, the government of the city of Bruges—to solve the problem of the poor. It is also one of the two occasions, the other being his collective program of educational reform, in which Vives descends from the lofty perch of theory and into the arena where practical problems are met with practical solutions. In that sense it is accurate to say that what remains of *De subventione* is a blueprint for the banishment of destitution and poverty from the commonwealth. Translated into political terms, what Vives is also suggesting here is that poverty and destitution are not only social and charitable (Christian) problems to be taken care of by the Church as the interpreter of the evangelical message of charity, but a political concern first and foremost, an issue for the solution of which the government exists and was created. And by this path we arrive at the reason that explains why the treatise is divided into two parts. In Book I, Vives had provided the theoretical background justifying the premise that charity is a concern of the government, one of the very reasons indeed that explains the creation of the polity. In Book II, he will outline the means to carry out that basic obligation. In other words, having first agreed that charity is an individual's obligation as a Christian, why it is so, and how that duty is to be discharged, the author is ready to maintain that charity is the community's burden as well. Again, and in this instance in the explicit context of charity, we find illustrated what is a constant landmark of Vives' thought: the endless interplay between the individual and the community sheltering him.

ii

The first question to answer in this search for remedies is: how to succor effectively such a vast multitude? Vives suggests two basic premises to serve, in turn, as the springboard to action. First, succor of the poor is the concern and responsibility of the government, in this instance the municipality of Bruges. Second, as preliminary steps to fulfill that responsibility, the municipal authorities shall conduct an exhaustive census of the poor who dwell within the city, an effort obviously predicated, in turn, on finding out where the poor live. According to

---

[35] Ibid. 468-69.

Vives they are found in one of the following places. (1) Hospitals, defined
by the author as institutions where the sick are healed, some needy live,
orphans are raised, the insane are locked up, and the blind spend their
lives. In other words, under the collective term "hospital" Vives brings
together hospices, orphanages, asylums for the mentally ill, homes for the
indigent elderly, and other similar institutions supported by private funds
and initiative but customarily managed and administered by the Church.
(2) Beyond the hospitals, Vives also finds that some among the poor beg
in public and thus presumably live in the streets. (3) Finally, still others
are said to live at home.[36] But before actually moving into the subject of
what shall be done with the poor once their residences have been
ascertained, Vives pauses to discuss the hospitals.

The hospitals are in effect the backbone of the welfare system as
practiced in Bruges. As such, all the specialized forms of care offered by
them are the business and concern of those who run the municipal
government. In this its overseeing capacity, therefore, the latter must see
to it that (1) the statutes and provisions made by the founder of the
hospital must remain inviolate and that no one be exempt from their
rules, and (2) the wills that provide for the creation of the hospitals must
always be interpreted, not literally, but in function of equity and in such
a fashion that the funds bequeathed for the maintenance of the hospital
and its services shall at all times be put to their best possible use. It would
appear that what Vives is aiming at when he reminds the civil authorities
that hospitals are their business, and in ensuing reflections concerning the
foundation of hospitals, is that, privately endowed or not, the latter must
be controlled by the state. And this in turn carries with it an unmistakable
message: in what concerns the administration of hospitals, the Church
must surrender its prerogatives to the municipality. What follows makes
the implications of the message, as far as the question of Church-state
relations is concerned, even more telling. Nothing within the
commonwealth, Vives claims, is endowed with such freedom that it
cannot be subject to the knowledge and overseeing of the political
authority. Freedom from subjection and obedience to the state is not a
rational freedom but an invitation to disorder and anarchy, a rather
understandable conclusion if we remember our previous discussion of
man's individuality and its relation to the social whole. And, moreover,
no one can exempt his goods or even his life from the care and
jurisdiction of the government without simultaneously placing his own
self outside that jurisdiction. The reason is simple enough: a private

---

[36] Ibid. 469.

citizen's property can only be acquired with the cooperation of the community and preserved through its protection.[37] Given such compelling circumstances, it is clear that there is no reason to exempt privately-endowed hospitals from government oversight and control. True enough, the thrust of Vives' argument is ostensibly aimed at justifying the subordination of individual rights to collective needs. But the target of his point is clearly the hospitals, and the hospitals are administered by the Church. Is it possible, under the circumstances, to exempt the Church as an institution from the logical consequences of a reasoning presumably fashioned to apply to individuals, and still justify bringing the hospitals under secular control? Obviously not. No matter how Vives may try to sweeten the pill the fact remains that his proposals will adversely affect the Church.

Returning now to the matter of the census, Vives proposes that for the practical purpose of overseeing the activities taking place in hospitals a commission composed of two representatives from the municipal government and one secretary shall be named to visit and inspect those establishments where the needy live. The commission's first care shall be to take stock of the hospital's income and its actual cash flow; it will, furthermore, record the names of the inmates the establishment supports and the reasons for their institutionalization. All this information the commission must then pass on to the city government.[38] But obviously not all the needy live in hospitals. To the end of bringing those who live at home within the fold of the projected census, Vives suggests that they be visited by the two government officials assigned to the parish where their residence is located. In their reports those officials are required to itemize the needs of the poor in their jurisdictions, the manner of their living, and the reasons that might have forced them into their present state. All these items of information, which as in the case of the hospitals will be placed in the hands of the municipality, should not come directly from the interested parties but be gleaned instead from reports provided by the neighbors concerning the kind of person the pauper in question is and what sort of life he leads—of course, no pauper will be allowed to give information concerning another pauper. As for the beggars without fixed domicile but in good health, they shall be required to appear before the full municipal governing body to give their names and to state the reasons why they beg; but it must be done, Vives the hypochondriac cautions, in open and well-ventilated premises for fear of contagion from the many

---

[37] Ibid. 469-70.

[38] Ibid. 470.

diseases that such rabble are known to carry. And, always prudent, the author is even more so when the indigents to be questioned are in poor health. In that case the city fathers must be effectively shielded from contagion by a phalanx of less exalted—and presumably more expendable—officials who, themselves assisted and advised by a physician, will conduct the actual examination. Finally, Vives insists that whatever officials the city chooses to carry out the census ought to be given broad jurisdictional authority, including the power to compel and even imprison those reluctant to comply.[39]

Once the number and location of the indigent living in the city of Bruges are reasonably familiar to the municipality, and the hospitals have been placed under its supervision and control, two additional preliminary steps remain before the actual plan of reform can be implemented. First, measures will be taken to uproot idleness. After the Fall, Vives reminds us, the Lord demanded of man that he earn his daily bread through work; the city, therefore, cannot tolerate the presence of malingerers in its mist, for, "as in a well-ordered house," in the community everyone must occupy his own place and tend to his own job. To be sure, Vives accepts the possibility that some may be unable to work. In that case those who by reason of age or infirmity are effectively incapacitated will be exempted from the general, and otherwise inflexible, policy; but to ferret out pretexts and prevent cheating a physician must give faith that the infirm are truly so and unable to earn a living.[40] Second, foreign beggars must be expelled from the city, but only after being provided with funds for the return trip home, a necessary precaution in Vives' view, for otherwise they might be forced to steal to survive and become a scourge of the neighboring countryside. But even in this instance an exception can be made for those non-citizens from neighboring villages afflicted by war, for charity plainly demands that these be given refuge and comfort in the city.[41]

Having in this fashion cleared the decks, Vives is now in a position to outline the remedies to be applied toward the solution of the remaining core problem: what to do with beggars who are both citizens and of sound body? If they have no trade of their own the municipality will take the necessary steps to teach them one suited, whenever possible, to their individual natural talents. But even here Vives is not willing to set aside

---

[39] Ibid.

[40] Ibid.

[41] Ibid. II iii 471.

his stern determination that we must all face up to the consequences of our actions. He makes it abundantly clear that if a pauper was beggared through his own improvidence and wicked habits the state will burden him with the most onerous chores and feed him the roughest fare. In this fashion they will be taught responsibility and, it is hoped, serve as an object lesson to others.[42] The decision on who works where and how rests exclusively in the hands of the municipal authorities, and Vives is quick to point out how the factories of Bruges suffer from want of workers. Should, moreover, any of the beggars assigned to a municipality-sponsored program show unusual talents, the city government ought to help them open their own shops; and to them, in turn, the municipality ought to entrust the city's public works.[43] Finally, but strictly on a temporary basis, those able-bodied indigents for whom no gainful employment has yet been found will be supported by the alms collected in the districts where they reside.[44] All this, needless to say, applies to the indigent who enjoy good health. But what of those who do not? To answer that question Vives must now return to the hospitals. The next item in his unfolding program of reform, therefore, is their reorganization. Before anything else, he demands, it is imperative that those among the institutionalized poor of sound mind and body be discharged and forced to work; and even in such exceptional cases in which healthy inmates are allowed continued residence in the hospital, it must be with the explicit understanding that they will simultaneously be gainfully employed in the outside. Next, the workers who are in residence in the hospital to provide round-the-clock care for the sick must be strictly supervised and compelled to do the jobs for which they were hired; they must not, in other words, be allowed under any circumstances to take over the institution, and control its workings. Once these measures are in place, Vives continues, the next goal is to structure properly the status of those indigents who have legitimate reasons for living in the hospital. The needy who while at the hospital are able to work must be compelled to do so. The blind, the infirm, the old: all are grist to the mill of Vives' work ethic, for "none is so helpless that he completely lacks the strength to do anything."[45] If, Vives promises, these guidelines are followed and the financial administration is carefully scrutinized and ruthlessly purged of

---

[42] Ibid. 472.

[43] Ibid. 473.

[44] Ibid.

[45] Ibid. 474.

all superfluous expenditures, the hospital will become the efficient and lean institution whose resources can be focused on providing care for those who in truth are helpless and mentally ill.[46]

Pueri expositi are Vives' next urgent care. They must have their own hospices and those who have mothers should remain under their care until the age of six, when they will be taken to public schools and there fed and taught to read and write. The running of those schools must be entrusted to competent and upright men whose very example shall serve to mold the character of the children of the poor, and see to it that they receive a useful upbringing consisting in, besides the elementary education already mentioned, good habits, cleanliness of body and soul, and Christian piety. While Vives proposes that all the children be exposed to this broad curriculum, he also suggests that the most promising among them should be given additional instruction and kept in school so that they, in turn, can become teachers of other children.[47] Obviously, all this would soon become meaningless if proper supervision were not provided for. Vives' plan, in short, would promptly founder if bereft of some means of coercion. The author therefore calls for the appointment of two *censores* who, chosen from the ranks of public officials, will seek out and punish any among the poor who indulge in activities threatening to plunge them once more into the misery of destitution. And in a gesture revealing how kindred a spirit Vives is to the likes of Erasmus and More as they place order and outward social harmony high above what we today cherish as personal liberty and privacy, the author witsfully remarks that he would wish those officials to have the necessary authority to investigate the conduct of all other citizens as well. How, in what fashion, with what endeavors and activities they occupy their time: this is what Vives would like all citizens, poor and rich alike, to be accountable for before the city government. After all, what are the city's magistrates if not the fathers of all citizens?[48]

iii

Such, then, is the broad outline of Vives' plan for reforming a city's welfare structure. But of course no such proposal can be complete without an answer to the following question: how to pay for it? Vives begins with a brief survey of how the Church itself, from the earliest

---

[46] Ibid.

[47] Ibid. II iv 476.

[48] Ibid. 477-78. Again, this is Vives' belief that each individual is subordinate to the community that nurtures and protects him.

times, fulfilled its mission of charity. The faithful, he claims, placed their riches at the disposal of the Apostles, who then proceeded to distribute them among the needy. But in time the Apostles came to devote all their efforts to the task of preaching, and all charitable activities devolved by default into the hands of deacons. Still later the same obligation was passed on to the members of the Christian community itself, until at a still later date the Church, bishops and priests, once again shouldered the responsibility for carrying out charitable work. And now comes the argument, no less powerful for being implicit, that in effect justifies in practice the transfer of the care of the poor from the Church to the state. Eventually, Vives sorrowfully acknowledges, the Church "began to emulate the world in pomp and luxury." Its expenses grew on this account and so did its need for money, meaning that eventually bishops converted into their own the property originally earmarked for the poor. Is it any wonder, the humanist seems to be saying, that I should have advised the municipality to take charge of privately-funded charities heretofore managed by the Church? Dangerously close to the abyss, however, Vives stops. No question, he says, that ecclesiastics are not doing all they ought to in devoting their resources to poor relief. But he recoils from the final pilloring with a "let them render account of their misdeeds to Christ"; whether from personal fear of the consequences or from reluctance to incite to social discord, it is difficult to tell. His own testimony would seem to point to the second alternative. "Civil discord is a worse evil than retaining for one's use the money belonging to the poor, for no amount of money, regardless of the quantity, justifies recourse to arms." At all times the public tranquillity must take precedence. In this fashion Vives, in an age of revolution, takes the revolutionary edge off his harsh accusations against the Church and ultimately opts for an unjust peace rather than a just war—but not before "disarming" the enemy by taking the hospitals away from its control.[49]

Following this broadside *manquée* aimed at a Church that has forgotten its traditional obligation to charity Vives returns to the subject at hand, the financing of his reform. If, Vives advises, every year the income of the various hospitals were to be pooled and added to the yield derived from those among the inmates who can work, there would be sufficient capital at hand to care for the needs of both those who live in the hospitals and those outside them. In short, if the resources of charitable institutions "were scrupulously administered," there would doubtless be enough money to succor all the ordinary and extraordinary

---

[49] Ibid. II vi 478-80.

needs of indigent citizens.[50] In further pursuit of financial reform Vives suggests that the rich hospitals ought to surrender their excess capital to the poorer establishments, and that if after defraying routine expenses anything were left the money should be distributed among the more deserving indigent, meaning of course those who are poor through circumstances not of their own making, as opposed to the professional beggars. An additional, and rather original, means of raising funds suggested by Vives is to exhort the well-to-do citizens to bequeath to the poor the money that would otherwise pay for excessively sumptuous funerals. But should these measures fail to meet the financial demands of his plan, Vives' creativity supplies three additional possibilities: (1) Collection boxes to be installed in the three or four most frequented churches in Bruges. Devout citizens will surely opt for depositing their alms there rather than directly into the hands of the beggars themselves. But to emphasize the strictly temporary nature of this recourse, Vives insists that it shall be resorted to only when the need is pressing.[51] (2) If a time comes when all these steps prove inadequate to meet the expenses incurred in taking care of the poor, Vives suggests that the rich be asked to make up the difference. Anticipating the latter's reluctance to give freely, the humanist further proposes the following novel idea: the government will commit itself, if and when the monies from alms become more abundant, to refund the contributions extorted from the wealthy. (3) The government itself ought to cut down on frivolous expenses of a public nature—banquets, annual festivals, trips, unnecessary pomp—and apply the sums thus saved to poor relief.[52] Vives closes his recommendations with one stern warning. In collecting alms no manner of coercion should be considered, much less applied. Even when they are given indirectly through a state agency, alms must be given freely or not be given at all.[53]

Such are the measures proposed by Vives to raise the wherewithal needed to fund his plan. Two more aspects of the latter, however, remain to be considered. The first concerns the protection from malfeasance the monies raised by the various devices already mentioned, to devise a means whereby the funds will reach their destination. To that end Vives suggests that not all the money available at any one time be placed at once at the

---

[50] Ibid. 480.

[51] Ibid. 481.

[52] Ibid. 482.

[53] Ibid. 482.

disposal of those entrusted with it. Knowing full well how corrupt the administration of the hospitals is, for instance, the author fears that in view of the large sums involved, the officials in charge of their dispersion and proper utilization will divert them toward their own pockets. Vives outlines several solutions to cope with this problem. For one thing, no purchases of real estate in the name of the poor should be allowed. It would seem that this was a device commonly used by directors of hospitals to pocket the funds destined to the needs of the inmates. Adducing the need to accumulate the price of a given piece of real property, a corrupt hospital administrator could successfully and indefinitely prevent much-needed cash from reaching its rightful destination. Additionally, when for whatever reason and in any part of the city a large sum comes to any official entrusted with alms requested in the name of the government, at least a portion of that sum must be immediately sent elsewhere, to those places where the need is greatest. Above all, the municipality must take care that the monies earmarked for charity not be frozen; the needs of the poor are obviously constant and so must the flow of funds in their direction be. Finally, no ecclesiastic is to be allowed, under the pretext of celebrating masses in the name of the poor, to divert to his own use money explicitly given to aid the needy.[54] Vives is fully confident that if (1) the measures outlined earlier for the raising of funds and (2) those suggested above to protect the collected money are implemented, all the wherewithal required for a successful system of poor relief will become available.[55] The second remaining point mentioned above remains. Vives' plan for the reform of poor relief aims fundamentally at eradicating two kinds of poverty: the real poverty of men and women who for reasons of fate and their own improvidence find themselves destitute; and the fraudulent poverty of the confidence man and professional beggar who have one thing in common: unwillingness to work. But the humanist's program also makes room for those who are temporarily in dire straits: victims of a fire, shipwreck, illness, war. The same officials to whom the government entrusted the census of the poor living in their own home shall be simultaneously responsible for bringing to the attention of both the city fathers and the rich these "hidden" cases of temporary need or indigence; the names of these unfortunates, however, must remain confidential.[56]

---

[54] Ibid. 481-82.

[55] Ibid. 483.

[56] Ibid. 484-85.

The Critics

i

And now, we consider the critics. Vives is fully aware that the program just outlined will have detractors. Some will claim that it is inhuman to expel the beggars from Bruges. In truth, he explains, his war is not against the poor but against poverty; he wants to eradicate the condition, not those who suffer from it.[57] Then there will be other critics who, adopting theological airs, will zealously lay their hands on Biblical passages—concretely, Christ's statement that there will always be poor among men.[58] Still others will not fail to pillory the plan simply because they invariably reject whatever has not issued from themselves.[59] Vives is obviously not unduly concerned by such verdicts. What worries him, however, is the kind of opposition he foresees coming from two different quarters. First, the men for whose benefit the plan was conceived to begin with; in other words, those among the poor so deeply sunk in their own squalor that they will resent any and all attempts to rescue them from it.[60] Vives' answer to this threat provides us with another interesting glimpse into his approach to the relations between the individual and the state. No matter, he argues, that the poor may oppose what is intended for their benefit; what is of true import is not what people want to do but what they ought to do, not what pleases them but what is good for them. With the characteristic humanist arrogance displayed whenever the "vulgar" are concerned, Vives smugly concludes that sooner or later they will perceive the truth and thank the city of Bruges for forcing them away from their sloth; conversely, if the city failed to act and instead temporized with their wishes, they would curse the government for not having pushed them toward the right path.[61] The implicit political message here is that the state exists to bring about the good of the citizens and that good, sometimes clearly perceived by the community at large but not by some of its members, must be imposed on the recalcitrant—presumably by force, if necessary. In fact, Vives is quite explicit on this: "it is the duty of the republic's governor to lend a deaf ear to the opinions held by one or two or a few concerning the laws and the government, provided that they issue from a previous consultation and general concern for the good of the

---

[57] Ibid. 486.

[58] Ibid.

[59] Ibid. 488.

[60] Ibid.

[61] Ibid. 489.

whole body social. The laws are useful even for the wicked, either so that they will mend their ways or will not ultimately persevere in their wickedness."[62] Second, those at present in administrative control of the hospitals, the institution most affected by the reforms, are surely bound to complain. After all, they will shortly, as a result of Vives' plan, be deprived of a very lucrative business. The state will now scrutinize the financial condition of the hospitals and make sure that the provisions listed in the will of the hospital's founder or benefactor are followed and not broken, as heretofore, for the benefit of those managing the hospital. In this instance, however, Vives is being disingenuous. True, individual shady characters systematically milking different hospitals of their revenues may suffer personally from state intervention. But, what kind of serious opposition can they mount against the municipality? It would seem that Vives should have been far more fearful of the Church's wrath, for the latter was indeed bound to suffer the most at the hands of a plan aimed at secularizing charity.[63]

ii

And Vives was indeed right. There were critics, although there is no record that any of them belonged to the groups ostensibly feared by the humanist. Reduced to its simplest elements, let us say it again, Vives' plan involved two basic assumptions: (1) The government alone is the proper and suitable institution to deal with the problem of welfare within the community; (2) Beggary is not an acceptable solution to the problem of destitution; if "deserving" poor a man will, on both natural and religious grounds, be given all the needed assistance by the secular authorities. If, on the other hand, an able-bodied man resorts to mendicancy because he is unwilling to work, the state will see to it that he is denied that alternative to honest employment. On both counts the traditional role of the solicitor and dispenser of charity is correspondingly diminished, a fact not lost on those who, directly or indirectly, rejected Vives' proposal.[64] And to be sure, although Vives' tone was decidedly moderate, the implications of his recommendations seemed to have caused considerable alarm in some ecclesiastical circles. In a letter to his friend Cranevelt dated 16 August 1527, Vives mentions that a Franciscan, Nicolas de Burreau, bishop of Sarepto, was threatening to make an issue of *De subventione*,

---

[62] Ibid.

[63] Ibid. 489-90.

[64] Bataillon, op. cit.

labeling it a heretical piece supportive of Lutheran views. And although Vives had prudently, perhaps fearing the wrath of the powerful mendicant orders, refrained from mentioning mendicant begging, *De subventione* again came under attack twenty-four years after his death. The occasion was Bruges' attempt (1562) to set in motion a welfare system designed along lines similar to those suggested by Vives' own plan. In response, Lorenzo de Villavicencio, a Spanish Augustinian monk, wrote a *De oeconomia sacra circa pauperum curam* (1564), and cited Vives' book as a remote antecedent of what he judged to be the heretical position adopted by the city in matters of welfare. Vives' earlier proposal that municipal control be established over both hospitals and their charges is interpreted by Villavicencio as a clear infringement of ecclesiastical prerogatives. And, asks the monk, if the state were allowed to take control of foundations set up by private individuals for pious ends and therefore rightfully controlled by the Church, what next? Perhaps the property of the Church itself? Not unexpectedly, he finds in Vives' remark that through the centuries the Church had failed to devote all the revenues collected for the care of the needy to poor relief ample proof that this was precisely the humanist's intention.[65] It is thus fair to say that Vives' two main goals in *De subventione*—to make welfare properly the business of the state, and to eradicate beggary—struck a very sensitive chord in the ecclesiastical soul. The first frightened some because it was feared that depriving Church authorities of their monopoly over welfare was but a thinly-disguised first salvo prelude to an all-out attack aimed at secularizing Church property. The second goal, to extirpate mendicancy from the Christian commonwealth, also met with opposition. One concrete example of that opposition is of interest to us here.

Although this monograph is plainly not intended as a forum for the discussion of sixteenth-century attempts at welfare reform, there is one instance whose mention, because it involved Domingo de Soto, one of the day's Neoscholastic luminaries, may shed some additional light on the theoretical premises used by Vives to shore up the foundations of his welfare reform plan. The occasion for Soto's bilingual treatise— *Deliberación de la causa de los pobres/In causa pauperum deliberatio* (Salamanca, 1545)[66]—was the poor law enacted in Castile in 1540. Attempting to bring some measure of order to the system of poor relief variously practiced in the cities of the kingdom and to prevent the able

---

[65] Ibid.

[66] Cited hereafter as *Deliberación*. The edition used here is that of the Instituto de Estudios Políticos (Madrid, 1965).

bodied from begging, the authorities spelled "out the administration of a licensed begging system."[67] Although such was indeed the heart and soul of the law, and indeed Soto does devote lengthy pages to discussing what he outlines as its propositions or *artículos*, the Dominican theologian reserved the choicest comments for the final remarks that end the legal text of the law. And although those remarks are obviously but an incidental observation—whether begging is in practice the best means of providing for the poor—it is clear that Soto chose to interpret them as proof that the ultimate intention of the drafters of the law was to prohibit begging.[68]

iii

According to Soto's interpretation of the provisions of the law of 1540, the first *artículo* instructed public officials to investigate the claims to poverty adduced by those who earned their living by requesting alms in the name of God. In Soto's judgment the goal aimed at by the authors of the law was twofold: (1) to find out whether a man's poverty was true or feigned; (2) to inquire into the life and morals of the poor.[69] Vives, we have seen, considered a similar objective to be essential to his own plan. And both he and Soto wholeheartedly agree that it is imperative to distinguish between those who are truly poor and those who, falsely claiming to be needy, in effect perpetrate a fraud upon the charitable public. But Vives felt no need to go into the reasons that justify depriving the false poor of access to charity. By contrast Soto, theologian and Thomist (although in this instance he expressly promises to refrain from reasoning after the "scholastic" fashion), insists on explaining, with the backing of the usual authorities, that by divine, natural, common, and Castilian law able-bodied men who refuse to work, preferring instead to live off the charity of others, "must not be tolerated in the commonwealth."[70] But after studying the problem more closely, it would appear, Soto changed his mind. It is interesting to mention, moreover, that this volte-face simultaneously inaugurates an approach to the law of 1540 characterized by a rigorous cross-examination of every possible

---

[67] L. Martz, *Poverty and Welfare in Habsburg Spain* (Cambridge, 1983), 20.

[68] Soto's critical remarks were answered by the Benedictine abbot of San Vicente, Juan de Robles, in *De la orden que en algunos pueblos de España se ha puesto en la limosna: para remedio de los verdaderos pobres* (Salamanca, 1545). Robles' treatise can be found in the edition of Soto's work cited earlier.

[69] *Deliberación* 71.

[70] Ibid. 31.

aspect and consequence, explicit or implicit, that Soto's imagination can attach to the law's rather simple and straightforward provisions. In short, *reductio ad absurdum* soon becomes Soto's preferred approach to a subject that in a very real sense has now become a target.

It is worth following Soto's reasoning in some detail because it adds a new dimension to the issue of the feigned poor, one, furthermore, never considered by Vives in his extensive discussion of *caritas*. Two different virtues, Soto claims, are involved in this particular issue: *misericordia* (which could be easily translated as *caritas*; Soto defines it as "the culmination and perfection of all virtues") and justice.[71] Although both are joined as one in God, among men they are very different. Whereas *misericordia* was entrusted by God to all men, and all must therefore practice it, "few are the ministers of justice."[72] It is hardly an exaggeration to say that this statement is the justification for all the liberties that Soto will take with the law of 1540. True, he will argue again and again, the provisions of the law meet the demands of human justice, but they clearly subvert *misericordia*. And with this refrain in mind and *misericordia* as a wondrous catch-all, the theologian happily embarks upon the task of demonstrating that, considerations of human justice aside, the law of 1540 is a needless, monstrous, and even malevolent absurdity. The ministers of justice, who are already in place within the commonwealth, must be entrusted with the task of ferreting out the false poor. There is no need, in other words, to create an additional mechanism of investigation to separate the true from the feigned needy. To do otherwise, Soto slyly intimates, would suggest that what in truth motivates the authors of the law is not "love and *misericordia*" of the real poor but "some hatred aimed collectively at all who are members of that wretched class."[73] Having thus created a rational platform of doubt that openly questions the Christian motives of the law's supporters, Soto launches himself into further mischief-making.

His first target is *justicia*, one of the two virtues involved in the *artículo* under consideration. He is not convinced, he claims, that the poor will be given a fair hearing by the law. For one thing, they are notoriously helpless. The rich, when accused and convicted, can still defend themselves by means of "bribery or with weapons in hand"; the poor man to whom the right to beg has been denied is left with

---

[71] Ibid. 72.

[72] Ibid.

[73] Ibid. 72-73.

nothing—"no hole to crawl into other than the grave."[74] For another, it is obvious that to be poor a man does not have to be absolutely destitute. He may easily be partially incapacitated, able to work indeed but not to the extent needed to provide full support for himself or his family. Such a man plainly needs to supplement his income with alms. Will the ministers of justice charged with overseeing the poor be willing or able to take into account such subtleties in the condition of their charges? Soto thinks not. They will instead pronounce such cases to be instances of fraudulent poverty. Care must be taken, he adds sententiously, that in our zeal to pull the tares we do not uproot the wheat as well (Matthew 13:29). Moreover, what if a man who can work today lacks the strength to do so tomorrow? Must he appear every other day before a local official to have his condition as indigent validated? And what if, even though willing to work, he cannot find employment? Should the commonwealth not delay its sentence on eligibility until such time as it has made certain that all who want to work will in fact find an occupation?[75] Soto's last question addresses itself to an issue thorny indeed, one that even Vives did not fail to consider. His plan for welfare reform does in fact provide for the creation of jobs for the indigent, both in the public and private (Bruges' textile industry) sectors. In this sense, and given Soto's objection that a man cannot in justice be denied the right to beg by a government that fails to provide him with an alternative means to make a living, Vives, having met the conditions of the objection, can fairly say that his recommendations concerning the need to exclude healthy men from access to alms are neither impractical nor unjust. Finally, and here Soto's reasoning (seeking perhaps to make the law look ridiculous) leans a bit toward the bizarre, there are those who despite their distinguished birth became, through loss of patrimony or failure to learn a useful trade, indigent. Rather than compelling such men to earn a living in menial jobs and thereby compromising their honor, permission should be granted them to beg.[76] At least insofar as those who lost their patrimony through personal profligacy (good birth notwithstanding, it would seem) are concerned, Vives harbors no sympathy whatsoever. In obvious opposition to Soto, he argues instead that they should indeed be fed the roughest fare and burdened with the most onerous occupations.

    What has transpired so far in the above paragraph, it must be

---

[74] Ibid. 73.

[75] Ibid. 75-76.

[76] Ibid. 76-77.

remembered, has to do with the justice side of the *artículo* under consideration. But, what of *misericordia*? On this question Soto lets St. Chrysostom speak for him. How dare the well-fed, who at night sleep in a warm and comfortable bed, complain about the poor who feign illnesses and even mutilate themselves to survive? Their own indifference, cruelty, and inhumanity are precisely the cause of such abominations—by now, of course, Soto has completely blurred the lines between true and feigned poor. What else can the needy do when total destitution is the only alternative left to them? The poors' fraud is the loudest indictment of the richs' culpable indifference. Had the latter not failed to show them *misericordia*, the poor would have no need to debase themselves with such trickery. "In conclusion, since you the rich failed to learn and practice *misericordia* the disinherited, in the same measure that they cripple their own bodies, stoke up the fires of hell for themselves and you."[77] Soto's casuistry now surfaces in all its glory. The point of St. Chrysostom's formidable accusations, he explains, is that even those who fraudulently pass themselves for needy are in no sense different from those who, living in other levels of society, are guilty of equivalent sins and prevarications. "And against them we do not mass such formidable artillery."[78] Who in Spain, he further asks, has financially suffered at the hands of those *vagabundos*, who merely ask for what can easily be refused? On the other hand, there are those who have stolen far more than all the poor of the kingdom put together; but because they are powerful we endure their depredations. The poor alone, because they are powerless, we refuse to tolerate.[79] Finally, Soto brings to a close his observations on the first *artículo* by reminding, by way of a veiled threat, the authorities that the real motive behind the law is their fear of urban crime. And as always he manages to do so by conveying the impression that their measures will have precisely the opposite effect of that intended. If we chase the vagabonds (the feigned poor) from the cities of Castile, he warns, they will spread over the neighboring countryside and its villages. There the petty deceits they practice in the cities to extort alms will become serious crimes. The message is loud and clear: beware lest wishing to uproot a minor problem, a major one, far more difficult to control, be created.

We now move to the second aspect of the first *artículo* being

---

[77] Ibid. 80.

[78] Ibid. 82.

[79] Ibid. 83.

analyzed by Soto: that the life and morals of the poor be investigated by the authorities. In principle, Soto agrees, there is nothing wrong with fraternally admonishing the poor to edification; we can all profit from some guidance. But he objects to the idea of putting charity and moralizing under the same tent. The function of the former, in its guise as "bodily *misericordia*," is merely to feed the hungry, clothe the naked, and lodge the pilgrim; it has nothing to do with "brotherly advice."[80] Soto's point is once more, and St. Chrysostom again comes to the rescue with his inimitable homilies, that there is a conspiracy afoot: linking charity with morality is but another excuse used by the rich to withhold charity from the poor. There can be no other explanation, for to reason that charity and morality belong somehow together is patently absurd. The meaning of *caritas* as *misericordia* is plain enough: to help whoever asks, regardless of whether he truly needs it or whether he leads an upright life. Thus it is in Soto that we find an uncompromising translation into reality of the theoretical definition of *caritas* that Vives (who also insists in his plan that the mores of the poor must be looked into) gave us earlier, and which he would again reaffirm in his scathing indictment of the Anabaptists. If you agree to define *caritas* as something owed by every man to every other man as mandated by God, the theologian seems to be asking the humanist, why retreat from that position where the urban poor are concerned? Are you perhaps the spokesman for the interests of Bruges' oligarchy? Citing instances found in both Laws, Soto relentlessly drives home the point that the mores of the beneficiary are irrelevant to the practice of charity. The Christian tradition unqualifiedly teaches that *misericorida* is owed even to the wicked. "What the Fathers teach is that it is not incumbent upon *misericordia* to differentiate between the good and the wicked. That task is reserved to the ministers of justice. The burden of *misericordia* is to succor all."[81] How, then, asks Soto sarcastically, can we hope to reconcile the Christian introduction prefacing the law of 1540 with what the law then demands: deny charity to the feigned poor, scrutinize the mores of the needy, expel non-native beggars from the city?[82] *Misericordia* is to do good unto the unworthy, for what is done unto the deserving is but justice.[83] True, Soto concedes, all other things being equal in matters

---

[80] Ibid. 85-86.

[81] Ibid. 91.

[82] Ibid. 92.

[83] Ibid. 93.

concerning help to the needy, it might be more desirable to succor the good than the wicked. "But just because you do not wish to help those whom you do not consider worthy of assistance do not make a law to prevent others who want to succor them from so doing."[84]

Those responsible for the law of 1540, however, wanted more than to separate feigned from true poor and to inquire into the conduct of the latter. According to Soto the law's second *artículo* aimed at banishing from the city beggars not native to it. We remember that Vives himself had argued that only indigenous beggars (meaning in this instance those native to the city of Bruges) should be tolerated. To those acquainted with the high-minded tone and loftiness of purpose that invariably characterize the humanist's approach whenever he discourses on the issues variously associated with the human condition, it seems a surprisingly intolerant condition. But then, this aspect of *De subventione* addressed itself to the pressing realities of life in Bruges, a practical problem to be dealt with in pragmatic terms. And Vives was obviously determined to rise to the occasion. Soto, on the other hand, feels in this instance unencumbered by the burden of reality limiting Vives' options, or perhaps he simply feels that it is abhorrent to deny the bounty of Christian charity to men whose only fault was to have originated in a place other than the one in which they presently found themselves. Be that as it may, the fact remains that the theologian takes issue with that particular provision of the law of 1540—and in the process, and this is what interests us here, sternly, albeit implicitly, rebukes the humanist as well. Soto reminds Prince Philip (to whom the work is dedicated) that the provision in question has no precedent in divine, natural, common, or Castilian law. Is it possible, he asks facetiously, that mankind could have heretofore been so neglectful as to have failed to issue legislation barring to foreign beggars access to local charity?[85] Surely not, he concludes. The fact of the matter is that such legislation was never before enacted for five reasons, reasons that in effect make the second *artículo* of the law of 1540 unacceptable. To begin with, no man can be banished without due cause. Soto reprises here the argument adduced by his master, Francisco de Vitoria, in support of the concept of human fellowship. And it is worth observing how remarkable it is that a man like Vives, otherwise so attuned to the moral teachings of Roman Stoicism, and indeed in all other respects so sensitive to the idea of human solidarity, should have been so preoccupied with the outward trappings of welfare in Bruges that he could fail to notice the moral

---

[84] Ibid. 94.

[85] Ibid. 33.

quandary in which he placed himself by denying a human being access to
this aspect of *caritas* solely on such flimsy grounds. Undoubtedly, in this
instance at least the theologian has the moral advantage over the
humanist. By *ius naturale* and *ius gentium*, then, man enjoys total
freedom to travel so long as he is not a declared enemy or guilty of a
crime. Hence he who is truly poor and begs for alms in the name of the
Lord cannot, since he is guilty of no crime, be expelled.[86] Moreover, Soto
adds, there is no law that can prevent an indigent man from leaving his
place of origin to seek more abundant charity elsewhere; unless, of course,
the local community were to commit itself to support the poor in their
own midst. To do otherwise would clearly amount to condemning the
needy, unjustly, to suffer from want.[87] There is in addition a third reason
that adds further weight to the argument just proposed: a kingdom is a
single "body." Some of its members—the cities—will, by the very nature
of things, be more prosperous than others. To keep the whole in proper
balance, therefore, it is obvious that a rich city is under obligation to aid
the poor of another city enjoying lesser means. In point of fact, Soto
concludes, the binding nature of that constraint is such that it transcends
the artificial limitations set by the kingdom's boundaries. Because
Christendom is itself but one body (I Corinthians 12:12-13), the needy
from one Christian kingdom have therefore the right to beg in the name
of God in any other Christian kingdom.[88] And furthermore, he insists, it
is a fact of life that for varied reasons charity is not practiced everywhere
with the same devotion; clearly, then, the poor would be forced to endure
unjustified privations if unable to move from where charity is scarce to
where it is abundant.[89] Finally, the theologian concludes, two more
reasons must be kept in mind if we are to judge properly how unjustified
this provision of the law truly is: (1) both pagans and Christians have
traditionally held hospitality to be a sacred duty; (2) neither the Old
Testament nor the New ever makes a distinction between native and
foreign poor.[90]

The last of the *artículos* itemized by Soto that bears any resemblance
to the provisions of Vives' plan is perhaps the most interesting, for the
theologian sees it as the one on which the authors of the 1540 law insist

---

[86] Ibid. 35.

[87] Ibid. 37.

[88] Ibid. 38.

[89] Ibid. 39.

[90] Ibid. 39-42.

most. But the *artículo* in question (whether begging is indeed the most effective means of feeding the poor), I have already pointed out, was merely an afterthought and never a formal provision of the law. The presumed conspiracy, in other words, was strictly a straw man of Soto's own making. The spurious nature of the *artículo* notwithstanding, the facts remain that (1) Soto apparently did fear that the entire thrust of the law of 1540 was to deny the poor the right to beg; and (2) Vives' own plan of welfare reform is in effect an attempt at finding a practical alternative to urban beggary. Under the circumstances, we are keenly interested in Soto's objections to any proposal that, explicitly or implicitly, may call for the abolition of mendicancy. As on an earlier occasion, he begins by observing that the problem must be approached from two different perspectives: what is rightful and what is equitable. Both are implied in the premises he now proceeds to outline. First of all, divine and natural law have endowed the poor with the privilege of attempting to satisfy their own needs by begging; and that privilege remains in force as long as the poor suffer from want.[91] Additionally, of course, no one has the right to prevent anyone else from practicing charity as he sees fit. Both premises lead Soto to the reason against outlawing beggary that he considers weightiest, which he admonishes the authors of the law to keep in mind. Anyone depriving a poor man of his right to beg in the name of God must provide him with whatever the poor man would garner if his right to beg had not been denied him.[92] In other words, if a city decides to prohibit begging within its limits—and it must be emphasized that the law of 1540 provided for no such thing—it must be simultaneously prepared to supply the poor thus affected with room, board, clothing, or anything else that they could themselves acquire by begging. It is of fundamental importance to note that Soto, who on an earlier occasion had demanded that the state provide employment opportunities for the indigent, is here completely silent on that issue, which is of course the *sine qua non* condition of Vives' own plan. But Soto is of course not serious, for he hastens to add that in practice the conditions that he has outlined are impossible to fulfill. He offers two reasons: (1) It is hopeless to try to find out what the needs of the poor are or what the citizens must individually contribute to cover those needs—"Who, indeed, is to judge what the needs of one man are as opposed to those of another; even in the matter of food alone men have different wants, and one may need twice

---

[91] Ibid. 104-05.

[92] Ibid. 109.

or three times as much bread as another";[93] (2) Men cannot be constrained by force to give alms (the money needed to support the poor; the money, in other words, that Vives sees no difficulty in raising), as they would have to be if the needy were deprived of their right to beg.[94] Soto's conclusion is hardly unexpected: it is impossible, in justice, to deprive the poor of their right to beg. Of course, this is by no means the end of Soto's attack against the mythical threat posed by the law of 1540. His additional arguments, however, are pure sophistry designed to expose any attempt at suggesting alternatives to begging as grotesquely impractical. Of greater interest is his argument from *misericordia*. First, what is truly important about begging is the inestimable opportunity it affords to the giver. The spiritual compassion felt toward the poor that issues into the giving of alms is what counts most in God's judgment.[95] Second, it is essential to inculcate in the young the theory and practice of *misericordia*, a task impossible to fulfill without the presence of the poor.[96] Third, obedience to Christ compels His followers to practice *misericordia* directly. No one can be truly Christian without sharing himself with the poor. To take the needy away from the Christian community, therefore, deprives its members of the opportunity to reaffirm their own Christian nature. It would in effect take the very heart out of Christianity.

To conclude. It is plain from all the above that, unlike Vives, Soto is not interested either in the problem of welfare or in finding a practical solution to it. To provide the poor with necessities and to allay begging and its attendant ills to a manageable level are social and political issues, which affect and concern urban government exclusively. Strictly speaking, then, welfare does not become a spiritual problem until its reform becomes a Lutheran initiative threatening (1) to spill over into Catholic areas and (2) to do away with mendicancy altogether. Then and only then does it turn into what in modern terminology would be called a civil rights issue, and as such becomes worthy of the attention of a theologian. The specter of a world where an effective system of welfare controlled by the secular authorities has caused begging to be either banned or obsolete (or both) is profoundly shocking to the sensibilities of Soto the theologian. The reason is not hard to find. In a society conceived and executed by God as the environment uniquely suitable to afford man

---

[93] Ibid. 111.

[94] Ibid. 110.

[95] Ibid. 121.

[96] Ibid. 122-23.

the opportunity to prepare himself for everlasting salvation, the beggar plays an indispensable role. Take him away and important opportunities for the ordinary Christian to earn merit in the eyes of the Lord vanish as well. But is this not also Vives' definition of society? Why, then, does the humanist believe that he can banish the beggar from the stage and not do damage to God's second provision? The logic of everything that we have said about Vives' views on the subject of society would seem to lead to placing him and Soto on the same side. And yet, we have seen, they could hardly be further apart when it comes to the indigent and their care. Why? The reason, I think, may be found in the eternal problem of the thinker turned practical planner. Both Vives and Soto are men of ideas, men most at ease when dealing with abstractions. But while Soto remains throughout true to his calling, Vives, moved perhaps by the pressing needs of his beloved Bruges, ventures into the unfamiliar seas of practical reality. He founders, and Soto is most helpful in showing us how. The key lies with *caritas*. Vives had implicitly defined it as the pervasive glue that keeps society together. But, as Soto demonstrates, *caritas*, if it is indeed to be the earthly embodiment of the love divine, must be absolute and absolutely applied. In his welfare reform plan Vives' *caritas* fails that test. Is it *caritas* to compel a man to work for a living when he would rather beg for his daily bread? How can we be said to be offering loving succor to a beggar whom we force to leave the city solely on the grounds that it is not the place of his birth? Are we showing charity to the citizens of Bruges as we force them to contribute to defraying the expenses that the municipality must face because it forbids the needy to beg? (Is this not tantamount to forcing charity on the good burghers of Bruges, something that Vives will harshly rebuke the Anabaptists for suggesting?) In what sense can the ordinance that tells the hospital to whom they can or cannot offer refuge be interpreted as an expression of *caritas*? In all cases the failure of Vives' plan to answer these questions satisfactorily is attributable to Vives' fear and distrust of that *locus* of human ambition and unruly passions: his individuality. By contrast, Soto, despite his frequent recourse to sophistry to discredit what he single-mindedly opposes, invariably emphasizes the fate awaiting the individual beggar in the collective arrangement suggested by the likes of Vives. Perhaps unconsciously but nonetheless unmistakably, Soto has driven home a fundamental fact regrettably ignored by the humanist and other architects of social planning before and since: collective measures have unexpected and painful consequences, which invariably and adversely affect the individual part of the whole they are designed to benefit.

The Community of Goods

We have seen that Vives' understanding of *caritas* goes beyond the idea that a Christian, to keep society in being, is duty-bound by natural law and the injunctions of his faith to support the poor. Nonetheless, it is clear that for Vives *caritas* does imply an obligation on the part of a Christian to share his bounty with his less fortunate brethren. And that very fact suggests the following question: to what extent does that obligation shape Vives' views on private property? Or, to say it differently, does *caritas* necessarily mandate the community of goods? The question has of course always been a recurrent puzzle, which the advent of Christianity, with its emphasis on sharing, brotherhood, and contempt for the material world, often made more intractable. And in the first half of the sixteenth century, the problem was once again, through the good offices of the Radical Reformation, endowed with the utmost reality.

i

Barely three years before the publication of *De subventione* the growing radicalizing tendencies within Protestantism had spawned in Zürich that bewildering kaleidoscope of religious extremism known collectively as Anabaptism. Escaping from persecution, which after 1529 had become particularly savage everywhere, a group of Dutch Melchiorite Anabaptists under the leadership of Jan Matthys fled the Netherlands to Germany. In Münster, a city whose governing council had shown strong evangelical sympathies since 1533, the fleeing Melchiorites found a haven. Shortly afterward, however, the prince-bishop of Münster gathered an army and laid siege to the city; wholesale baptizings soon followed within the encircled town, and some tentative steps were taken in the direction of an enforced community of goods. Matthys, who in the short intervening period since his arrival had carried out a complete social, political, and religious revolution within the city, was killed during a sortie against the besiegers. The leadership of the Melchiorites now fell on the shoulders of Jan Bockelson, who promptly proclaimed himself king and—after the example of the prophets of the Old Testament—instituted polygamy as a means of providing for the women of Münster, who greatly outnumbered the men. Despite the fierce resistance of the besieged, the town was taken by assault in 1535 by the bishop's troops, and its inhabitants were put to the sword. The tale of the grim drama enacted in Münster soon spread and grew with the telling, especially in what pertained to the Münsterites dabbling in communist practices and polygamy. A wave of revulsion engulfed Europe, further blackening the reputation of the Anabaptists. And it is to this real and perceived horror centering around the Münster episode that Vives seems to have reacted in 1535 with *De communione rerum ad germanos inferiores*.

Vives begins the treatise with a pessimistic approach to the nature of man already familiar to us: because of our inclination we move in the direction of vice with the same ease that a boat moves with the current. The effort becomes considerable indeed, however, when we attempt to navigate in the opposite direction.[97] He then moves on to survey the recent history of "lower Germany," beginning with the time when German society was staunchly religious. In those days matters of piety were not trifled with, and no one thought it licit to question what generations had accepted as established truths.[98] But then things began to change. Someone—obviously Vives means Luther—had the temerity to question some of those truths, not, however, in order to discuss them, but with the clear intention of denying, abolishing, and suppressing them.[99] But in Vives' scheme of things Luther represents merely the first step taken in the direction of anarchy. What began as a struggle involving divine truths soon degenerated into open warfare under the pretext of fictitious liberty and the iniquitous pretension of equating the inferior with the superior—Vives is here referring to the 1525 uprising of the German peasants, which eventually came to be known as the Peasants' War. And the march of ambitious rebelliousness did not stop here, for eventually the unruly aspirations of the peasants were replaced by something even worse, the bold pretensions of the Anabaptists.

Who are the Anabaptists? Vives describes them as follows. They are men who demand and proclaim not only the equality of all men, but also that all things be held in common. To bring about that end, these "super Christians" have not hesitated to conspire and to take up arms against legally constituted authority. Their plan, however, does not end there, for Vives is certain that once they have unleashed fear and loosened anarchy upon the land they will fall upon the goods and fortunes of all.[100] And this is precisely what he believes to be the secret and ultimate intention of the Anabaptists; it certainly is the goal of their leaders: to steal the property of others and to enjoy it themselves. For Vives, therefore, the Anabaptists

---

[97] DCR *Opera* V 464.

[98] Ibid. 465.

[99] Ibid.

[100] Ibid.

will never be more than a horde of outlaws whose religious posturings, a smoke screen to mask their true motives (to loot the property of others), need not be taken seriously. In fact, as reported by Vives, the reasoning of the Anabaptists reduces itself to the following claim. Nothing could be more in agreement with Jesus' teachings than the common sharing of goods; if He were among us this is undoubtedly what He would command us to do.[101] But the truth of the matter, retorts Vives, is that their only argument is violence, and that is precisely what makes them into, not a sect, but a band of robbers. And at this point Vives, the sworn enemy of discord and war, adopts a surprisingly belligerent attitude. Having identified to his own satisfaction the Anabaptists as outlaws who have willingly placed themselves beyond the pale, he explains that reasoning is wasted on them and force is of the essence: force alone tames force, weapons must be subdued with weapons, deceit must be answered with deceit. What else is there to be done with those who leave none in peace and attack meek men with iron and fire?[102] And so it comes to pass that the Anabaptists force the hand of the ruler in the direction of violence, for clearly in failing to use force the prince would be derelict in his duty, imposed upon him by God, to protect his people.[103] Vives does not hesitate to liken the Anabaptist problem to an internal one of law and order within the Christian commonwealth: will the magistrate not sacrifice a man who threatens the public peace, on the altar of the entire community's safety?[104] And surely the Anabaptists are far worse than a mere isolated instance of human criminality. Night and day they draw up the cruelest plans on how to steal, how to destroy, how to tear to pieces.[105] But what Vives finds most galling, for hypocrisy is intolerable to a man of his temper, is that these miscreants hide all their detestable plans under the cover of Christian piety.[106] Detestable though the Anabaptists obviously are in his eyes, Vives is not unwilling to admit that not all are equally culpable of the felonies broadly attributable to the movement as a whole. In fact, he is more than ready to distinguish three distinct groups within it, which carry varying degrees of guilt. First stand the leaders, men of few scruples whose intentions are thoroughly suspect

---

[101] Ibid.

[102] Ibid. 466.

[103] Ibid.

[104] Ibid.

[105] Ibid.

[106] Ibid.

in Vives' eyes: their aim is to gain control of the mob and to use it either to quench their own thirst for riches or to satisfy some personal and unmentionable urge.[107] Next we have the unsavory adventurers, the footloose who foolishly squandered their patrimonies, or who refuse to toil for their daily bread, or who still possess a measure of personal wealth, which they hope to increase with their share of the expected loot.[108] But it is the third group that will monopolize the author's attention. Its members are the blind mass of followers, men who are sinners not through a conscious act of the will, but simply as a consequence of their low intelligence; men, in short, who will accept and act upon whatever interpretation of Scripture a clever deceiver places before them. Charity automatically makes all goods common, Christ commands that he who owns two coats surrender one to him who has none, in the primitive Church all property was held in common: these precepts, the Anabaptist rank and file are taught by their unscrupulous leaders, must be observed literally, for otherwise we shall remain unable to comply with the commands of the Christian religion.[109]

These hapless victims are Vives' target. Having identified the problem as one of ignorance, the author, in the best Christian humanist tradition, now dons his best pedagogical vestments and proceeds to enlighten the misguided wretches, who will abandon their wicked ways and return to the fold of humanity.[110] In the process Vives is forced to conduct his debate with the Anabaptists simultaneously along two fronts: one that leads him to reassert the views on the meaning and nature of charity already explained in *De subventione*, and another that causes him to conduct a spirited defense of private property. And it is perhaps for that very reason that Vives chooses to divide *De communione* into two parts. In the first he proves that the community of goods has not been

---

[107] Ibid. 466-67.

[108] Ibid. 467.

[109] Ibid. Of these three breeds of men the first are simply thieves and ought to be dealt with as such. Against them, and in accordance with established law, must proceed the man who not without cause wields the sword, for, if he brandishes it against thieves, adulterers, and cheats, why not use it also against men who are pits of wickedness? Ibid. The rapacity of the second kind of men found among the Anabaptists can be easily thwarted, although not by legal punishment because there are no sanctions under civil law for greed; but no matter, God Himself will take care of their guilt. Ibid.

[110] Understood in this sense, *De communione rerum* is a splendid example of the most enduring characteristic of Christian humanism: the belief that education is the most potent weapon in the arsenal of those seeking to transform society.

decreed by any, let alone evangelical, law because charity is not, and does not imply, communism. In the second the format changes, moving away from charity as the possible foundation endowing communism with a mandatory character, to proving that even if the community of goods were a desirable idea, it could not be implemented in practice. Obviously both paths transit over a common ground: individual ownership of material things. It becomes, therefore, imperative that before joining Vives in his journey along them, we return to *De subventione* to understand his views on private property. The very nature of the goals he pursues in that work demands that beyond placing the problem of charity squarely on a philosophical foundation, he justify as well the need to aid the poor in terms of an answer to the following question: if man has come by his material goods in a legal and honorable fashion, why should he be compelled to share them with other men too incompetent to emulate his accomplishments? In other words, Vives must address himself to the issue and nature of property privately held. And this is precisely what he does in Chapter IX.

ii

His initial argument is one in which, to all appearances, private property stands condemned root and branch. Underlining the intimate relationship binding nature and God together—"nature is none other than the will and the command divines."[111]—Vives insists that everything that exists in the former was placed "so that all creatures engendered by it could share in the common bounty."[112] Echoing Plato, who damned as nefarious the words "mine" and "yours," Vives argues that using a shallow pretext—"inasmuch as I have invested my effort and industry, I ought to be allowed ownership"[113]—we monopolize that which nature intended to be free and open to all, thereby depriving others of that to which by natural law they have identical rights; we defend it, we put it beyond their reach with walls, gates, locks, irons, weapons, laws.[114] In this fashion human avarice and malice—for plainly the practice of hoarding by the few the bounty meant for the many could not possibly have originated in nature—introduced two alien scourges: famine and scarcity.[115] Falling back

---

[111] DSP *Opera* IV 451.

[112] Ibid.

[113] Ibid.

[114] Ibid.

[115] Ibid.

on an analogy popular among Christian humanists and immortalized by
Erasmus in his thunderings against war, Vives insists that the animals
themselves teach us a different lesson with their example. They take what
nature freely provides only to the extent of satisfying their needs, leaving
for the use of others what they do not require for their survival. Thus,
Vives concludes, man alone, in perpetual violation of nature's own
precepts, insists on both consuming more than he needs and on
monopolizing what he does not consume. Consequently, private property
can be justified only when there is a willingness to share it. "Let whoever
has taken possession of the gifts of nature know that if he shares them
with his indigent brother he possesses them in justice and in accordance
with nature's will and instruction; otherwise, he is a thief and a plunderer,
convicted and damned by natural law as one who has seized and keeps
what nature did not create for him alone. . . . Let none be therefore
unaware that his body, life, money have not been given to him for his
own private use and convenience, but that he is their steward and that to
no other end does he receive them from God."[116] As the Ancients
themselves well understood—although, Vives pointedly qualifies, vaguely
and in a shadowy fashion—only after man has discharged his primary
obligations to others is he allowed to care for his own self. "Laws were
enacted for the citizens in order to impress upon them the fact that all
owed everything to the city and that the latter had the authority to
dispose of their bodies, lives, and fortunes."[117] And of course, Vives
concludes again echoing More, what even those ignorant of the true faith
were able to fathom, ought to be plain to men who call themselves
Christians. And it is precisely for that reason that Vives, who until now
has "mixed the human and the divine" in an effort to awaken those
"submerged in the deepest darkness" to the realities of charity, will in
Chapter X list the compulsions operating upon Christians in that
direction purely in relation to God's commands as they are witnessed to
by both Testaments. With all this in mind let us now return to *De
communione*.

The first argument commonly adduced in defense of the community
of goods, Vives begins, is the example of the Apostles, in whose day
Christians presumably held things in common and did not have private
property.[118] Two passages from Acts seem to have been bandied about by

---

[116] Ibid. 451-52.

[117] Ibid. 452.

[118] Ibid. 468.

the Anabaptists to justify their paradigmatic use of Apostolic custom. The first (4:32)—"Now the company of those who believed were of one heart and soul, and no one said that any of the things which he possessed was his own, but they had everything in common"—Vives interprets in the sense that all things were used to satisfy the common needs, and only after this fashion can things be said to have been held in common. As for the second (4:34-35)—"as many as were possessors of lands or houses sold them, and brought the proceeds of what was sold and laid it at the apostles' feet, and distribution was made to each as any had need"—Vives explains that nowhere is it recorded that all did it; in fact, it is explicitly stated only that Barnabas acted in this fashion.[119] But even more telling, he adds, was that those who indeed sold their property and gave their money to the Apostles did so on their own initiative and not because they had been told to do so.[120] And such is precisely the thrust of Vives' reply to the claims of the Anabaptists. The common sharing of goods might in fact have been practiced by the Apostles, but if so it clearly resulted from the individual initiative of some recently baptized Christians whose fervent charity led them along the path of total sharing. But neither Christ nor His closest disciples demanded it of them; what the Lord indeed requires of every man is that he be ready to share what he has with his needy neighbor. It was, in short, spontaneously zealous charity, not mandated communism, that moved early Christians to practice the community of goods.[121]

The second argument often took the form of a question: does charity not in fact make the sharing of goods obligatory? As explained by Vives the Anabaptists certainly believed such to be the case and justified their conviction on the basis of (1) Luke 3:10-11,[122] (2) the Old Testament teaching that those who refuse to be charitable of their own free will must be compelled by force, an interpretation that presumably justified the acts of violence committed by the Anabaptists, and (3) natural and divine law, which made all things common. Vives answers the first Anabaptist claim by pointing out that indiscriminate sharing was never the intention of the Lord, for He clearly did not intend the recipient of the extra garment to be a man whose indolent nature and debauched life-style were the cause of the loss of his own. Otherwise, He would be implicitly counseling us

---

[119] Ibid. 472.

[120] Ibid.

[121] Ibid. 468.

[122] "He who has two coats, let him share with him who has none."

to reward slothfulness with our charity.[123] On this point, Vives insists, there can be no debate, inasmuch as St. Paul unmistakably asserts that he who does not wish to work shall not eat.[124] Moreover, when Christ suggested sharing the extra coat, He said "to give" not "to steal,"[125] which is precisely what the Anabaptists want to do—"to extort it with violence, with arson, with death."[126] No one is obligated to share his goods in common, only to give that which is superfluous while keeping for his own private use what is necessary; but precisely this, objects Vives, is what the Anabaptists stubbornly refuse to accept. They want everything, regardless of whether it is necessary or not, refusing to consider whether the goods they steal belong to the young or the old, the rich or the poor, single men or individuals burdened with family obligations. The Anabaptists, in short, do not take the proffered extra robe; they steal both garments.[127] As for the man who refuses to lend an ear to Christ's exhortations and ignores the plight of those who need what he owns in excess, Vives answers the Anabaptist proposition that the Old Testament teaches that he must be forced to comply, with a retort that is both simple and fundamental, not only to the issues now under discussion but to his thought in general: it is not possible to force man to be charitable against his will.[128] Moreover, he adds contemptuously, the Old Testament examples adduced are simply the reflection of a physical reality that is but a metaphor for the New Testament's own spirituality.[129] Finally, does the

---

[123] Ibid. 469.

[124] Ibid.

[125] Ibid.

[126] Ibid.

[127] Ibid.

[128] Ibid. 470.

[129] Ibid. 469-70. At this point, it is worth quoting the following passage from Luther's *Against the Robbing and Murdering Hordes of Peasants*, the violent diatribe in which he condemns the revolt of the German peasants in 1525. "It does not help the peasants when they pretend that according to Genesis 1 and 2 all things were created free and common, and that all of us alike have been baptized. For under the New Testament Moses does not count, for there stands our Master, Christ, and subjects us, along with our bodies and our property, to the Emperor and the law of this world, when He says, 'Render to Caesar the things that are Caesar's' (Luke 20:25). Paul, too, speaking in Romans (13:1) to all baptized Christians, says, 'Let every person be subject to the governing authorities.' And Peter says, 'Be subject to every ordinance of man' (1 Pet. 2:13). We are bound to live according to this teaching of Christ, as the Father commands from heaven, saying, 'This is my beloved Son, listen to Him' (Matt. 17:5). For baptism does not make man free in body

natural law implicit in the concept of friendship make all things common? Vives replies that indeed charity, meaning here the love shared by friends, causes things to be commonly shared for love of friendship; but such sharing must be understood in terms of access to their use when the need arises, not in terms of possession.[130] And never must the sharing take place against the will of the legitimate owner. For a definition of true charity (as opposed to the Anabaptists', which he calls that of thieves and pirates) Vives now goes to St. Paul.[131] Charity, he concludes, is something that man puts into effect when he helps his fellows within the measure of his own possibilities; when he favors them in soul, body, possessions, by words, by deeds, insofar as he can.[132] When a man, however, scrutinizes what another man gives, keeps, or possesses, then that man's actions are not motivated by charity but by envy and wicked passions; because charity, by contrast, willingly suffers all and everything, and chooses to believe nothing but good of him whom it loves.[133]

Evidently, then, Christian charity does not necessarily lead to communism. And so Vives brings the first part of De communione to a close. It now remains to show that from a practical point of view communism is also an impossibility. In the process Vives unleashes a vigorous attack on all forms of utopianism. Let us, Vives proceeds,

---

and property, but in soul; and the Gospel does not make goods common, except in the case of those who, of their own free will, do what the apostles and disciples did in Acts 4:32-37. They did not demand, as do our insane peasants in their raging, that the goods of others should be common, but only their own goods. Our peasants, however, want to make the goods of other men common, and keep their own from themselves. Fine Christians, they are! I think there is no devil left in hell; they have all gone into the peasants. Their raving has gone beyond all measure." *Against*, in *Luther's Works*, vol. 46 (Philadelphia, 1967), page 51.

[130] DCR *Opera* V 472. Inasmuch as the Anabaptists are so respectful of charity and Christian perfection, why, sneers Vives, instead of pouncing upon what belongs to others, do they not give away their own goods? When Christ says, give to the poor what you have, he means not that the Anabaptists should take or even ask for, but that they should give. Ibid. 471. Vives' unspoken corollary here is clearly implied: Christ's very injunction to charity in effect makes the community of goods impossible because those who would seemingly benefit from the loss of goods by those who have them are also commanded not to keep them.

[131] "Love is patient and kind; love is not jealous or boastful; it is not arrogant or rude. Love does not insist on its own way; it is not irritable or resentful; it does not rejoice at wrong, but rejoices in the right. Love bears all things, hopes all things, endures all things." 1 Corinthians 13:4-7.

[132] DCR *Opera* V 473.

[133] Ibid.

examine the implications of the Anabaptists' central desire: that all things be shared in common (*vultis esse communa omnia*). But to do that both realistically and effectively, Vives suggests that the remote age of man when he lived in innocence be set aside, and that the discussion be limited to man in his present state: a fallen creature prone to vice and besieged by a multitude of ills.[134] In this the real world of man Vives observes that its objects can be divided into three possible categories. First, those elements of creation that are indeed *communes*. Second, those that only a madman would insist could be held in common. And third, the objects that, following the conventions of private property, may be classified as being a man's collective wealth.

Natural law decrees that the sky above, the heavenly bodies, the air that we breathe, undoubtedly belong to us all; and fish, fowl, and deer are equally shared in common until caught by a fisherman or hunter. In addition, there are other things that are common to all men by mandate of human law: untilled fields, owned by all and none until such time as they are claimed by an occupant; the seats in temple and theater, free to all until taken by the earliest arrival. But, Vives cautions, these things are common simply because in one fashion or another they are open, in some instances as long as no claim is laid to them, to common use; they are not, however, collectively owned, and here the key word is *usus* as opposed to *possessione*. Even in this instance, therefore, Vives strictly qualifies the manner in which things may be said to be held in common.[135] But there is another category of things that cannot possibly be common, either in the sense of use or in the sense of possession. And yet, Vives points out, were the claims of the Anabaptists to be taken seriously, those very things would indeed have to be shared. Shall, for instance, the soul's virtues (talent, experience, prudence, memory) be common? And what of the body, its health, vigor, beauty, age? I am a man of learning, you are a soldier; is it fitting that my books be yours and your weapons mine? "Is it meet that the infirm be given what the healthy need and vice versa?" Vives does not doubt the absurdity of answering these questions in the affirmative.[136] But the next aspect of the problem that Vives touches upon is of greater significance and certainly of considerable interest to us. The humanist argues that in addition to bearing in mind that there are certain things that human beings could not possibly share, the Anabaptists would

---

[134] Ibid.

[135] Ibid.

[136] Ibid, 474.

do well to remember that some men are naturally lords and others servants (*heri, famuli*)—"do you perchance think that all men should be magistrates?" Christ's law, Vives answers, retained untouched the hierarchical distinctions between lords and servants, magistrates and private persons. There has to be an order of obedience, for a common-wealth with no one to govern over the rest is like a headless body, a rudderless ship. There is no greater inequality than such equality.[137] And obviously the idea that women should be held in common is not only preposterous but fraught with perils.[138] If, then, in neither of the two categories examined so far the community of goods is a practicable idea, what is left? What is left is precisely what to some contemporaries seemed to be a not altogether inappropriate application of the principle of the community of goods: external wealth. Vives begins his rebuttal of Anabaptist pretensions on this score with the all-important question: "What do you want, what goals do your demands pursue?" True, to each must be made available whatever he needs. But, Vives qualifies in the same spirit that guided his proposals in *De subventione*, a needy man is one who lacks both what he needs and the means—by cause of age, physical weakness, or ignorance—to acquire it. That unmistakably indicates that the man who squandered his patrimony and now shamelessly asks or demands that he be provided with what he requires to live cannot be included in this category. Neither must a man who refuses to work be considered needy.[139] The result of Vives' critical approach to the battle cry of the Anabaptists is the creation of a criterion of need that guides the author as he tries to discriminate between those among the destitute who deserve help and those who must instead be treated in a manner befitting parasites; a task that Vives, the would-be reformer of welfare, has no choice but to undertake. He is therefore now ready to examine, on the basis of an approach to private property conditioned by that premise, the various forms that wealth takes.

First, the house and the property generally associated with the family. It is impossible to share[140] this manner of wealth in common because of the temperamental differences that characterize, distinguish, and in fact separate one human being from another.[141] Some men are

---

[137] Ibid. 474.

[138] Ibid.

[139] Ibid. 475.

[140] Ibid.

[141] As Vives outlines one by one all the obstacles in the path of realizing the Anabaptist

loners; others are gregarious by nature; still others are busy with
preparations for war. There are those who occupy themselves with the
business of marrying off a daughter; many concentrate on the study of
human learning; and not a few are concerned with matters divine. All
these temperaments, which coexist with difficulty even when bound by
family ties,[142] would find, when strangers are involved, impossible the task
of getting along while sharing common identical physical space. And what
of individuals who, in addition to being mutually strangers, also dislike
each other, how are they going to function if compelled to share home
and hearth? There is no question in Vives' mind that the result will be
enmity and discord. And equally important in this respect, he reminds the
Anabaptists, is the need felt at one time or another by all men—with
varying intensity, to be sure—to be alone, to withdraw into themselves;
and at such times no greater injury can be inflicted than to violate this
yearning for privacy.[143] And the physical space represented by real estate
is but the tip of the iceberg. Take for instance, Vives suggests, one's
wardrobe. Should it be shared? Apparently Vives thinks that the
Anabaptists insisted it should be. But is it in fact possible to do so? In
Vives' view the idea is simply preposterous, for it implies a bizarre
contradiction: he who owns the garment cannot wear it when it pleases
him to do so, while he who does not own it may enjoy its use whenever
and for however long he pleases. Again, as in the case of the forced lack
of privacy, the author suspects that this manner of sharing will unleash
that most feared of monsters in the Christian humanist bestiary: discord.
And money? Vives cannot possibly bring himself to admit that what a
man has gathered with his intelligence, work, and industry should be
shared, against his will, by idlers and parasites; that the wherewithal won
through honest toil must now be used to encourage sloth and

---

dream, it eventually emerges that this would-be reformer of society is by no means a
revolutionary. And it would seem that he could offer some strong criticisms to More
along the same lines. In what sense is Vives therefore a social reformer? In the sense, I
think, of wishing to *improve*, not radically *change*, the existing institutional framework.

[142] And yet the discipline of Utopian society seems able to overcome these difficulties.
More seems to have found the way of establishing iron social discipline, but this was to
be done by: (1) crushing the passions; (2) total submersion of the individual into the
whole. The first is plainly unacceptable to Vives; the second, even though he believes that
sin damaged man's individuality, Vives is unwilling to sacrifice it altogether. The
following is emerging: More is a radical, Vives a moderate, reformer.

[143] Ibid. 475-76. To further emphasize the importance of these considerations, Vives is not
averse to going in some detail into the relation between privacy and the performance of
bodily functions.

irresponsibility. To be thus compelled to share what one has come by honestly will surely arouse anger, create resentment and friction, and eventually plunge society into discord.[144]

Clearly, then, no manner of sharing material wealth is conducive to anything other than social strife. Instead of bringing forth amity and a collective well-being, it engenders enmity, tension, and the eventual disruption of the social fabric. Charity Anabaptist-style will indeed bring about precisely the opposite of what, according to Vives, charity must do for society: it will be a solvent instead of its glue. Let us now see in what sense the nature of man makes a pipe-dream out of the sharing of goods.

To start with, Vives begins, we must consider the different temperaments with which men have been endowed.[145] It is clear that although God in fact created all things for man's own use, necessity itself begot the fashion of their utilization; and reason, after the creation of political society, in turn rules *necessitas* as the pilot guides the ship. But inasmuch as all men do not have the same needs or enjoy the same rational powers (in short, they have different mentalities), what, asks Vives, is the justification for demanding that all shall use things in the same manner? For example, and now the political implications of communism stand revealed, it is obvious that justice and wisdom are conditions essential to the governance of the human community; evidently, then, the man who possesses both is the most suitable candidate for the task. But the internal logic of the Anabaptist plan demands that the task of governing be shared by the just and wise man with the witless and juvenile, the ruffian without scruples, the bold pirate, and the butchering gladiator. Could it perchance be that for the Anabaptists it makes no difference whether the commonwealth is ruled by a prudent man or by an unscrupulous adventurer? Given that men are so different among themselves, Vives concludes, it stands to reason that they should enjoy differently the possession and use of things.[146] And beyond the dissimilarities in mental faculties of human beings, nature has placed a further and insuperable obstacle in the path of communism. "Do you not see that some are children, others youngsters, old, males, females, strong, weak, healthy, ill, tall, short? And you wish to apply identical standards to such disparate entities? . . . Nature finds your attitude utterly

---

[144] Ibid. 476.

[145] Ibid. 477.

[146] Ibid. 477-78.

repugnant."[147] Even if a powerful prince at the head of a mighty army were to succeed in imposing a system akin to that advocated by the Anabaptists, the new order would crumble into dust within two days. Some men would immediately squander their share while others would judiciously manage[148] to increase theirs; and, needless to say, since the former would instantly demand to partake of the augmented wealth, and the latter would naturally resist their attempts, violence would inevitably follow.[149] But the Anabaptist plan does not offend nature at the economic level alone, politically, the consequences will be equally unnatural and disastrous.[150] It is an inescapable characteristic of the Anabaptist utopia that in such a commonwealth none obey but all seek to command.[151] Obviously Vives believes that the community of goods is inseparable from some sort of anarchy; princes and magistrates will increase in number a thousandfold, for everyone will be the equal of everyone else. And instead of the tyranny of one, we will therefore have a far worse form of despotism: the tyranny of the many, the tyranny of all.[152] But no matter what the true and ultimate goals of the Anabaptists are, Vives continues, one thing is certain: the real nature of their intentions is easily deduced from their deeds. Honorable men would choose to perish of want rather than turn the commonwealth upside down for the sake of satisfying their own needs, no matter how justifiable those might be. The Anabaptist leaders, by contrast, demand nothing but sedition, killings, burnings, and universal chaos;[153] they are ignorant men, lacking in heart and judgment. How can those men therefore pretend to discriminate among ideas as important as the ones involved in the subject of private property? In truth they are the scum of the earth, and to them soon

---

[147] Ibid. 478.

[148] In other words, private property is the result of man's own nature.

[149] Ibid. And, Vives goes on to ask, if today we are besieged by idlers who would rather perish than work, what will happen in this egalitarian world dreamed up by the Anabaptists? Surely, either we shall all perish as a consequence of the total penury issuing from everyone's unwillingness to work or we should be plunged into a ferocious conflict after which the victor will force the vanquished to work. Ibid. 478-79.

[150] If Vives is so afraid of idlers and indigents, how does he propose to solve the problem? After all, without them there would be no Anabaptist crisis. In part two of *De subventione pauperum* he gives a solution at the local level—Bruges.

[151] DCR *Opera* V 478.

[152] Ibid. 479.

[153] Ibid.

enough the soldiers will add their own contribution. Will a soldier, a man who kills in war for a few coins and in times of peace blithely murders another on account of a gesture interpreted as contemptuous, be a suitable teacher of piety? Will, finally, the injunctions of such a man be weightier than the laws of the land, the faith owed to princes, the exhortations of the Church Fathers, human and divine right?[154] True, Vives concedes, there have been scoundrels before, who have moved war and sedition to free themselves from the clutches of poverty; but none have before used the sacred name of charity to justify their thievery.[155] The Anabaptists pose as the new Apostles. Indeed, replies Vives indignantly, these new Apostles steal what belongs to others. The old ones obeyed magistrates and princes for the sake of Christ, while the new ones set traps for them for the sake of their own bellies.[156] After heaping scorn on the wretched followers of those miscreants, Vives leaves them with the following thought: "If your cause were to triumph, do you think that those whom you follow would be more forgiving toward you than they are toward the rest of mankind? Once finished with the latter they would turn their rage and thievery against you, your wives, and your children . . . everything that you own and hold dear would be turned over to them, not to the best but to the most violent. The cruelest and most atrocious tyranny would be called government, while robbery, public and with impunity, would be decreed as law by brute force."[157]

iii

It can be persuasively argued that the first part of *De communione* is specifically aimed at a gathering of zealots, a villainous lot for whom Vives has scant respect. But it is equally true that in the second part, the humanist casts his net far more widely, to include in fact all who in one fashion or another, coarsely or elegantly, in brutally direct fashion or subtly under cover of weighty discourse, and by way of the community of goods insist that it is possible to bring back man's age of innocence. Seen in this light, Vives' treatise becomes an uncompromising diatribe designed to warn contemporaries against the disastrous social, economic, and political disruptions implicit in any and all forms of utopianism.

As understood by Vives, the Anabaptists based their conclusion that

---

[154] Ibid. 480.

[155] Ibid.

[156] Ibid. 480-81.

[157] Ibid.

worldly goods ought to be shared in common on two underlying premises: private property did not exist among early Christians; charity makes the sharing of goods obligatory. The humanist of course rejects both as false. And once the premises are proven worthless, all that the Anabaptists try to build on their foundation of necessity crumbles as well. But the impact of Vives' discussion does not lie with his rejection of Anabaptist claims concerning the nature of private property or with his questioning of the Scriptural sources cited to uphold those claims. The main thrust of his wrath aims much deeper, at the Anabaptist vision of society and the consequences attendant on their efforts as they are applied in the direction of bringing that vision into being. What is truly significant about *De communione*, in other words, is that the Anabaptist episode is merely a pretext for the author, once again, to emphasize the reality of society. Society is not an historical, disembodied construct, but a reality at every turn conditioned by its own historical development. And plunging even farther along the historicist path, Vives insists that anything proposed at any given moment to heal the ills afflicting society, at that same moment carries with it, if applied, concrete consequences of which all must be extremely mindful. For that reason, and if the latter are not to be perilously alien to the end pursued, the measures/remedies must be inflexibly relevant to the historical moment lived by the patient. The Anabaptists, for instance, maintain that the Old Testament compels man to charity, an injunction which they insist remains equally binding in the society of their own day. But, objects Vives, that point of view, if applied in practice, would entail dire consequences, because the injunctions of the Law obeyed historical circumstances no longer extant. Today's society, Vives further reminds his adversaries, is demonstrably more the child of the New Testament than of the Old, and the former exhorts, rather than commands, man to charity. Vives' point is clear. Society is most certainly not a field of dreams to be used as playground by the feverish imagination of ideologues, be they respectable philosophers or boldly ambitious knaves parading as zealous Christians. His true target, then, is utopianism at large and in whatever guise it might choose to clothe itself. Under the circumstances, we have no choice but to answer the following question. What do these utopians—be they Anabaptists or the Platos, Mores, Montaignes, or Charrons of this world—want? They want to give mankind a Golden Age, a project Vives sees as nothing short of absurd. And interestingly enough the reasons put forth by the humanist to support his sweeping judgment read like an abbreviated roll-call of he key Vivesian ideas that we have reviewed in this monograph.

Let us begin with the Fall. The enthusiasm—or self-interest—of those who wish to bring back an age of innocence to mankind blinds them into disregarding a crucial historical event: man's fall from grace. Vives, the drama coach who in the *Fabula* committed himself to instructing the human actor on how to perform on the stage created for him by the Father of the Gods, knows that God's plan was changed by His creature's disobedience. Are we to assume that a handful of dreamers can in some way invalidate the new divine plan and resurrect the old one? As in some past occasions, Vives chooses to play the Augustinian card for all its worth. The society painfully built by man (mediately, of course, a creation of the Father) after his rebellion is the spawn of the first sin, and hence irrevocably conditioned (i.e. tarnished) by the very reality that caused it to be in the first place. How, then, can anyone possibly propose that out of the base material of a creation rooted in sin, there will issue a noble state of innocence? To do so would be tantamount to believing that man can perform miracles (workings contrary to nature): to bring perfection (the state of innocence or Golden Age) out of something by definition imperfect (society). Even in alchemy, the tradition of learning that in the Renaissance came closest to fulfilling (at least such was the commitment implicit in its claims) the promise of radically revolutionary change, the adept can create nobility out of baseness because the ancient theory of the unity of all matter taught him that metallic nature is one and that lead does have the natural potential to become gold. No comparable assumption, making the state of innocence and society into two evolutionary phases of the same unique whole, is acceptable to Vives. For the humanist they represent two entirely different realms separated by an unbridgeable chasm. Only that which is part of a historical continuum can be said to belong to a single whole. But the state of innocence has no history. It goes without saying, of course, that in the end the state of innocence will once more be realized, but not in this world. And so Vives bluntly advises the miracle workers (Plato explicitly and all others implicitly) to be sure that before they undertake to bring about the state of innocence they take care to start out from the state of innocence.

Granted that the Anabaptists (or some among them, at any rate) may at bottom be well-intentioned, if misguided, ideologues. It may also indeed be praiseworthy to yearn for a return to man's age of gold, or even to mourn the passing of practices said to have been common among early Christians. But only a fool or a knave, and both are certainly well represented among Vives' Anabaptists, would in fact attempt to infuse life into a dream. But, we have noted earlier, the hapless Anabaptists are not the only—perhaps not even the main—target aimed at by Vives. Why, then, do so many men persist in pursuing such a chimera? The answer brings us once more to the humanist's bitter complaint against those who forget duty to self, family, and society for the sake of chasing after a pipe-dream—the men, in other words, who allow themselves to be seduced by the undeniable charms of the *ratio contemplativa*. To those so motivated, society is not a practical and historical reality ruled by criteria as inflexible for Vives as Newton's laws would one day be for future generations. Rather, it is an abstract and putty-like notion to be molded into whatever the artisan's fancy dictates—reprehensible intellectual anarchy made possible, it is to be emphasized, by the wantonness to which contemplation is prone. Such men, Vives does not hesitate to imply, are willing in their enthusiasm to treat natural reason as if it had not been flawed by the Fall—indeed, they behave as if man had never lapsed from grace. Of course, Vives would be hard put to pin on his Anabaptists the sin of excessive intellectual sophistication. But although by now they have obviously been left far behind, the manner in which he disposes of their dream turned nightmare is strongly reminiscent of how he derails (1) More's claim that the Utopians built their society with the aid of reason alone. What reason, Vives would ask? Surely not practical reason; and (2) the ultimate fideism insisted upon by the French skeptics of the late sixteenth century. Because in the event both Montaigne and Charron will maintain that man's search for knowledge will be doomed to failure as long as he insists on using a flawed instrument, what they call artificial reason. Only by rejecting it and surrendering instead to "natural" reason will man discover that true knowledge that God alone can impart. And it is not hard to conclude from this that as far as Montaigne and Charron are concerned, the only true hope for man lies in a society elaborated in terms of man's natural—plainly Vives' own *ratio speculativa*—reason. For a man who like Vives places all his hopes in practical reason (undoubtedly the very instrument dubbed "artificial" by French skepticism) as the only means to fulfill man's earthly destiny as mandated by God and without the need to appeal directly to Him and to His word, this conclusion is unacceptable. And fideism becomes, in this sense, merely another form of epistemological dogmatism, albeit clothed in skepticism and (a most peculiar hybrid) making its ultimate appeal to God's Word. For Vives, then, a society thus envisioned in fideistic terms could be nothing but a state of innocence in no wise different from the Anabaptist kingdom of the saints.

Finally, nature in general and the very nature of man in particular make the Anabaptists dream impossible. The collective sharing of goods would be a viable proposition if and only if the Anabaptists first took care to suppress man's passions; for Vives has shown what personal and public disorders would ensue if, with their passions allowed to remain unfettered, men were subjected to the rigors of total sharing. Bring about, he challenges, Plato's republic (contrary to nature though it is) and the community of goods might in turn be a viable proposition. Short of achieving these conditions, what the Anabaptists demand is fraught with hatreds, discord, strife, and war; because, simply stated, it is against man's own nature. But, on the other hand, the humanist has already cautioned us against the Stoics' injunction to crush the passions; they must instead be brought under control. And, it must be owned, it is a sound warning, for to eradicate the passions means to empty the vessel that is man. To appreciate how seriously Vives' words to the wise must be taken we need only to remember charity. *Caritas* is the love divine made passion, the most sublime passion designed to be the mistress of all passions. Kill the passions, then, and charity necessarily dies. And charity, and herein lies the great irony, the same charity that the Anabaptists thought made communism mandatory, becomes the latter's first victim. The community of goods, contrary to More's assumption (economically, politically, or spiritually) does not make Utopia possible. On the contrary, it destroys charity and with it the bond, one mandated by God and therefore of nature, that keeps society in being.

BIBLIOGRAPHY

PRIMARY SOURCES

Agrippa, Cornelius. *Of the Vanitie and Uncertaintie of Artes and Sciences*, ed. C .M. Dunn (Northridge, 1974).

Aquinas, St. Thomas. *Summa Theologiae.*

Aristotle. *Metaphysics*, The Loeb Classical Library, trans. H. Tredennick (2 vols., Cambridge, Mass., 1961).

————. *Prior Analytics*, The Loeb Classical Library, trans. H. Tredennick (Cambridge, Mass. 1962).

————. *Posterior Analytics*, The Loeb Classical Library, trans. H. Tredennick (Cambridge, Mass., 1960).

————. *Topica*, The Loeb Classical Library, trans. E.S. Forster (Cambridge, Mass., 1960).

————. *Nicomachean Ethics*, The Loeb Classical Library, trans. H. Rackham (Cambridge, Mass., 1962).

Cicero. *Academica*, The Loeb Classical Library, trans. H. Rackham (Cambridge, Mass., 1979).

————. *De inventione*, The Loeb Classical Library, trans. H.M. Hubbell (Cambridge, Mass., 1976).

————. *Topica*, The Loeb Classical Library, trans. H.M. Hubbell (Cambridge, Mass., 1976).

————. *De oratore*, The Loeb Classical Library, trans. E.W. Sutton and H. Rackham (2 vols. Cambridge, Mass., 1976).

Diogenes Laertius. *Lives of Eminent Philosophers*, trans. R.D. Hicks (2 vols., London, 1925).

Erasmus, Desiderius. "The Free Will," in *Discourse on Free Will*, trans. E.F. Winter (New York, 1961).

Lucretius. *On Nature.* Edition of R.M. Geer (Indianapolis, 1965).

Luther, Martin. "The Bondage of the Will," in *Discourse on Free Will*, trans. E.F. Winter (New York, 1961).

————. *Against the Robbing and Murdering Hordes of Peasants. Luther's Works* (Philadelphia, 1967) vol. 46.

Melanchthon, Philip. *Loci communes theologici* (1521-1522), trans. L.J. Satre, in *Melanchthon and Bucer*, ed. W. Pauck (Philadelphia, 1969).

Montaigne, Michel de. *Les Essais de Michel de Montaigne*, ed. P. Villey (Paris, 1965).

————. *The Complete Essays of Montaigne*, trans. Donald P. Frame (Stanford, 1965).

More, Thomas. *Utopia.* Ed. E. Surtz (New Haven, 1964).

Sextus Empiricus. *Sextus Empiricus*, trans. R.G. Bury, The Loeb Classical
    Library (4 vols., Cambridge, Mass. 1976).
Soto, Domingo de. *Deliberación de la causa de los pobres.* Modern edition of the
    Instituto de Estudios Políticos (Madrid, 1965).
Tacitus, Cornelius. *The Complete Works of Tacitus.* The Church and Brodribb
    trans. Ed. by M. Hadas (New York, 1942).
Vives, Juan Luis.   *Opera omnia*, ed. Mayans y Síscar (8 vols., Valencia,
    1782-1790). There is a new edition of the complete works in progress by
    the Institució Valenciana d'Estudis i Investigación.
————. *Obras completas*, ed. and trans. L. Riber (2 vols., Madrid, 1948).
————. *In Pseudodialecticos*. Ed. and trans. de C. Fantazzi (Leiden, 1979).
————. *Selected Works of Juan Luis Vives*. Gen ed.. C. Matheeussen. *De initiis
    sectis et laudibus philosophiae; Veritas fucata; Anima senis; Pompeius fugiens.*
    Introduction, critical edition, translation and notes. Eds. C. Matheeussen,
    C. Fantazzi, E. George (Leiden, 1985).
————. *Epistolario*. Ed. and trans. J. Jiménez Delgado (Madrid, 1978).

SECONDARY SOURCES

Abbott, D.P.   "Juan Luis Vives: Tradition and Innovation in Renaissance
    Rhetoric." *Central States Speech Journal* (1986): 193- 203.
Abellán, J.L. *Historia crítica del pensamiento español* (4 vols., Madrid, 1979).
Adams, J.L. *The Better Part of Valor* (Seattle, 1962).
Adams, M.M. "Intuitive Cognition, Certainty, and Scepticism in William of
    Ockham." *Traditio* 26 (1970): 389-398.
Alcayde Vilar, F. et al. *Colección de artículos* (Ofrenda en el IV Centenario de la
    muerte de Vives). Cátedra de Luis Vives en la Facultad de Filosofía y
    Letras de la Universidad de Valencia (Valencia, 1940).
Allen, D.C. *Doubt's Boundless Sea. Skepticism and Faith in the Renaissance*
    (Baltimore, 1964).
Atkinson, W. C. "Luis Vives and Poor Relief." *Dublin Review* (1935).
Baker, H. *The Wars of Truth* (Cambridge, Mass., 1952).
Baker-Smith, D. "Juan Vives and the *Somnium Scipionis*," in Bolgar's *Classical
    Influences on European Culture.*
Bataillon, M. *Erasme et l'Espagne* (Paris, 1937).
————. "Autour de Luis Vivès et d'Iñigo de Loyola." *Bulletin Hispanique* 30
    (1928): 184-186.
————. "Du nouveau sur J.L. Vives." *Bulletin Hispanique* 32 (1930): 97-114.
————. "Luis Vives, réformateur de la bienfaissance." *Bibliothèque d'Human-
    isme et Renaissance* 14 (1952): 141-158.
Batle, M. *Introducción, programa y bibliografía sobre J.L. Vives* (Murcia, 1942).
Batllori, M. "Joan-Lluís Vives en l'Europa d'avui." *Miscellania Sanchis Guarner.
    Quaderns de Filologia.* Universitat de Valencia (1984): 33-39.

Baxter, E. *The Educational Thought of J.L. Vives*. Doctoral dissertation, Harvard University (1943).

Belarte Forment, J.M. "Aproximación al estudio de la teología humanista de Juan Luis Vives," in Mestre's *Volumen introductorio*.

Bevan, E. *Stoics and Sceptics* (Oxford, 1913).

Blanco, R. *La pedagogía científica y la instrucción de la mujer* (Madrid, 1935).

Böhmer, E. *Spanish Reformers* (London, 1970).

Bolgar, R.R. (ed.). *Classical Influences on European Culture. 1500-1700* (Cambridge, 1976).

————. "Humanism as a Value System, with Reference to Budé and Vives." in Levi's *Humanism in France*.

Bonilla y San Martín, A. *Luis Vives y la filosofía del Renacimiento* (Madrid, 1903)

Briesemeister, D. "Die gedruckten deutschen Uebersetzungen von Vives' Werken im 16. Jahrhundert," in Buck's *Juan Luis Vives*.

Broachard, V. *Les sceptiques grecs* (Paris, 1959).

Buck, A. (ed.). *Juan Luis Vives. Wolfenbütteler Arbeitsgesprach* (Hamburg, 1981).

Bullón y Fernández, E. *Los precursores españoles de Bacon y Descartes* (Salamanca, 1905).

Burnyeat, N., ed. *The Skeptical Tradition* (Berkeley, 1983).

Carreras y Artau, T. y J. *La filosofía moral y jurídica de J.L. Vives* (Barcelona, 1911).

————. *Luis Vives, philosophe de l'humanisme* (Louvain, 1962).

Carriazo, J.M. *Las ideas sociales de J.L. Vives* (Madrid, 1927).

Casanova, R.A. *Soixante lettres de Juan Luis Vives traduites du latin* (Paris, 1943).

Casas, J.M. "Luis Vives y sus comentarios a la *Civitas Dei*." *La ciudad de Dios* 168(1957): 615-619.

Cassirer, E. et al. (eds.). *The Renaissance Philosophy of Man* (Chicago, 1948).

Castro, A. "Escepticismo y contradicción en Quevedo." *Humanidades* XIII (1928): 12-13.

Chisholm, R. "Sextus Empiricus and Modern Empiricism." *Philosophy of Science* 8 n. 3 (1941): 371-384.

Clemens, R.D. "The Role of J.L. Vives in the Development of Modern Medical Science." Doctoral dissertation (1965). The University of Chicago .

Colish, M. "The Mime of God: Vives on the Nature of Man." *Journal of the History of Ideas* 23 (1962): 3-21.

Cooney, J.F. "*De ratione dicendi*, a Treatise on Rhetoric by J.L. Vives." Doctoral dissertation (1966). Ohio State University (1966).

Daly, W. *The Educational Psychology of Juan Luis Vives* (Washington, D.C., 1924).

Dalcourt, G.J. "The Primary Cardinal Virtue: Wisdom or Prudence?" *International Philosophical Quarterly* III (1963): 55- 79.

Dantín Gallego, J. "La filosofía natural en Huarte de San Juan." *Estudios de Historia Social de España* II (1952): 153-208.

Del Arco, R. *La erudición española en el siglo XVII* (2 vols., Madrid, 1950).

Díaz-Jiménez y Molleda, E. *Escritores españoles del siglo X al XVI. Los fundamentos psicológicos, éticos y religiosos de la pedagogía de Vives* (Madrid, 1929).

Escosura, P. de la. "La beneficencia en el siglo XVI: consideraciones sobre el opúsculo de J.L. Vives *Del socorro de los pobres.*" *Revista de España,*(1876), 9: 193-210, 339-356, 462-481; (part two), 68-87, 187-204.

Estelrich, J. *Vives. Exposition organisée à la Bibliothèque Nationale* (Paris, January-March, 1941).

Etchegaray Crus, A. "Juan Luis Vives según Erasmo de Rotterdam," in *Homenaje a Luis Vives. VI congreso de estudios clásicos*, (Madrid, 1977).

Fantazzi, C. "Vives, More, and Erasmus," in Buck's *Juan Luis Vives.*

Febvre, L. *Le problème de l'incroyance au XVIe siècle* (Paris, 1942).

Fernández-Santamaría, J.A. *Juan Luis Vives. Escepticismo y prudencia en el Renacimiento* (Salamanca, 1990).

————. "The Foundations of Vives' Social and Political Thought," in Mestre's *Volumen introductorio.*

Fontán, A. "El latín de Luis Vives," in *Homenaje.*

————. "Juan Luis Vives, un español fuera de España." *Revista de Occidente* 145(1975): 37-52.

————. "La política europea en la perspectiva de Vives," in Ijsewijn's *Erasmus in Hispania.*

Frame, D. *Montaigne's Discovery of Man* (New York, 1955).

García Cárcel, R. "La familia de Luis Vives y la Inquisición," in Mestre's *Volumen introductorio.*

Gariglio, T. and Sottili, A. "Zum nachleben von Juan Luis Vives in der Italienischen Renaissance," in Buck's *Juan Luis Vives.*

Garrido R. and Ferrer, J. *Luis Vives y la psicología educativa* (Valencia, 1944).

George, E.W. "Imitatio in the *Somnium Scipionis*," in Buck's *Juan Luis Vives.*

————. "Rhetoric in Vives," in Mestre's *Volumen introductorio.*

Gilbert, N.A. *Renaissance Concepts of Method* (New York, 1960).

Gómez, H. "Los fundamentos filosóficos del humanismo de Luis Vives." *Verdad y Vida* 12 (1954): 339-385.

Gómez-Hortiguela Amillo, A. *Luis Vives entre líneas. El humanista valenciano en su contexto* (Valencia, 1993).

Gomis, J.B. *Criterio Social de Luis Vives* (Madrid, 1946).

González y González, E. *Joan Lluís Vives. De la escolástica al humanismo* (Valencia, 1987).

————. "La lectura de Vives, del siglo XIX a nuestros días," in Mestre's *Volumen introductorio.*

Gotdon, J. *Luis Vives* (Madrid, 1945).

Green, Otis H. *Spain and the Western Tradition* (4 vols., Madison, 1968).

Guerlac, R. (ed.). "Vives and the Education of Gargantua," *Etudes Rabelaisiennes* II (1974).

————. (ed.). *Juan Luis Vives Against the Pseudodialecticians. A Humanist Attack on Medieval Logic* (Dordrecht, 1979).

Guy, A. *Vivès ou l'humanisme engagé* (Paris, 1972).

Haydn, H. *The Counter-Renaissance* (New York, 1950).

Henry, M.Y. *The Relation of Dogmaticism and Scepticism in the Philosophical Treatises of Cicero* (Geneva, N.Y., 1925).

Hoopes, R. "Fideism and Skepticism During the Renaissance: Three Major Witnesses." *The Huntington Library Quarterly* 4 (August, 1951): 319-347.

Howell, W.S. *Logic and Rhetoric in England, 1500-1700* (New York York, 1961).

Ijsewijn, J. *Erasmus in Hispania. Vives in Belgica. Colloquia Europalia* I. Acta Colloquii Brugensis, 1985. Eds. J. Ijsewijn and A. Losada (Louvain, 1986).

————. J. L. Vives in 1512-1517. "A Reconsideration of Evidence." *Humanistica Lovaniensia* 26(1977): 82-100.

————. "Zu einer kritischen Edition der Werke des J.L. Vives," in Buck's *Juan Luis Vives*.

———— "Vives and Humanist Philology," in Mestre's *Volumen introductorio*.

Iriarte, J. "Francisco Sánchez el Escéptico disfrazado de Carnéades en discusión epistolar con Cristóbal Clavio." *Gregoriarum* XXI (1940): 413-451.

Iriarte, M. de. *El doctor Huarte de San Juan y su "Examen de ingenios"* (Madrid, 1948).

Janssen, H. *Montaigne fideiste* (Utrecht, 1930).

Jardine, L. "Lorenzo Valla and the Origins of Humanist Dialectic." *Journal of the History of Philosophy* 15(1977): 143-164.

Kahn, Victoria. *Rhetoric, Prudence, and Skepticism in the Renaissance* (Ithaca, 1985).

Kaufman, G. "Juan Luis Vives on the Education of Women." *Signs. Journal of Women in Culture and Society* 3-4 (1978): 891-896.

Kohut, K. "Literaturtheorie und Literaturkritik bei Juan Luis Vives," in Buck's *Juan Luis Vives*.

Kristeller, P.O. "The Myth of Renaissance Atheism and the French Tradition of Free Thought." *Journal of the History of Philosophy* 6 (1968): 233-243.

Landa, Rubén. *Luis Vives y nuestro tiempo* (Mexico, 1969).

Levi, A.H.T. (ed.) *Humanism in France at the End of the Middle Ages and in the Early Renaissance* (New York, 1970).

Losada, A. "La huella de Vives en América," in Ijsewijn's *Erasmus in Hispania*.

Lucas, J. de. "Notas para la historia de la tolerancia. Una lectura de J. Luis Vives." *Estudios dedicados a Juan Peset Aleixandre* (Valencia, 1982).

Maccoll, N. *The Greek Skeptics* (New York, 1929).

McCully, G.E. "Juan Luis Vives (1493-1540) and the Problem of Evil in his Time." Doctoral dissertation (1967). Columbia University.

Marañón, G. *Luis Vives. Un español fuera de España* (Madrid, 1942).

Margolin, J-C. "Conscience européene et réaction à la menace turque d'après le *De dissidiis Europae et bello turcico* de Vivès (1526)," in Buck's *Juan Luis Vives*.

————. "Vivès, lecteur et critique de Platon et d'Aristote," in Bolgar's *Classical Influences*.

Martí, A. *La preceptiva retórica española en el Siglo de Oro* (Madrid, 1972).

Mateu y Llopis, F. *Catálogo de la Exposición Bibliográfica celebrada con motivo del IV Centenario de la muerte de Luis Vives (15 May-15 June 1940)* (Barcelona, 1940).

Matheeussen, C. "Das rechtsphilosophische Früwerk des Vives," in Buck's *Juan Luis Vives*.

————. "Quelques remarques sur le *De subventione pauperum*," in Ijsewijn's *Erasmus in Hispania*.

Menéndez Pelayo. M. "De los orígenes del Criticismo y del Escepticismo y especialmente de los Precursores españoles de Kant," and "Apuntamientos biográficos y bibliográficos de Pedro de Valencia." Both essays in *Ensayos de crítica filosófica*, Edición Nacional de las Obras Completas de Menéndez Pelayo (Santander, 1948).

Mestre, A. (ed.). *Ioannis Lodovici Vivis. Opera Omnia. Volumen introductorio* (Valencia, 1992).

————"La espiritualidad de Juan Luis Vives," in Mestre's *Volumen introductorio*.

Monsegú, B.G. *Filosofía del humanismo de Juan Luis Vives* (Madrid, l961).

Monzón i Arazo, A. "El Derecho en Joan Lluís Vives." Doctoral Dissertation (1986), Universidad de Valencia.

————. "Juan Luis Vives y la enseñanza del Derecho." *Revista de la Facultad de Derecho.* Universidad de Madrid 5 (1982): 241-247.

————. "Humanismo y Derecho en Joan Lluís Vives," in Mestre's *Volumen introductorio*.

————. "Bibliografia vivista recent. Balanç i perspective." *L'Espill* 27(1988): 109-112.

Moral, B. del. "Estudio comparativo del 'Ingenio' en Luis Vives y Huarte de San Juan." *Analecta Calansaciana* 18 (1976): 65-143.

Nauert, Jr., C.G. *Agrippa and the Crisis of Renaissance Thought* (Urbana, Ill., 1965).

————. "Magic and Scepticism in Agrippa's Thought." *Journal of the History of Ideas* VIII (1957): 161-182.

Nelson, B. "Probabilists, Anti-Probabilists and the Quest for Certitude in the 16th and 17th Centuries." *Proceedings of the Xth International Congress of the History of Science* (Paris, 1965): 268-273.

————. "The Early Modern Revolution in Science and Philosophy: Fictionalism, Probabilism, Fideism, and Catholic Prophetism." *Boston Studies in the Philosophy of Science*, vol. III (1967): 1-40.

Nero, V del. "Pedagogia e psicologia nel pensiero di Vives," in Mestre's *Volumen Introductorio*.

————. "Recenti studi su Juan Luis Vives (1970-1985)." *Cultura e Scuola* 102 (1987): 121-141.

Noreña, C.G. *Juan Luis Vives* (The Hague, 1970).

————. *Studies in Spanish Renaissance Thought* (The Hague, 1975).

————. *Juan Luis Vives and the Passions* (Carbondale, 1989).

————. "Vives and Agricola in the Low Countries," in Ijsewijn's *Erasmus in Hispania*.

————. "Was Juan Luis Vives a Disciple of Erasmus?" *Journal of the History of Ideas* 7(1969): 263-272.

————. *A Vives Bibliography* (Lewiston, 1990).

Ong, W.J. *Ramus: Method and the Decay of Dialogue* (Cambridge, Mass., 1958).

Owen, J. *The Skeptics of the French Renaissance* (London, 1893).

————. *The Skeptics of the Italian Renaissance* (London, 1893).

Patrick, M.M. *The Greek Skeptics* (New York, 1929).

Piñera, H. *El pensamiento español de los siglos XVI y XVII* (New York, 1970).

Popkin, R.H. *The History of Scepticism from Erasmus to Descartes* (Assen, 1964).

Price, J.V. "Scepticism in Cicero and Hume." *Journal of the History of Ideas* 25 (1964): 97-106.

Puigdollers, M. *La filosofía española de Juan Luis Vives* (Barcelona, 1940).

Randall, Jr., J.H. "The Developement of Scientific Method in the School of Padua." *Journal of the History of Ideas* I (1940): 177- 206.

Rey Altuna, L. "La ética del Renacimiento: Luis Vives." *Revista de Filosofía* 5 (1946).

Rice, E.F., Jr. *The Renaissance Idea of Wisdom* (Cambridge, Mass., 1958).

Rico Verdú, J. *La retórica española de los siglos XVI y XVII* (Madrid, 1957).

Riley, A.M. "Political Theories of J.L. Vives." Doctoral dissertation (1955). University of New Mexico.

Ríos y Portilla, F. *J.L. Vives en sus tres libros "De prima philosophia"* (Madrid, 1864).

Robin, L. *Pyrrhon et le scepticisme grec* (Paris, 1944).

Romuáldez, A.V. "Towards a History of the Renaissance Idea of Wisdom." *Studies in the Renaissance* XI (1964): 133-150.

Sancipriano, M. "Il sentimento dell'Europa en Juan Luis Vives." *Humanitas* 12(1957): 629-635.

————. "La pensée anthropologique de J.L. Vives: l'entelechie," in Buck's *Juan Luis Vives*.

Sanz, V. *Vigencia actual de Vives* (Montevideo, 1967).

Saunders, J.L. *Justus Lipsius: the Philosophy of Renaissance Stoicism* (New York, 1955).

Schmitt, C.B. *Cicero scepticus* (The Hague, 1972).

————. "Giulio Castellani (1528-1586): A Sixteenth-Century Opponent of Scepticism." *Journal of the History of Philosophy* 5 (1967): 15-39.

Senchet, E. *Essai sur la Methode de Francisco Sánchez* (Paris, 1904).

Serrano y Sanz, M. *Pedro de Valencia, estudio biográfico-crítico* (Badajoz, 1910).

Sinz, W. "The Elaboration of Vives' Treatise on the Arts." *Studies in the Renaissance* 10 (1963): 68-90.

Solana, M. *Historia de la filosofía española. Epoca del Renacimiento* (3 vols., Madrid, 1941).

Steppe, J.K. "Mencía de Mendoza et ses relations avec Erasme, Giles de Busleyden et Jean-Louis Vivès." *Scrinium Erasmianum* 2(1969): 449-506.

Strough, C.L. *Greek Skepticism* (Berkeley, 1969).

Stupperich, R. "Das Problem der Armenfürsorge bei Juan Luis Vives," in Buck's *Juan Luis Vives*.

Swift, L.J. "Sommium Vivis y el *El sueño de Escipión*," en *Homenaje a Luis Vives*.

Telechea Idígoras, J.I. "Sobre la ortodoxia de Vives. Una censura inédita de su obra (1536)," in Mestre's *Volumen introductorio*.

Thomas, M.J "The Rhetoric of J.L. Vives." Doctoral dissertation (1967) Pennsylvania State University.

Tobrinner, A. "Juan Luis Vives and Erasmus." *Moreana* 24(1969): 35-44.

Trinkaus, C. "The Problem of Free Will in the Renaissance and Reformation." *Journal of the History of Ideas* X (January, 1949): 51-61.

Uhlig C., and Arnold, C.K. "Vives in England," in Buck's *Juan Luis Vives*.

Urmeneta, F. *La doctrina psicológica y pedagógica de Luis Vives* (Barcelona, 1949).

————. "Senequismo y Vivismo." *Agustinus* 10 (1965): 373-383.

Vasoli, C. "G.L. Vives e la polemica antiescolastica nello *In pseudodialecticos.*" *Miscelánea de estudios a Joaquín Carvalho* 7 (1961).

———— . "La première querelle des 'anciens' et des 'modernes' aux origins de la Renaissance," in Bolgar's *Classical Influences*.

Versenyi, L. *Socratic Humanism* (New Haven, 1963).

Villoslada, R.G. *La Universidad de Paris durante los estudios de Francisco de Vitoria* (Rome, 1938).

Walsh, J.J. "Is Buridan a Sceptic About Free Will?" *Vivarium* 2 (1964): 50-61.

Waswo, R. "The Reaction of J.L. Vives to Valla's Philosophy of Language." *Bibliotèque d'Humanisme et Renaissance* 42 (1980): 595- 609.

Watson, F. *Vives and the Renascence Education of Women* (London, 1912).

————. *J.L. Vives: A Scholar of the Renascence, 1942-1540* (London, 1920).

Zanta, L. *La renaissance du stoicisme au XVe. siècle* (Paris, 1914).

Zeller, E. *Stoics, Epicureans, and Sceptics*, trans. O.J. Reichel (London, 1880).

INDEX